2015 Edition

UP YOUR SCORE

SAT

378.1662 BER
Berger, Larry
Up your score

CENTRAL $13.95
319940152246827

THE UNDERGROUND GUIDE

by Larry Berger, Michael Colton, Manek Mistry,
Paul Rossi, and Ada Throckmorton

Illustrations by Chris Kalb

WORKMAN PUBLISHING • NEW YORK

Library of Congress Cataloging-in-Publication Data is available.

ISBN 978-0-7611-7976-4

SAT questions selected from the following publications of the College Entrance Examination Board: 5 SATs (1981); 6 SATs (1982); 10 SATs (1983, 1986, 1990). Reprinted by permission of the Educational Testing Service, the copyright owner of the test questions.

Permission to reprint the SAT material does not constitute review or endorsement by the Educational Testing Service or the College Board of this publication as a whole or of any other testing information it may contain.

SAT is the registered trademark of the College Board, which has not endorsed this publication.

Grateful acknowledgment is made for permission to reprint the following:

You Can Call Me Al by Paul Simon © 1986 Paul Simon.

Workman books are available at special discount when purchased in bulk for special premiums and sales promotions as well as for fund-raising or educational use. Special editions or book excerpts can also be created to specification. For details, contact the Special Sales Director at the address below or send an email to specialmarkets@workman.com.

Workman Publishing Company, Inc.
225 Varick Street
New York, NY 10014-4381
workman.com

Printed in the United States of America

First printing June 2014
10 9 8 7 6 5 4 3 2 1

To Our Parents

FLORENCE AND TOBY BERGER
ELLEN AND CLARK COLTON
VIRGINIA AND NARIMAN MISTRY
CHARLINE AND FAUST ROSSI
TERESA THROCKMORTON

Acknowledgments

There are many people who have helped us with *Up Your Score*. Listed in alphabetical order, the following people deserve our deep gratitude:

Matt Alisch, Kara Klinke, John Murphy, Matt Pagel, Kabir Seth, Aaron Van Oosterhout, and Ying Zhang for their cultural expertise and numerous suggestions over the lunch table

Doris Berger, for her devoted promotional work

Florence Berger, Cornell University professor, for helping with the memory and concentration chapters, and for revealing her secret recipe for Sweet and Tasty 800 Bars

Toby Berger, electrical engineering professor at Cornell University, for calculating the statistics that prove our methods work, advising us on the math section, and correcting our mistayckes

David Bock, Ithaca High School, for being a terrific math teacher, for the valuable ideas he gave us for the guessing section, and for his editing assistance

Belle Cohen, for being the best PR and Marketing grandmother in the business

Brian Colton, for being himself

Clark Colton, for superb editing and negotiating

Ellen and Jill Colton, for support, encouragement, and TLC

Jason Colton, for his business savvy

Randy A. Faigin, for her suggestions and supportiveness

Dennis Ferguson, for his excellent proofreading

Nous remercions bien cordialement les Fougerays d'avoir si aimablement hébergé Paul, et les Warchols d'avoir hébergé Michael.

Florence Harris, for her generous editing assistance and advice

Lynn C. Harris, for her extraordinary support, outstanding advice, and hilarious contributions

Sharon Herbstman, for helping with astuteness and zeal and everything in between

All our friends in the Ithaca High School Class of '86, and the Newton North High School Class of '93, for their all-around greatness, encouragement, and suggestions

Milton Kagan, one of the few SAT coaches who really knows his stuff, for sharing some of his excellent ideas with us

Andrea Kochie, Ithaca High School, for being an amazing college admissions advisor, and for helping us acquire so much of the information that we needed

Dr. Elizabeth Mandell, for her medical consultation for the "Little Circles" section

Kevin McMahon, Ithaca High School math teacher, for his suggestions about the math section

James Pullman, amazing English teacher at IHS, for helping us plan the writing section

Rita Rosenkranz, the agent John Grisham wishes he had, for scoring a perfect 2400 on the Super Agent Test

Charline and Faust Rossi, for the many kind efforts they have made on our behalf

Bob Schaeffer and FairTest, for advice and information

David Schwarz, for his insightful editorial guidance

Linda Shapiro, for recommending Michael and launching his literary career

Helen Smith, for teaching Michael how to write good

Paul Sondel, Williamsville East High School, for helping with the new math topics, and for knowing that equations have emotions, too, just like everybody else

Teresa Throckmorton, for encouraging Ada to always pursue being her best as a person or in any activity, Keith Parrish and Lucas and Ari Throckmorton for being the best brothers a girl could want, and Christopher Burrows for being the type of teacher who makes kids want to learn

The folks at Workman Publishing, for their astuteness, audacity, alacrity, and ardor—Margot Herrera and Heather Schwedel for their brilliant editing, Peter Workman for taking us on, Carol White for her attention to detail, and Orlando Adiao for great design work

The Yale Class of '90: Deborah Bloom, Jeff Dolven, Amelia Eisch, David Franklin, James Hanaham, Chris Kincade, Julian Kleindorfer, Andrew Michaelson, Jim Rosenfeld, Zachary Silverstein, SM 1845J, Mike Warren, and Jay Withgott, for their contributions, humor, and support.

A BRIEF HISTORY OF THIS BOOK

**ONE
AFTERNOON
IN THE
ITHACA
HIGH
SCHOOL
CAFETERIA
WAY BACK
IN THE
LATE '80S**

**YEARS
LATER . . .**

"This book really stinks," Paul yawned as he pulled the crust off his sandwich, scattering Miracle Whip all over page 12 of Barron's SAT guide.

"Yeah, what's the point of the SAT anyway?"

"To cause us pain and suffering," Manek mumbled.

"You know what's wrong with these SAT review books?"

"No, what?" asked Larry.

"They're all written by embalmed educators who were born before the invention of the number 2 pencil, before the SAT itself, and before *The Brady Bunch* went on the air."

"If I wrote an SAT review book, it wouldn't be so boring."

"I know what you mean. If I wrote an SAT review book, it would be erudite, yet not bombastic, it would elucidate the turbid depths of this baneful examination, and carry students to new heights of academic self-actualization . . ."

"Yeah, and have lots of skin."

"You know, Larry's right. If we could write an awesome manual telling confused, bored, and frustrated students like us across this great land how to rock on the SAT we would—"

"We would be making a contribution to society that . . ."

". . . that could bring us enough funds to pay for college."

". . . and a chance to get on *The Tonight Show.*"

"*Tonight?* Do you really think so?"

A few months later, after Larry, Manek, and Paul each scored over 1500 on the SAT (excellent scores at the time), they began work on a review book that shared their secrets of SAT success. It was called *Up Your Score*, and it helped many students get into prestigious colleges that cost more than they could afford.

Over the next six years, Larry, Manek, and Paul grew old and joined bingo and shuffleboard leagues, and the SAT also changed. Because too many students had read *Up Your Score* and outsmarted the test, the SAT was revised. In order to meet

this new challenge, Larry, Manek, and Paul decided to seek out some young blood, and searched long and hard for a new coauthor to update the book. Eventually, they decided upon Michael Colton, a brilliant young rebel from Massachusetts who achieved a perfect 1600 by reading *Up Your Score* and who also baked award-winning chocolate chip cookies.

Michael's revision of the book enabled a generation of youngsters to follow in his footsteps at Harvard, but age eventually took its toll on him, too. His hair grayed, and he forgot who Jennifer Lawrence was. Students reading *Up Your Score* were confused by his references to *The Cosby Show* and Vanilla Ice. The book was losing its edge. To keep the book fresh, the by-now creaking, wheezing *Up Your Score* crew decided that every two years they would bring in a guest author who would sweep away the cobwebs, add his or her own SAT strategies, and report on the latest changes to the test.

Grabbing his cane, Michael embarked upon a nationwide quest to find the next SAT genius. He met Lisa Exler, an *Up Your Score* disciple who had also used the book and earned a 1600. Lisa revitalized *Up Your Score* and gave it a much-needed feminine perspective.

Nonetheless, the inevitable happened. Even Lisa grew staid and stale. So Michael, now too old to search for fresh talent, convinced the publisher to hold a national contest to find the next guest author. Countless whiz kids submitted applications and many were exemplary. The finalists were given a series of horrific tasks that included marathon 24-hour practice testing and calculating pi to the 314th decimal.

Only two applicants made it through the grueling process: Hannah Bowen and Adam Jed, both of whom had used *Up Your Score* to achieve 1600s. Adam and Hannah were a dynamic duo, but before long, sections in the book like "Rush Scores by Pony Express" and "Slide Rule Tricks" became outdated. Another contest was announced on the *Up Your Score* website.

From the masses emerged Joe Jewell, the one destined to lead *Up Your Score* into the twenty-first century. Soon, however, Joe noticed his peers at college referring to him as ye olde

Master Jewell. Aged as he got, he didn't totally lose touch; he went on to cofound his own test prep company.

A new search located Jason Abaluck and Smitha Prabhuswamy. These two so comprehensively decimated the SAT that the ETS admitted defeat and changed the test! Janet Xu then rose up from the masses of forlorn students and defeated the reincarnation of the SAT . . . but the task was so straining, that afterward she completely forgot how to read. Luckily, Jean Huang and Swetha Kambhampati magically appeared to save the day, but they eventually grew old and weary and were sent off to college to rest. The same fate befell our next test slayers, Ginger Jiang, Jarey Wang, and Alan Hatfield. Then JaJa Liao bravely stepped forward to carry on the battle against the ETS. She fought valiantly on behalf of test takers everywhere, but her brain finally gave out and she now spends her days lounging comfortably in a quiet dorm room. So we held a contest to find someone who was up to the challenge of leading *Up Your Score* into the future. And guess what? We found a totally superheroic gal who scored an impressive 2400.

Months Later . . .

Hey, readers of *Up Your Score*, I'm Ada—the superheroic (mess of a) gal mentioned above—and I'm the new guest editor. This means that the comments and dumb jokes in the margins are my doing. Together, we'll be embarking on a little journey of SAT preparation. Whether you see the SAT as a killer of all happiness, an impossible-to-climb mountain, a rite of passage (yeah, right), and/or your personal life-terrorizing monster, it's our goal to make the killer/mountain/monster as docile as possible (and to use advanced words like "docile" in the process). To prepare, you can load up on 5-hour ENERGY the night before the test and hope for the best. You can create a comprehensive study regime 18 months in advance. Or, you can leaf through *Up Your Score* and follow the tips that sound like they will be most helpful to you. It's your choice, but we're here because every kid needs to find his or her own way to conquer that universal tormenter, the SAT.

CHAPTER 1

ABOUT
THE SAT

BEFORE WE BEGIN, ANY QUESTIONS?

Why do I have to read this book if I want to go to college?
Good question. The answer is, you don't. You can choose not to read this book and halfway through the SAT have a nervous breakdown from which you never quite recover despite decades of psychiatric care, which will lead to all of your several marriages ending in bitter divorces that cost you every penny you make as a mediocre professional bowler, until your life is cut short by an agonizing disease for which they find a cure a week after no one comes to your funeral. Next question?

What is the SAT?
The SAT was developed in 1927 because colleges wanted an objective way of comparing students. It used to be that they had no way of knowing that Eggbert's D average at Impossible High School was actually much more impressive than Betty's B average at Easy Academy. Supposedly, the SAT gives an accurate measure of a student's ability to do college work. Certain teenage review book authors think that it fails miserably in its attempt to do this, but the fact remains that it is a very important part of the college application process. Your SAT score can make the difference between acceptance to and rejection from a college.

What exactly is on the SAT?
The **SAT I** is 3 hours and 45 minutes long. It has 70 minutes of critical reading testing (two sections of 25 minutes and one section of 20 minutes), 70 minutes of math testing (same breakdown as verbal), and a 60-minute writing test (a 25-minute essay, and 25-minute and 10-minute multiple-choice sections). Plus, there's a 25-minute experimental section in either math, critical reading, or writing that won't count toward your score. Only catch, you won't know which section is experimental. (And, no, guessing which one is experimental isn't a good idea.)

The **SAT II** tests cover individual subjects such as literature, foreign languages, history, math, and science.

Note: We usually refer to the SAT I simply as "the SAT."

Ada says:
While this book focuses on the SAT I, it is important to figure out which SAT II tests (if any) you want to take based on your career interests and the requirements of specific colleges.

. . . for now, that is. Aren't they changing the test?

Right you are: The College Board plans to roll out an over-hauled SAT in spring 2016. This book will help you study for any SAT given before the big changeover, but if you're taking the test after spring 2016, be warned: It's going to be out of date. Supposedly, the new test will address many of the complaints critics have lodged against the test over the years, and cover material more like what you actually learn in high school. In the new regime, the maximum score will once again be 1600 (goodbye, 2400) as the essay will be optional; the math section will be more narrowly focused; and the "evidence-based read-ing and writing section" will do away with obscure vocab and focus instead on "relevant words in context." Plus, the penalty for wrong answers will be gone, and you'll be able to take the test on paper or, at some locations, on computer. With these changes, could it be that the ETS is finally . . . admitting defeat? Not so fast. We can only presume that it's simply evolving new and unexpected ways to wreak havoc, unfortunately. If you're on the cusp and have to choose between the old and new ver-sions, take practice tests of both and see which one gives you a higher score.

What is a "good score" on the SAT?

Each section of the test is scored on a scale of 200 to 800. So the perfect combined score is 2400 (math plus critical reading plus writing), and the score you really, really don't want to get is a 600.

No, seriously, what score should I shoot for?

Well, that depends. First, you have to consider what your goals are. Some of you are reading this book because the NCAA rules require that you get a certain minimum score in order to be eligible to play on an intercollegiate team as a freshman. Some of you want to end up at Harvard so you'll want to score in the 2300s on the SAT. Schools usually offer the SAT score range of the middle 50 percent of their freshman class to give an idea of what type of score they're looking for. For instance,

The "College Search" tool on collegeboard.org can be very helpful.
— Ada

A long time ago, we asked Jim Wroth, then a sophomore at Yale, what his combined math and verbal scores were on the SAT. He said 1760. When we responded that it's impossible to score above 1600 (because it was at the time), he explained that he has Yale relatives who date back to the year 1760, so it didn't really matter what his scores were.

Columbia recently had a composite score range of 2140–2330. Macalester College had a range of 1890–2190, and Lake Forest College had a range of 1580–1920. Usually, you can find this information on a college's website.

And remember, these numbers are typical of the scores of the students entering these schools. They are not minimum requirements, nor do they guarantee admission.

Admissions officers consider many other factors. High school grades and courses, work experience, extracurricular activities, application essays, leadership qualities, the admissions interview, ethnic background, athletic prowess, legacy (having relatives who went to the school you are applying to), and many other things all have an impact on whether or not you get in. Although these other factors are important, your SAT score may be the most crucial. If you are president of every club in your school, the admissions officers may be so impressed with your extracurricular activities that they'll accept you even if you scored noticeably below the school's average SAT score. But if you don't have legacy, your grades are ho-hum, and you have a boring list of extracurriculars, then you will need SAT scores well above the average. (For more on college admissions, see page 323.) Many admissions officers would try to deny this claim, but the admissions records show that if you have an SAT score above the average for the school to which you are applying, and there's nothing flagrantly wrong with the rest of your application, then you will usually get in. While the other factors on your application are subjective, your SAT score is a big, fat, hairy, "objective" *number*. Even an admissions officer who claims that the SAT score is not particularly important is going to be subconsciously influenced by this number. It categorizes your application in the admissions officer's mind as "smart kid" or "dumb kid." It has an impact on the way an admissions officer interprets virtually everything else on your application.

What about the PSAT?
If you've already taken the PSAT and you didn't study for it, don't read this. It will only depress you.

The PSAT follows a format similar to the SAT, but it supposedly contains fewer of the most difficult questions, and it's only 2 hours and 10 minutes instead of 3 hours and 45 minutes. As in the SAT, you'll see math (two 25-minute sections), critical reading (two 25-minute sections), and writing (one 30-minute section). Quantitative comparisons and analogies from the old PSAT have been eliminated and short reading passages have been added. You won't, however, see any of the third-year college preparatory math that will be on the SAT (though some of the questions will require higher-level skills than the old PSAT did). The PSAT's writing section will mirror the SAT's writing section, but the ETS is reserving the real torture and pain for the actual SAT: *There is no official essay on the PSAT.* They are *too* kind! Another difference is that, while SAT does not have a *P* as its first letter, PSAT does. Here's why . . .

The *P* in PSAT stands for three things. The first is easy—Preliminary. The PSAT is a preliminary look at the real SAT. It's a sneak preview of what the real thing is going to be like and a good chance to practice (which also begins with a *P* . . .). In fact, your PSAT score report will come with your test book and a computer printout telling you, for each question, the correct answer, your answer, and the level of difficulty of the question. You can use this information to help prepare for the SAT.

But the PSAT is more than just a chance to practice. The second thing the *P* stands for is Programs, as in scholarships and special programs. A good score on the PSAT makes you eligible for all sorts of scholarship programs, the most famous of which is the National Merit Scholarship Program. The National Merit Scholarship is based on your *selection index,* which is your math score plus your critical reading score plus your writing score. Recognition by the National Merit Program is a big plus on your college applications and it can even win you some money. The top 50,000 scorers are recognized by the Merit Program. The top 16,000 scorers become semifinalists, and 15,000 of *them* become finalists. About 8,200 of the finalists get big bucks toward college.

A good score on the PSAT makes you eligible for all sorts of scholarship programs, the most famous of which is the National Merit Scholarship Program.

Sometimes, even if you don't become a finalist, or you're not one of the finalists to receive a scholarship from the National Merit Corporation, you still may be eligible to get money from one of your parents' companies. Also, if you score well on the PSAT but don't make the final cut, some colleges still might offer you scholarships to attend their school—they can get bragging rights to educating the greatest number of National Merit semifinalists or finalists, and you get your college education for less than you planned on spending—sometimes for free. This program is described in depth in the "PSAT/NMSQT Student Bulletin," which also lists the corporate and college sponsors of the program. You can pick up a copy in any guidance counselor's office.

The third thing the *P* stands for is *Ap*plications. The ETS says the PSAT is not used as a college admissions test. But some schools have a space for PSAT scores on their applications. Of course, it's optional whether or not you tell them your PSAT scores, but it's impressive if you have good ones.

I've also heard about the ACT. What's that?

Like the SAT, the ACT is a college admissions test, which for many years had the reputation of being the test of choice in the Midwest, while students on the coasts took the SAT. In recent years, that distinction has been erased. Colleges across the country accept both tests, so you can take either or both. What's the difference between the tests? In brief: The ACT is a little shorter, has a science section, and is supposed to be more knowledge-based than the SAT, which is a reasoning test, but that's just the beginning. Visit upyourscore.com to download a chart comparing the two tests in detail. A good way to figure out which test is for you is to try practice tests of both, and see which one you do better on.

Back to the SAT. What about Sunday test dates?

The ETS offers the SAT seven times a year between October and June; most students take the test on a Saturday morning. However, those students who cannot take the SAT on a

Saturday for religious reasons have the option of taking it on Sunday, usually the day after the scheduled Saturday test. The Sunday test doesn't cost extra, but on your registration form you need to fill in the special 01000 test center code, and you must also send in a signed letter from your clergyperson on official letterhead explaining that religious convictions prevent you from taking the SAT on a Saturday. When you sign up for one Sunday test, you must take the rest of your tests on Sundays as well.

Because the test given on Sunday is exactly the same as the Saturday test, you cannot register for both. The test is scored on the same scale, and percentages are calculated the same way for Sunday test takers as for Saturday test takers. In the end, therefore, there is no advantage or disadvantage to registering for a Sunday test. Only do it if you have to.

What if I want to apply for Early Decision or Early Action?
Many students now take the SAT in October and November of their senior year in order to meet the deadlines for Early Decision or Early Action. Under these programs, seniors generally know by the end of December whether they will have a low-stress second semester. By applying for Early Decision, you commit to attending the school if your application is successful. (This means that you can apply for Early Decision at only one school.) There is no such restriction with Early Action policies, which in general means you can apply for Early Action to more than one school. Some schools, however, have a "Single-Choice Early Action" policy—you aren't obligated to accept their offer of admission, but you can't apply to any other schools under Early Action. If you're seeking early admission anywhere, make sure you know what the school's policy is.

Note: Some schools that are eager to attract good students may send you their "Priority" or "Distinguished Student" applications. These can also count as early admission options. If you've already applied for Early Decision or Single-Choice Early Action elsewhere, check to see that these don't violate the agreement. Don't be one of those "almost broke the early

Ada says: Why not get the SAT over with earlier? Taking it in your junior year can cut down on stress and make maximum use of any studying you did for the PSAT. You also then have time for a do-over (not that you'll need it, of course).

admission rule and got themselves blacklisted" kids. Soooo not cool.

What special skills will I need to take the SAT?

Several abilities are necessary. First, you must be able to stay awake, which can be difficult even though you will be sitting for almost four hours in the most uncomfortable chair imaginable. (This is the reason for the sections on yoga and concentration in Chapter 6.) Second, you have to be able to sign a statement alleging that you, not some cyborg clone, are taking the test (see page 311 for practice). Third, you must be able to read. (And if you're reading this, you've probably already cleared that hurdle, unless you're just looking at the pretty design of the pages.) Fourth, you must know a lot of math and reading and writing stuff so that you can answer the questions correctly. (That's what most of this book is about.) Fifth, you need to understand the proper strategies for taking the SAT and the many ways you can outsmart the test. (We explain all the tricks.) Sixth, you need to be able to fill in all the little circles on the computerized answer sheet, without going out of the lines. (We've provided several columns of little circles for practice and have done extensive experimentation to identify the most efficient way to fill them in. See page 307.)

For more on snacking successfully, see Chapter 6.

Other useful skills are eating for endurance and stealth snacking. These skills are covered in Chapter 6.

How do I get psyched to study for the SAT?

You cannot study for the SAT unless you are mentally and physically prepared. Listed here are several ways of psyching yourself up.

1. Try to convince yourself that it is fun and challenging to learn new words and mathematical facts. (Good luck.)
2. Try to convince yourself that the things you learn in today's study session will enable you to think critically

and to sound articulate for the rest of your life. (This technique does not work either.)

3. Realize that the opposite sex is often attracted to equations and big words. (Nope.)

4. Note that the average teenager burns approximately 115 calories during an hour of intense studying. (Maybe so, but walking up and down stairs for an hour is much more interesting and burns 350 calories.)

The above techniques do not work because they use positive thinking. The SAT does not inspire positive thinking. You must learn to think negatively. For example:

1. Recognize that if you do not do well on the SAT you will not get into a good college. You will have to go to school in the Australian outback and your college years will be disrupted by kangaroo migrations.

2. Go to the kitchen. Press your tongue against the metal freezer tray and hold it there for 10 minutes. Then rapidly yank it away. By comparison, studying for the SAT may actually be pleasurable.

3. Realize that the ETS is a wicked organization. By reading our book you are beating the system because you will score higher than you would otherwise.

4. Most of the dweebs who deserve to get into the colleges of their choice are probably too busy playing with their TI-89 calculators to have time to read this book. It's fun to watch dweebs get mad when they don't get into a college that you get into.

5. The SAT is expensive:

$51.00	test fee for the SAT
13.95	this book
21.99	*The Official SAT Study Guide*
5.00	transportation to and from test
.50	four number 2 pencils
4.00	food brought into test
$96.44	Total

You must learn to dwell on these negative thoughts. Let

them gnaw at your insides. Begin to feel a hatred of this test and all it stands for. Hate is a powerful emotion: It will give you the drive and determination you need for intense study.

Before we begin we must make one important point. In the extremely unlikely event that you read this book and still do miserably on the SAT, do not whine. Just make the best of going to college in the Australian outback. In addition, there are a number of small details that could go wrong during the test regardless of what you learn (or do not learn) from this book. A few examples:

1. You lose your admission ticket, so they never even let you into the testing center.
2. You fall asleep during the critical reading passage about the history of celery.
3. You fall asleep while the proctor is reading the directions.
4. You fall asleep the night before the test and do not wake up until it is over.
5. You don't know the answer to question 6 on the test, so you skip it. However, you forget to leave number 6 blank on your answer sheet. Then, you put the answer to question 7 in the space for question 6, the answer to question 8 in the space for question 7, etc. You don't realize that you have done this until you wake up in the middle of the passage about the history of celery and try to find your place. (Seriously, if you mess up your answer sheet like that, the proctor will probably give you some time to rearrange your answers after the test is over. Raise your hand and ask.)
6. All four of your number 2 pencils break, and you end up having to use chalk.

Some distractions can be remedied. For example, if your desk squeaks, it's too hot, there's a fan blowing your papers

If you take the SAT at your own school, there is a good chance you will know your proctor!

—Ada

around, or you're left-handed and the desks are made for right-handed people—tell the proctor! Although some proctors bite, most don't carry any dangerous diseases, and the occasional proctor will even try to help you. (See "Proctors: Mindless Slaves of the ETS" in Chapter 6.)

How should I prepare the day before the SAT?

There is much disagreement about the ideal way to prepare for the SAT. Each of the authors of this book has a favorite method. Choose the one that is best suited to your personality.

1. Larry's Method: Be Prepared. Preparedness is the key. Have a healthy breakfast of juice, toast, milk, and organic cereal. Walk briskly to school so that you have time to giggle with your friends and clean your teacher's blackboard. Pay attention in all your classes. Go to the Honor Society meetings. While you are at varsity track practice, try your hardest to demonstrate your dedication to the coach and your pride in the school. Go home. Do your homework.

Spend the night before the test relaxing—see a movie, practice your clarinet, play Scrabble. Don't bother with last-minute studying except to look at your list of the 10 words that have given you the most trouble. Put four number 2 pencils with unblemished erasers, your ID, two calculators, and your admission ticket by the door. Say your prayers, and go to bed early.

2. Manek's Method: Be Mellow. Tranquility is the key. Skip school the day before and relax—turn off your phone, lock the door, and put a cloth over your goldfish bowl so you won't be distracted. Lie down on the floor with your favorite potato and breathe deeply. Starting with your toes and progressing to your earlobes, calm your entire body; feel yourself losing control of your muscles. When you're marvelously mellow, put your most prized possessions in the microwave and melt them. If you feel alarmed at this stage, then you're not totally tranquil—go back to the beginning and try biofeedback.

When you are entirely free of tension, center your

thoughts on how wonderful it will feel to be done with the test, while pronouncing solemn and meditative syllables of wisdom. Close your eyes. Sleep.

3. Paul's Method: Get Pumped. Adrenaline is the key. Do not prepare for the SAT the day before. Instead, try to build up as much anxiety and fury as possible in your tortured, nerve-racked body. Do calisthenics. Mosh to hardcore ska. Invite a few friends over and engage in a primal screaming session. Beat your body repeatedly with knotted cords and whips. Break lots of glass. When morning comes, make sure that your pulse is above 250 beats per minute, then break open the test center doors and destroy the test with your awesome animal energy.

Organizing materials such as your pencils, ID, admission ticket, and prayer manual the night before does not improve your score or general well-being. Disorganization forces you to think fast and deal rationally with unusual situations and problems such as those tricky questions that will undoubtedly appear on the SAT. Finally, don't go to bed the night before the test. You can catch up on your sleep the first year that you're dead.

4. Michael's Method: Be Superstitious. Superstition is the key. Find three live mice, a number 2 pencil, a proctor, and a college brochure. On the last full moon before the test, boil all of these together in a Teflon cauldron; simmer until golden brown. Chant the following:

> "O great *Up Your Score* lords, give me the strength to defeat the ETS! I am the Gatekeeper, and I will do as you command!"

If a black cat crosses your path, shoot a mirror with a silver bullet.

The clothes you wear on the test day are very important: If the test is on a rainy day, wear a raincoat. However, if the test is on a day when the Red Sox are playing at home, wear two pairs of socks. If there has been an earthquake during the

past week anywhere in Canada, make sure you wear a blindfold during the test (you can take it off during the breaks). Follow these rules, and you are destined to score well.

5. Ada's Method: Be Determined. Determination is the key. You have to know what you want, and be confident that you're going to get it (according to a lot of con artists, this attitude can get you through the rest of life, too).

Of course, attitude is no substitute for hard work, but by the time you're striding into the testing center, the work will be behind you! Keep your eye on the prize and tell yourself that the SAT is going to be four short hours and before you know it, it'll be over. You've done the studying, you've done the preparation, you've read *Up Your Score*. So you just have to show all that to the ETS—and if you can do it well the first time, you won't have to go through all the heartache of studying for a retake.

So on the day of the test, find a friend to hang out with in line. Don't talk about how afraid you are; talk about the latest gossip or what you have been watching on Netflix. When you're in the room and the tests finally get passed out, sign your name and fill in those bubbles with confidence. Do it like it's the last time you'll ever have to sign your name or fill in bubbles—it could be!

6. Larry, Manek, Paul, Michael, and Ada's Method: Be Together. Togetherness is the key. The SAT is a dismal, lonely ordeal. You are isolated not only during the almost-four pathetic hours of solitude that is the test, but also during long, bleak minutes of studying with nothing but this book to keep you company. We have confirmed that the ETS has offshore investments that profit right around testing time, when millions of students rush out to buy Prozac and inflatable companions.

BUT YOU ARE NOT REALLY ALONE! There are millions just like you who no longer need to suffer in silence! Comrades, on the night before the test, find a computer that is connected to the Internet and share your feelings about the ETS with your fellow test takers. Vent your thoughts by sending a pointed email message to the ETS at sat@ets.org, then become a fan of *Up Your Score* on Facebook. There you can find updates from Ada, trade tips, and commiserate with other poor suckers like you who are preparing to vanquish the ETS. Together we will be strong! And when the sun rises on Saturday morning—we will prevail!

Each of these methods has its merits. People using the first method tend to get higher scores, people using the second method get spiritually enriched, people using the third method die young, people using the fourth method get locked up, people using the fifth method get charged up, and people using the sixth method get a warm fuzzy feeling. No matter which method you use, be sure to read the wisdom on page 324 on the night before the test. Don't peek at it before then.

Tempting,
I know . . .
— Ada

Who Makes Up the SAT?

The conventional answer to this question is that it is made up by the Educational Testing Service, a company based in New Jersey. However, we have discovered that this answer is a cover-up. The real truth about who makes up the SAT is revealed here for the first time in history. . . .

The Story of the Evil Testing Serpent

In the beginning, there was no SAT. Students frolicked in their high school paradise without knowledge of evil, able to pick freely from the Tree of College.

But then the Evil Testing Serpent (ETS) silently slithered into the high school through the hot-lunch loading dock. The ETS was the most nefarious, loathsome, malevolent, malicious, odious, insidious, cunning, beguiling, deceitful serpent that ever existed. (It was because of this serpent that high school students have had to learn vocabulary words like the ones in the previous sentence.) The ETS, an unfathomably long, mighty, mucus-encrusted beastie, was determined to bring evil and pain into the paradise. So it devised a plan that would put an end to the happiness of high school students.

This is how the Serpent's plan was to work. For over three hours students would have to answer an incessant string of multiple-choice questions. The questions would be both boring and tricky. Students who gave too many wrong answers would have miserable futures and then die. He called this hideous ordeal the Slimy and Atrocious Torture (SAT).

The ETS inflicted the SAT on the oppressed masses of students for many years, and the Serpent's power increased as it drained their meager life forces. Gradually, all resistance was crushed and the tormented youths became accustomed to taking the SAT. Parents and teachers began to view the SAT as a national institution. Long, bleak years of misery appeared to lie ahead for civilization.

Could no one defeat the ETS? Would this merciless Serpent continue to strangle its victims into submission? Would *Saturday Night Live* ever be funny again? Was there no hope for humanity? Well, it turned out there was. Five ordinary students, born under the tyranny of the ETS, suffered through the unholy SAT with the rest of their comrades. But afterward, they made a secret blood vow to avenge the misery they had suffered at the fangs of the Evil Testing Serpent. They delved into the mysteries of the SAT in the hope of uncovering its weaknesses and defeating it. They soon discovered many ways of psyching out the ETS and outsmarting the SAT. They transcribed their revelations in a stirring document wherein they demonstrated that although the ETS was mean, their readers would be above the mean. The high school paradise was soon restored and students once again were able to pick freely from the Tree of College.

Just when peace was restored, the ETS realized that kids were flocking back to their happy paradise, and its scales shimmered with hatred. One night, as it lay stewing in its miserable New Jersey cave, an idea formed in its so-called mind. Why not make the test *harder*? Maybe add more math questions using terms most adults wouldn't even understand! Add more insipid reading passages! And maybe even an essay! Combined, the Slimy and Atrocious Torture would last 3 hours and 45 minutes, a half hour longer than ever before. The ETS quivered with delight! But not to worry. The five gallant fighters vowed to fight the Serpent, no matter what form it took. So they stealthily searched its cave, and with greater success than the search for weapons of mass destruction, they found its secrets and revised the document. *It is that document you now hold in your sweaty, trembling hands.*

Here, the cruel tricks of the ETS will be revealed and you will be shown how to use your understanding of the Serpent's methods to your own advantage. Throughout this book, the Serpent will make loathsome appearances and will secrete foul venom all over the pages to protest our revelations of its weaknesses and its trickeries. Soon you will be able to recognize the Serpent's infamous tricks and you will live forever free of the fear of the Slimy and Atrocious Torture.

SAT Scoring

Fewer people know how the ETS really derives an SAT score than know whether or not the government has UFOs buried in a bunker in Nevada. This information hovers in a cloud of confidentiality and "we'll call you back"s. The ETS claims that this information is known only by a few members of their statistics department and that no single person knows the entire system. On one occasion, they even told us that we can't call the department that could explain this system because they don't have a phone.

Despite this veil of secrecy, by piecing different information together, we were able to find out quite a bit about how the ETS takes the number of questions you got wrong and translates them into a percentile and SAT score.

What is a raw score?

The raw score is a number based solely on how many questions you got right minus a fraction of a point for each question you got wrong.

What is a percentile?

Your percentile is based on the percent of test takers who had a lower raw SAT score than you. If, for example, you're in the 64th percentile, your raw score was higher than the scores of 64 percent of the other people taking the test.

What about that other score—you know, the important one?

The other score you receive is the numerical score, which is on a scale of 200 to 800 for each section. This is the score that is shrouded in so much mystery.

Many people believe that SAT scores are set up on a bell curve, which means that most people would get a score just above or below a 500, and that an equal number of people would get scores an equal distance from the average. This would mean that if 620 people got an 800 on the math section, 620 people would also get a 200. And it would mean that the average score on the test should be 500. But none of these things is true. The ETS admits that the average score on each section is not 500. For the class of 2013, the average math score was 514, the average critical reading score was 496, and the average writing score was 488.

The ETS will not explain how they set up their curve, but the National Center for Fair and Open Testing, a watchdog group that believes that all of this information should be available to the public, says that the ETS takes a standard bell curve and shifts it up slightly, allowing more 800 than 200 scores. They also go through a complicated process of evaluating which questions on the test were the most difficult and comparing your performance to that of other people who took the same test and to other people who took the test in the last few years.

Are percentiles and SAT scores connected?

Your score and percentile are definitely connected, although the exact relationship will probably be discovered after the identity of the shooter on the grassy knoll. The ETS releases a chart that roughly matches scores with percentiles.

Score	Critical Reading Percentile	Math Percentile	Writing Percentile
800	99+	99	99+
750	98	97	98
700	95	93	96
650	90	86	90
600	80	75	82
550	67	62	70
500	51	46	54
450	34	29	37
400	18	15	21
350	8	7	8
300	3	2	3
250	1	1	1

How many questions can I get wrong and still get a perfect score?

That varies from year to year. There is always more leeway on the critical reading scores than the math scores. During an average year, you can get three or four critical reading questions wrong and still score 800, but you can miss only one math question and still get an 800.

Why are scores on a scale of 800 instead of 100?

When the SATs were first invented, the ETS decided that if scores were on a scale of 0 to 100, people might start to complain that their SAT scores were not on a par with their regular school grades: "I got a 96 in math but only a 90 on the SAT math section." To avoid problems like this (and in our opinion to make the test seem more grand and precise than it really is), they set it up on a scale of 200 to 800. Since no one ever gets a 705 or a 692, many people wonder why scores are not on a scale of 20 to 80, the same way PSAT scores are calculated. Again, this is probably a marketing ploy. It sounds better to get an 800 than an 80, and the SAT needed to set itself apart from other tests in order to get thousands of colleges to force kids to pay millions of dollars to take it.

SAT MISTAKES

The ETS is human after all! Well, not exactly "human," but it does make mistakes.

On the SAT I given in October 1996, the math section contained a flawed question. A student much like you realized that, depending on how one interpreted the unclear (and mean and nasty) problem, there could be different answers. The College Board acknowledged its treachery and rescored the exam, raising the scores of about 45,000 tormented students (13 percent of those taking the exam on that day) an average of 10 points.

For the SAT I in October 2005, about 4,600 tests were wrongly scored, due to scanning problems with the machines. While this affected only a tiny proportion of students taking the test that day, you can imagine how you'd feel if you were one of the unlucky ones.

These mistakes just prove that no one (not even the Evil Testing Serpent) is perfect. If you really think a question is unfair—not just that you don't know the answer, even though we all think those are unfair—there is a (slim) possibility that it is a mistake. The procedure for challenging a question is in the

Ada says: If you really think something went wrong with the grading of your test, the College Board offers a score verification service for $55.

registration bulletin, and your proctor should be able to help you as well.

SAT SERVICES

Scores Online or by Phone

Your scores will be available online about three weeks after you take the test. You can also hear them over the phone by calling (866) 756-7346, but you won't get them any earlier this way, and it also costs an extra $15. You might be wondering, how could it possibly cost $15 per student? According to our local phone company, the ETS is probably paying about 50 cents for each toll-free call—so most of the $14.50 left over would seem to be pure profit for the supposedly nonprofit Evil Testing Serpent. If every student in America used this service, the Serpent could make more than $20 million a year off it. That's enough to gold-plate the tennis courts on the ETS's 400-acre estate! (Yes, your test fees really do go to support a 400-acre estate with tennis courts.)

Why should you give the ETS even one more measly dollar? Hasn't the Serpent already wrung enough moolah out of you, not to mention blood, sweat, and tears? The better option, by far, is to get your scores over the Internet. For no additional fee, you can go to collegeboard.org, click on "SAT," put in your username and password, and click on "Scores" to see your entire score history. There is one hitch: You must sign up for a College Board account *before* you take the test. Make sure you do this!

Score Sender

When you register, you are given the option of requesting your score report to be sent to up to four colleges at about the same time the report is sent to you. You will need to send score reports when you apply to colleges, so if you have an idea of where you're going to apply when you take the test, you might as well use the Score Sender option. It saves a step later on. And it's free. However, if you don't know where you're applying and/or have time to get your scores first (and take the test again, if necessary), you can wait and request score reports for your colleges later. The score report is cumulative, and shows all of your scores for up to six SAT Is and six SAT II subject tests.

The College Board lets you request score reports over the phone or on the Internet, and once again the Internet is much more convenient. Using the College Board's site (sat.college board.org/scores/send-sat-scores), you can send as many reports as you want for the cost of $11.25 per report.

Remember, it takes about three weeks for your scores to be mailed after you request them. So if you have a college admissions deadline, plan ahead. But if you forget, there is a rush reporting service. It's available only online, and it costs $31.00, in addition to $11.25 for each report. Scores are mailed out within two business days of your request.

Tip: Be careful when you're tempted to use the rush reporting service. Some colleges specifically state that they will not accept rushed scores.

Score Choice

Though normally all of your SAT scores will be sent to a college when you send a score report, you can use a service called Score Choice to pick which SAT I and SAT II scores will be sent. While Score Choice doesn't cost any extra, it still has some pros and cons. In the pro column, if you took the SAT II in Biology twice, you can choose to send only your higher score. However, Score Choice only allows you to omit entire tests—meaning you can't choose to send your 800 in Critical Reading and not your 580 in Math from the same test. Additionally, some colleges don't allow Score Choice. But never fear! Most colleges will "super score" (or only look at the best score you have received in each section) anyway.

Registering Online or by Phone

If you have already registered for any SAT test, you can register for another by phone. Just call (866) 756-7346. But, if we haven't beaten it into you by now, here it is again: Registering online is a much better way to go. All you have to do is go to sat.collegeboard.org/register and follow the instructions.

Why should you register online? For one thing, it's a lot faster. (And cheaper! There's a $15 fee to register by phone.) Just a few clicks and you're done. You will also know the moment you sign up where your testing center is. In the event that you lose your admission ticket, all you have to do is print out a new one. And, just when it couldn't get any better, you can also see your scores online the day they come out, instead of waiting three weeks for the paper report to come. You can also see a copy of your own essay online, too.

For SAT services that help you practice, read on.

HOW TO PRACTICE

Some books are too easy, and some are too hard. Find your Goldilocks book!
— Ada

Read the explanations the booklet gives for every question (including the ones you got right). The more you read, the deeper you'll get into the evil brain of the ETS. It might give you the creeps, but it also makes the questions more predictable.

We didn't put many practice problems in our book. This does *not* mean that you don't need to practice. In fact, practice is critical, and we suggest that you do as much as you can possibly stand. And practice comes in many forms: Ada attributes her success to doing SAT practice tests with a great group of friends. (Doing miserable things can be more bearable when you do them with friends.) We want you to practice, but we didn't want to make up fake SAT questions when there are thousands of real SAT questions that have already been published by the ETS. Other review books contain tons of practice questions, but a lot of the questions are totally unlike the ones that are on the real SAT. Also, in many books, several of the given answers are *wrong*! The five of us got so frustrated with the questions in these books that we decided not to make the same mistake ourselves.

Our advice is to practice on real SAT questions. Here's how:

1. Get the "SAT Practice Booklet" and the "SAT Practice Test" published by the College Board. They should be available at no cost from your guidance counselor. The Practice Booklet contains sample critical reading, writing, and math questions and explanations, as well as preparation and test-taking tips. The Practice Test booklet contains one complete practice test and answer sheet.

2. Get the book *The Offical SAT Study Guide: Second Edition*, published by the College Board. This book contains ten practice SATs. It also has hundreds of extra practice questions, many with clear explanations. The hints and strategies it provides are also worth reading. Of course, because it is published by the College Board, the official sponsor of the SAT, it doesn't tell you how foolish the SAT can be, it doesn't show you any of the tricks on how to beat it, and it's not nearly as funny as we are.

3. Take advantage of the SAT and College Board services. Since many colleges consider only your highest score, you can take the SAT more than once. For example, if you are planning to take the test in May or June, you can also register for the January test date and sign up for one of the services that the College Board offers to help you learn from your first test (and to make themselves more money). The Question-and-Answer Service provides you with a copy of the test you took, your answers, the correct answers, scoring instructions, and information about the type and difficulty of each question. The service costs $18.00, and you can order it either when you register for the test or up to five months after your test date. It takes three to seven weeks after your test is scored for you to receive the materials, but if you're willing to pay the $18.00 and wait a bit, you'll know exactly which areas of the SAT you need to practice. Unfortunately, the College Board does not offer this valuable service for all of the test dates. If you want to use it, be sure it's offered on your test date.

For the test dates on which the Question-and-Answer Service is not available, the College Board offers the Student Answer Service. For $13.50 you receive a computer-generated report that tells you for each question what type it was (sentence completion, geometry, etc.), whether you answered it correctly or

After each practice test, make sure you understand every single question you got wrong. If you don't, chances are, you're going to miss a similar question in the future.

incorrectly or skipped it, and the level of difficulty on a scale of 1 to 5. You can order this service the same way you order the Question-and-Answer Service, and you'll receive the materials three to six weeks after your test is scored. Although it doesn't provide you with as much information, you can still use it to gauge the areas in which you need work.

GETTING IN GEAR

Now that you know how to practice, the question is, how you're going to get yourself to do it. Needless to say, there are thousands of things you'd rather do than prepare for the SAT, beginning with weeding and ending with sticking hypodermic needles in your eyes. But assuming that you recognize the necessity of preparing, how do you make yourself actually sit down and study?

Set score goals in each subject, not just a total score.

—Ada

1. **Set a Score Goal**

   Establish a specific score as your goal. Pick a score that you think you can achieve but that will require some preparation. (A good score goal is one a bit above the average SAT score for students at the schools you're considering.) Once you've set this goal, don't stop studying and learning vocabulary words until you consistently achieve the score on practice tests.

Literally make a calendar. Vocab List 2 on Saturday, Math Practice Test 4 on Monday, etc.

—Ada

2. **Block Out Time in Your Schedule**

   Make appointments with yourself to study and take practice tests. Don't compromise this time; treat it as a serious commitment that you can't break. Find a quiet, secluded place, and don't let yourself be disturbed—that means no food breaks, no texting, no checking Facebook, no pat-the-cat sessions. When you're finished, go outside and yell for a while to release your tension. Then reward your hard work and self-discipline by bathing in melted milk chocolate.

3. Study with Friends

Anything is more fun if you do it with friends (except maybe body piercing). Read this book out loud. The jokes will be funnier and the tips will make more sense. Another advantage to studying with friends is that you can help each other with some of the harder math concepts and test each other on vocabulary words. Just make sure that you don't get carried away fooling around and forget to study. Also, don't have too good a time or the Serpent will hunt you down, hide under your bed, and stab a number 2 pencil into your little toe while you sleep. The ETS doesn't like students to have any fun with the SAT.

4. Treat It Like the Real Thing

When you are taking the practice tests—just like you don't want to compromise your study time—don't go too soft on yourself. This means taking the practice test within the time limit and not letting it go on for three days. If time's up, time's up. Sorry, you just have to be your own proctor. Don't be tempted to cheat on the practice test (what's the point, anyway?), like sneakily whipping out a pocket dictionary at the sight of hard vocabulary. You can review the hard questions *after* the test. If you've been conditioned to easier standards, you'll just have a harder time when the real SAT comes around.

Remember, if you don't prepare the first time, you'll just have to take the test again, and eventually you'll have to study. Unless, of course, you're aiming for college in Greenland.

Ada says: Take practice tests in the morning if you can. You're never going to be taking the SAT at 8:00 P.M., unfortunately.

U_P Y_{OUR}
S_{CORE}
C_{HEAT}
S_{HEET}

You're welcome!
—Ada

For Those Pressed for Time and/or Motivation

Think a perfect score is a little out of your league? Not to worry, this book is still for you! If you have limited time or motivation, then you're probably not going to read the book cover to cover (although you won't regret it if you do). Being kind, empathic, generous people, we're giving you a break. Here's a list of where to find the essential, not-to-be-missed, utterly important information.

Chapter 1, About the SAT
Read:
- "How to Practice," pages 26–28
- "Getting in Gear," pages 28–29

Chapter 2, The Critical Reading Section
Read:
- "Four Key Rules and a Tip," pages 34–36
- "Sentence Completions," pages 36–41
- "Critical Reading Passages," pages 41–46
Skim:
- "The Reading Passages," pages 46–51
- "The Six Types of Questions," pages 52–54
Read:
- "The Short Reading Passages," pages 57–58
- "About SAT Words," pages 58–60
- "Useful Synonyms" and "Similar-Looking Words," pages 155–157

Chapter 3, The Math Section
Read:
- "Calculators," pages 171–175
- "Fractions/Units," pages 176–184 (focus on the examples and boldface words)
- "Word Problems," pages 184–194
- "Equations," pages 194–198
- "Relations, Functions, and Function Notation," pages 198–199

- "Solving a Quadratic Equation" and "Quadratic Formula," pages 201–204
- "Exponents," pages 206–208
- "Geometry," pages 209–222
- "Coordinate Geometry," pages 222–229
- "Grid-In Problems," pages 236–239

Chapter 4, The Writing Section
Read:
- "The Three Question Types," pages 244–248
- "The 13 Rules of the Writing Test," pages 249–263
- "The Essay," pages 267–277

Chapter 5, Guessing
Very important! Read:
- "The Six Rules of Guessing," pages 285–290

THE CRITICAL READING SECTION

FOUR KEY RULES AND A TIP

In this chapter, we will go over each type of question individually in order to familiarize you with the different question types, and then we'll show you some slick tricks. But first, here are some general rules for doing the critical reading section.

Rule 1: Know Your Speed

On the test, you are given only 70 minutes for the 75 or so questions on the two critical reading subsections. So you figure, "Great, I have about a minute per question." *Wrong.* You have to subtract about 20 minutes for the amount of time you need to spend reading the reading passages. Then subtract another minute from the total test time for the time you spend watching the kid in front of you pick his nose and maybe another half second for the time you spend picking your own nose. Now you have only about 40 seconds per problem. That's just about the amount of time most people need if they work efficiently. If you find yourself finishing 10 minutes early, then you're probably working too fast and being careless, or you didn't spend enough time picking your nose. If you aren't finishing all the questions before the time runs out, you might have to be a little less careful (or skip the last critical reading passages of each section, as described in Strategy 5 of the reading passage section of this chapter, page 45). In any case, it's essential that you have practiced enough to know exactly how fast you should be moving. Good control of your speed and timing must be second nature to you when you take the real test.

Or coughing, pen-twirling, foot-tapping, or any other distraction you prefer.
—Ada

Rule 2: Do the Subsections in the Best Order

All questions are worth the same number of points. Therefore, you want to have done as many problems as possible before you run out of time. Sentence completions take the least amount of time, so do them first. Then do the short reading passages. The long critical reading passages take the most time; do them last. The only exception to this rule would be if you consistently find that you score better on practice tests when you do things in a different order.

This is why practice tests are so important!
—Ada

Rule 3: Realize That Questions Get Harder

The Serpent gets more and more cruel as each subsection (a set of 10 sentence completions, for example) progresses, except in the questions following each critical reading passage. The first question in a subsection is usually easy. The last question in a subsection is usually hard. This is important to remember, because if you know that you're going to have to skip some questions, you might as well skip the hard ones.

This can also be used to outsmart the Serpent. You can use it to find correct answers to questions that you otherwise wouldn't be sure about. How? Since the first few questions in a subsection are always easy, the obvious or most tempting guess is probably correct. The middle questions are a little harder; on these questions the obvious or most tempting guess is sometimes right and sometimes wrong. On the last few questions in a subsection, the obvious, most tempting guess is probably wrong. This is *crucial*. A question is put at the beginning of a subsection if, in the Serpent's experience, most students get it right. It is put at the end if most students get it wrong. The trick is to learn to pick the answer that "most students" would pick on the questions at the beginning of the section and at the end of the section avoid the answer that "most students" would pick. What we have explained here is just the basics of how to apply this concept. In Chapter 5, we provide a more advanced explanation, with additional useful strategies and tricks.

Remember, the questions get harder within *sub*sections, not from section to section. So when you get to the sentence completions, you'll be starting with relatively easy ones.

If you want an in-depth explanation of this rule and its uses, read the 700-page book *Cracking the SAT* by Adam Robinson and John Katzman. They call it the Joe Bloggs principle and, frankly, they get a little too carried away about it.

Rule 4: Know the Directions

The directions are the same every year. Don't waste time reading them during the test. Memorize them from your copy of "Taking the SAT," available on the College Board website.

On the last few questions in a subsection, the most tempting answer is probably wrong.

Unlike us and our jokes!
—Ada

Quick Tip: If you skip a question because you don't know the answer, put a mark next to it in the test booklet. We suggest an X for the questions you don't think you'll be able to figure out and a ? for the ones you think you'd get with more time, if you have it later on. Also, try putting a star next to the ones you did answer but aren't sure you're correct. That way you can go back and puzzle over them some more if you have any time left at the end.

SENTENCE COMPLETIONS

Definition: Fill in the blank.
Priority: Do them first.
Comment: Not that bad once you get the hang of them.

For each sentence completion question, the ETS presents you with a nice, logical sentence. The trouble is that one or two words are missing from it. Your job is to pick the correct missing word(s) from among five choices. All of the possible answers make sense grammatically, but only one will make sense logically.

Some students consider sentence completions to be the hardest part of the verbal section because they test your sense of "sentence logic" in addition to testing your vocabulary. We think they are the easiest part because you have a context to help you figure out the answer. For example:

> The man was smelly so I plugged my _____.
> (A) ear
> (B) toe
> (C) eye
> (D) socket
> (E) nose

Each of these choices is okay grammatically, but why would you plug your eye, toe, ear, or socket if the man was smelly? You would plug your nose. Usually, the SAT questions are more sophisticated, but the logic is the same.

If you approach them properly, the sentence completion questions can be extremely gratifying. When you choose the right words to go in the blanks, the sentence will have a certain flow, a sort of magical aura that will suffuse your body with a warm, rapturous glow.

The Basic Pattern

You should follow a basic thought pattern whenever you attack a sentence completion question:

1. Read the sentence first, skipping over the blanks, just to get a feel for how the sentence is set up.

2. Read the sentence again, and this time when you get to the blanks, guess *on your own* what the missing words should be. You may not be able to come up with a specific word, but all you really need to determine is the answer's generic category—whether the word is a "negative" or a "positive" one. In the blank write a "+" or "–" to remind yourself what type of word you're looking for. When there are two blanks, you should at least decide whether the two missing words are synonyms or antonyms, "good" or "bad."

3. Compare your guesses with the answer choices provided and see if any of them fit your general idea of what the answer should be.

4. Plug in the answer that looks best and see if it makes sense.

5. If it clearly makes sense, then go with it. Otherwise, try all the other choices and pick the one that works best. If the question contains double blanks, make sure that you carefully read *both* words for every answer choice, and pick the *pair* that best fits the blanks. As you're trying choices, cross out the ones that you're sure don't fit. Then, if you get stuck and decide to come back to the question, you won't have to waste time reading all of the choices again.

Ada says:
Only skip a question if you have absolutely no idea! It's better to spend a few extra seconds coming up with a solid guess than to skip a question and lose all the progress you've made in solving it.

After some practice, these rules should become second nature, so you won't have to go through a three-minute process on each problem.

Okay, enough rules. Here is an example.

> She insulted Irving's appearance by saying, "Your face is _____."
> (A) cheerful
> (B) beautiful
> (C) handsome
> (D) charming
> (E) a wart-ridden, misshapen mass of snotty goo

That wasn't too tough. And did you notice that magical feeling when you chose (E)?

Let's try some from real SATs.

> Until Florence Nightingale made nursing _____, it was considered a _____ profession.
> (A) scientific . . . painstaking
> (B) essential . . . dangerous
> (C) noble . . . lofty
> (D) patriotic . . . worthy
> (E) respectable . . . degrading

You should read this question, "Until Florence Nightingale made nursing *something good*, it was considered a *something bad that's the opposite of whatever's in the first blank* profession." You can eliminate (C) and (D) because *lofty* and *worthy* are both words that mean something good. You can eliminate (A) and (B) because they aren't opposites. Now you know the answer is (E). Check it, and it makes sense. Yippee!

> Although they are _____ by traps, poison, and shotguns, predators _____ to feast on flocks of sheep.
> (A) lured . . . refuse
> (B) destroyed . . . cease
> (C) impeded . . . continue
> (D) encouraged . . . attempt
> (E) harmed . . . hesitate

Ada says: Questions like these are why it is important to study the connotation of vocab words even if you don't have the time to fully master their definitions. In other words, it is never too late to study vocab!

The correct answer here is (C). Any time you see *although*, the sentence will have two parts. The first part will say "blah blah blah." The second part of the sentence will say something that you wouldn't expect considering that "blah blah blah" is true. In the above example, the first part of the sentence says, "Nasty things are trying to stop these predators from pigging out." Therefore, you would expect that they would decide not to pig out. However, the *although* indicates that the second part of the sentence will say the opposite of what you expected it to say. So you have to choose an answer that indicates that they are still pigging out. The only answer that would fit this idea is (C).

> As a scientist, Leonardo da Vinci was capable of _____, but his mistakes are remarkably few in light of his _____.
> (A) error . . . accomplishments
> (B) artistry . . . failures
> (C) genius . . . works
> (D) trivia . . . lapses
> (E) innovation . . . achievements

In the same way that *although* was the key word in the previous example, *but* is the key word in this example. You should be able to figure out that the two missing words should be in the combination "bad thing . . . good thing." In other words, you should think to yourself, "As a scientist, Leo made some bad mistakes, *but* his screwups seem pretty minor when you look at the good things he did." Scanning the list of possible answers, you see that

> (A) is "bad" . . . "good"
> (B) is "good" . . . "bad"
> (C) is "good" . . . "irrelevant"
> (D) is "irrelevant" . . . "bad"
> (E) is "good" . . . "good"

Therefore, the correct answer must be (A).

These are also useful terms when negotiating with parents.
—Ada

Following are other key words (like *although* and *but*) that can change the logic of a sentence:

- despite
- except
- far from (*Far from* doing blah blah, the thing has done almost the opposite of blah blah.)
- in spite of
- instead of
- nevertheless
- unless
- while (*While* that is true, it is also true that this is true.)
- yet (That is true, *yet* we must also recognize that this is true.)

A Couple of Tricks

In the sentence completion section, as you will see in the reading comprehension section, the ETS tries to be politically correct. So if you see a sentence that mentions women or minorities, it is probably saying something good about them. For instance:

> Although few in number, women in Congress have had _____ impact on a variety of issues.
> (A) an arbitrary
> (B) a negligible
> (C) a substantial
> (D) a minor
> (E) an inadvertent

You could get this problem right without even reading more than the first few words in the sentence. All you have to realize is that "substantial" is the only positive word among the answer choices.

The ETS thinks that just knowing that congresswomen are influential on Capitol Hill will help every girl in SAT-Land do well on the test, get into her top-choice college, and then excel in her career.

Using the principle that the questions at the beginning of a subsection are easy, you should avoid choosing difficult vocabulary words at the beginning of a sentence completion subsection. For example, this question is the second one in its subsection:

> Just as congestion plagues every important highway, so it _____ the streets of every city.
> (A) delimits
> (B) delays
> (C) clogs
> (D) obviates
> (E) destroys

Delimits and *obviates* are difficult vocabulary words. If you had to know the meanings of these two words to answer this question correctly, then this question would be difficult and it would not be the second problem in the section. So eliminate (A) and (D). The correct answer is (C).

Definition:	Passages followed by questions.
Priority:	Do these last.
Comment:	Each consecutive passage is harder than the one before it. However, the questions following a particular passage are not arranged from easiest to hardest.

The reading passages make up the majority of the critical reading section, so make sure you can do these well. Unfortunately, it is the only part of the SAT that you can't sit down and study for in any direct way. Fortunately, however, it's also the part of the test for which you've been studying for the longest time. You've been reading and analyzing books since kindergarten (remember *The Giving Tree**?). The reading passages might seem difficult because they're so incredibly long and boring—let's face it, the passages that the ETS chooses don't exactly read like a Suzanne Collins book—but that is precisely why the ETS chooses them. They're so obscure and unpopular that no student in his or her right mind would ever have read

Underlining key words in the sentence can be helpful.

—Ada

Critical Reading Passages

* If you don't, read it now. It's worth it.

—Ada

them before. The sheer dullness of these passages would put your physics teacher to sleep, let alone a bunch of teenagers who usually sleep until noon on a Saturday. That's why you have to learn how to focus on reading these passages, how to pick up what's important, and, most importantly, how to get through them without nodding off.

The ability to read quickly can be a big advantage. So read only those words that start with *w*. "Hold it," you say, "but then I won't understand anything." To which we respond, "Oh yeah, you're right, sorry," and then suggest, "Try reading everything very carefully and make sure you comprehend it all." To which you respond, "But then I won't have time to finish the test."

This is the heart-wrenching conflict you must deal with on the critical reading section: to speed or not to speed. All we can say is, do as many practice tests as you possibly can so that you know how fast you can read and still understand as much as possible.

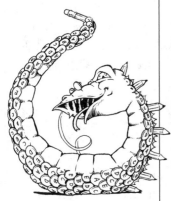

Fancy speed-reading tricks probably won't help much. Psychologists have found that speed-reading tricks really only teach you how to skim a text by skipping details. But for critical reading questions you have to know the details.

In order to improve your comprehension, we recommend that you expand your reading horizons. If your reading matter is presently limited to cereal boxes and the school's bathroom stalls, it's time to explore new possibilities. Caution: *Do not attempt to switch cold turkey!* Many a student has gone into intellectual shock after attempting to jump straight from *Teen Vogue* to *The Plasma Physicist's Quarterly*. We suggest that you work up to quality reading material using this one-week plan:

Day 1: *Outlaw Biker* (This is a real mag!)
Day 2: *WWE Magazine*
Day 3: *The National Enquirer*
Day 4: *Soap Opera Digest*
Day 5: *Seventeen*
Day 6: *People*
Day 7: *Rolling Stone*

If you like to keep up with the news, websites like Politico, The Huffington Post, or even BuzzFeed can help, too.

—Ada

Now you should be ready to tackle the kind of reading you are likely to find on the SAT. Read things like *The New York Times, The Economist, Time, The Atlantic, National Geographic, Sports Illustrated, The New Yorker, Harper's, Scientific American,* and *Forbes.*

Reading these publications is important for many reasons. First of all, you get to impress your friends with all the great vocabulary. ("Dude, evanescence is my MO—one minute I'm here, the next minute I'm gone.") Secondly, you'll do better on your writing section. And lastly, if you can survive an eight-page article on interest rates in the Middle East, you can survive anything the Serpent throws at you.

Of course, if you're feeling ambitious, you might also try reading a book.

Attitude

The reading passages are the one place where you should abandon negative thinking. As impossible as this may sound, it is important to assume a positive attitude toward the critical reading section. Why is this? Well, remember the chapter on oral hygiene in the health textbook you had in sixth grade? No, because it was boring and you didn't *want* to read it. But do you remember the chapter on sex? Yes, because you did want to read it. It's the same way with reading passages. You won't remember them if you have the attitude that they are boring and useless. (They *are* boring and useless, but that's beside the point.) Instead, you must convince yourself that you are dying to read them because you are passionately interested in whatever they are about. Get psyched to read them. Treat them as you would a love letter. Ponder them as you would a passage from a piece of great literature. Cherish them as you would a section of *Up Your Score.*

There is sound psychological backing for this claim. Scientists have shown that comprehension and retention levels are much higher when people are interested in what they are reading than when people aren't. Your brain just doesn't bother remembering stuff that it finds totally dull.

Strategies for the Critical Reading Passages

The following strategies may be useful when taking the test. You probably shouldn't use all of them because that would take a lot of time. The strategies you choose are a matter of personal preference. Try them all and see which ones you like.

Strategy 1

Skim the questions before reading the passage. This gives you an idea of what to look for while you read. Follow the four guidelines below if you use this method.

a. Read only the questions; don't read the answers, too. If the question is about a specific line in the passage, mark that line so that when you read the passage you will know to focus on the marked lines. (This is especially helpful for the vocabulary-in-context questions.)

b. When you see a question that asks for something general, such as "Which is the best title?" or "The main idea of the passage is . . . ," disregard it and go on to the next question. Why? Because you should always assume that there will be at least one question like that, so you don't even have to bother reading it.

c. As you read the passage, circle anything that is an answer to one of the questions. Don't immediately go and answer the question because that will break your concentration and interfere with your comprehension.

d. Make sure that when you read the passage, you don't get so caught up in looking for the answers to the questions that you fail to understand the overall meaning.

Strategy 2

After you read a paragraph, ask yourself, "Self, what was that paragraph about?" Spend two to six seconds summarizing the contents of the paragraph in your head. It helps to look at the paragraph while you are doing this because then you will remember where things are located in the passage. If you want, jot down notes and paraphrases in the margins or underline key phrases. This can save time later when you have to look for the answers. If you are a flake who, like Larry, can read

Ada says: Don't be afraid to write all over the page. They throw everything away at the end, anyway.

an entire passage before realizing that you weren't paying attention and that you have no idea what it was about, then this strategy might be of help in forcing you to concentrate.

Strategy 3

Usually the passage will be composed of a few sentences that state the author's main idea and others that contain facts to support the main idea. As you read the passage, underline any sentence that is purely a statement of the author's main idea. It is guaranteed that there will be at least one question relating to these sentences, and if you underline them, you won't have to waste time looking for them. We highly recommend that you use this strategy.

Strategy 4

While you are reading, underline the main sentence in each paragraph. The sound of your pencil will distract the other test takers, making them lose concentration and improving your score in comparison. And when you are answering the questions, the underlining will automatically draw your attention to the main idea of each paragraph.

Strategy 5

The Princeton Review suggests that if you are having trouble finishing the verbal subsections, you should skip the last (or longest) reading passage. The folks there argue that this passage takes several minutes, and since it's the hardest one, a lot of students get the questions wrong anyway. If you skip it, you will have more time to devote to the rest of the questions that take less time, are easier, and are worth the same number of points.

Strategy 6

Read the passage, then translate the whole thing into Swedish. (This will help only if you are Swedish.)

A few more pointers from Ada:

a. When you begin answering the questions after reading the passage, cover up the answer choices. Spend a few seconds thinking about the answer. Pretend that it is an open-ended question. A lot of the time, the answer you came up with will closely match one of the answer choices. Bingo.

    b. Lean toward the politically correct. Never pick an answer that seems too extreme. The ETS tries to be as politically correct and posh as possible.

    c. Don't be scared of searching for answers. The answer—or, at least, clues to it—is always in the passage, just sitting there, waiting for you to find it.

The Reading Passages

You can expect to see four long reading passages of between 450 and 850 words on the SAT. (There are actually five long passages because one is double—more on that later.) There will be 5 to 13 questions associated with each of the long passages. Each short reading passage of approximately 100 words will have two or three associated questions. There is always a passage on something scientific and a passage that is an excerpt from a narrative, which could be fiction or nonfiction. The other passage topics may include something historical, something about an art form, or something about a minority group.

This is why reading magazines is such good prep!
    —Ada

Each passage has a short introduction in italics. Read it carefully. It will help you understand the passage, and often it will define words or identify names that you need to know.

The Scientific Passage

Do not be intimidated by scientific jargon. The scientific passage will inevitably have some far-out scientific terms that you have never heard of. Don't worry. *You don't need to know scientific terms.* Either the terms will be totally irrelevant or they will be explained in the passage. Take for example the following excerpt from an actual SAT:

> ". . . Kinematic studies of such objects show them to be receding from us at a rate proportional to their distance . . ."

Some students might panic when reading this sentence because of the word *kinematic*. However, there is no need to panic. You don't have to know what *kinematic studies* are to answer the questions correctly.

The second reason this sentence could be intimidating is that it refers to proportions. Proportions are math, and math is scary. Once again, there is no need to worry. If you read the sentence that follows the difficult sentence, you'll see that it explains the math, so you don't have to do any thinking:

> "That is, those galaxies most distant from us
> have larger recessional velocities."

(You don't have to know what a *recessional velocity* is, either.) The expression "that is . . ." clues us in to the fact that this sentence is going to explain the previous sentence. You will frequently find this sort of thing in the scientific passages. If you don't understand a sentence, look at the sentences that precede and follow it. Chances are, one of them explains whatever it is you don't understand. Whatever you do, don't be daunted by the ETS!

The Historical Passage

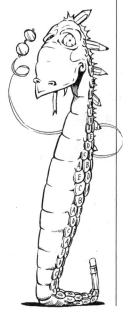

The historical passage will discuss a particular trend or period in history. The author will be making her own interpretation of that trend or period. She will support her interpretation with examples. When the author starts listing examples, read the first example, then skip the rest of the examples and write "EX" (for "example") in the margin near the list of examples. In many cases, the author will also support her interpretation by referring to other historians who agree with her. In other cases, she will refer to other historians who disagree with her so that she can refute their interpretation. Circle the names of historians the author refers to and decide whether they agree or disagree—there will probably be a question about them.

The Art Passage

The art passage will be about an art—literature, painting, sculpture, crafts, music, etc.—or a particular artist—musician, craftsman, writer, etc. In *all* the examples we looked at, the author had a positive attitude toward the artist or art form. The author might have some specific criticisms, but the overall point of the passage will be complimentary. The author will never say, "Beethoven sucks." (This rule does not apply to the double passage.)

The author will never say, "Beethoven sucks."

The Fiction Passage

The literature passage will be an excerpt from a piece of literary fiction. It is hard to predict what the passage will be like. Don't skim it too quickly. You have to read carefully to pick up the subtleties. However, when you start to answer the questions, do not read too deeply. You might have to interpret the figurative meanings of parts of the passage, but don't try to be profound and read things into the passage that aren't there. Also, make sure that you pay attention to the author's style and tone. There will almost certainly be a question about that. Practice in English class—teachers love it when you ask questions about style and tone (and remember, your grades count toward college, too).

The Minority Passage

The ETS has been accused of being biased against minorities. In the 1970s, the ETS decided to respond to these accusations by putting a reading passage about minorities in each SAT. This was a pointless politically correct gesture on their part because it didn't make the SAT any less culturally biased. (For more on the SAT and bias, see page 311.)

As far as we're concerned, the minority passage makes the SAT easier for everyone—minorities and majorities. This is because the passage is incredibly predictable. You know that the ETS is going to say good things about the minority group. That's the whole point of the passage. Therefore, many of the questions are giveaways, for example this one from a real SAT:

The author's attitude toward the Chinese achievements mentioned in lines 1–45 is best described as one of
(A) disbelief   (B) admiration
(C) anxiety   (D) ambivalence
(E) apathy

The only one of these choices that expresses a clearly positive attitude toward the Chinese is (B). Of course, (B) is the right answer.

The Double Passage
The double passage consists of two separate passages that, according to the ETS, "oppose, support, or in some way complement" each other.

The section is set up like this: an introduction, the first passage, the second passage, questions on the first passage, questions on the second passage, questions on both passages. **Don't do it in this order.** Here is our suggestion for the best order:

1. Read introduction.
2. Read *first* passage.
3. Do *first* passage questions.
4. Read *second* passage.
5. Do *second* passage questions.
6. Do *both* passage questions.

Our reasoning is that the questions on the first passage will have nothing to do with the second passage. Therefore, it makes more sense to do the first passage questions immediately after reading the first passage. Same for the second passage. Then, after you have read and answered questions on both passages, you will have such a thorough knowledge that you will ace the questions on both passages.

You should be able to tell easily whether the two passages agree or disagree. Often, the introduction will help by saying that the two passages have "much in common" (in which case they'll probably agree) or "present two views" (in which case they'll probably disagree).

If you're having trouble figuring out the relationship, follow this general rule: If the context and subject matter of the two passages seem different, then their main points will almost certainly be similar, and vice versa. For instance, in some of the double passages we've looked at, a speech from ancient Greece and a speech from the Civil War (two different historical eras and locales) had the same view on war, and an essay on silent film and one on mime (two different art forms) showed the similarities between the two forms. However, another selection had two passages on architecture, both from the twentieth century, and they disagreed. So if the two passages were written in different times or places or if they concern different subjects, they probably agree. If they talk about the same subject and were written in the same time or place, they probably disagree.

The Gigantic Passage

Late one night in an underground ETS laboratory, a critical reading passage was undergoing routine experimentation when it was accidentally exposed to a higher-than-usual dose of uranium 235. The laboratory assistants watched dumbfounded as the passage began to grow larger and larger and more and more grotesque, until it became the

At first the Gigantic Passage looks like an ordinary passage, but then it just keeps droning on and on and on and on—until its victims beg for mercy or fall asleep. Unlike a regular passage, where you can read it, answer the questions, and possibly have a minute or two left at the end to fix your hair, the Gigantic Passage is meant to bore and overwhelm you. While a regular passage is usually between 50 and 80 lines long, the Gigantic Passage can be as long as 110 lines, and there are no commercials to break it up.

Here's how to beat it: When you come to the Gigantic Passage, stand up, stretch, and get your blood pumping. People usually stay seated during the test, but the test directions don't forbid you to stand up and stretch (although you might want to be careful about not looking over anyone's shoulder while you're stretching). Next, take a Gigantic bite of your Sweet and Tasty 800 Bar (see page 319). Then realize that the questions following the Gigantic Passage tend to be in the order that the answers appear in the passage. That is, the answers to the first questions tend to be at the beginning of the passage, the answers to the middle questions tend to be in the middle of the passage, and the answers to the last questions tend to be at the end of the passage. This is usually true of reading questions, but it is almost always true of the Gigantic Passage. So if the answer to question 1 is about line 12 and the answer to question 3 is about line 20, then the answer to question 2 can be found between line 12 and line 20. This usually works even if a question is not asking about a particular line. For example, imagine three consecutive questions:

1. The reference to the "dusty" screen (line 65) most directly emphasizes . . .
2. The author of the passage believes that . . .
3. In line 73, "spirit" most nearly means . . .

Clearly the answer to question 1 is in line 65, and the answer to question 3 is in line 73. While you might think that the answer to question 2 could come from anywhere in the Gigantic Passage, the ETS knows that you don't have enough time to skim through several paragraphs in search of the answer. So there should be something between line 65 and line 73 that clearly supports one of the multiple-choice answers. This method usually works, but just in case, you should do your best to keep the entire passage in mind.

The Six Types of Questions

On "primary purpose" questions, key words like "persuade" or "explain" or "entertain" offer important clues.

Are you getting the pattern? Check the passage!

— Ada

The ETS is not particularly creative in making up the questions for the reading sections. It uses the same basic questions over and over. They fall into six main categories.

Type 1: General (Main Idea)

1. The author is primarily concerned with . . .
2. Which of the following titles best summarizes the passage?
3. The primary purpose of the passage is to . . .

Look at the topic paragraph and concluding paragraph, as well as the first sentence of each of the other paragraphs. It also helps to think of an idea before reading the answers.

Type 2: Explicit (Facts)

1. According to the fourth paragraph, some economists feel that . . .
2. According to the passage, an atom of which of the following substances will split, releasing energy and more neutrons?
3. According to the passage, Margaret asked Mrs. Horn's opinion because she . . .

These are pretty easy if you were paying attention. Plus, you can look back quickly to double-check.

Type 3: Implicit (Inferences, Reading Between the Lines)

1. It can be inferred that the guilds were organized as they were because . . .
2. It can be inferred that each of the following applies to the *perfecti* except . . .
3. With which of the following statements about marketing would the author most likely agree?

Again, think of your own idea first, and see which of the answers most closely resembles your thought. You will be less likely to go for the first of the impostor answers (see page 280) if you already have something in mind. For these implicit questions, the answer choice that is most obvious and merely restates a fact is probably wrong. You must read between the lines and pick the answer that takes the facts given in the passage to the next level and derives an appropriate conclusion from the provided details.

Type 4: Author's Logic

1. What tone does the author take toward the chickens?
2. Which of the following best describes the development of the passage?
3. The author cites specific examples of the work of slave artisans primarily to . . .

Pretend you're the author (but don't spend the time the real author ought to spend regretting ever having written such a boring, useless passage). As you're reading, circle adjectives and strong words that indicate the author's tone. To glean the author's attitude toward the subject, make note of how the author uses diction, sentence syntax, and imagery.

Annotate!
— Ada

Type 5: Vocabulary-in-Context

1. The word "obtrusive" is used in line 12 to mean . . .
2. The phrase "underlying themes" (line 7) refers to the . . .
3. Which of the following best captures the meaning of the word "alliance" in line 32?

Don't give up if you don't know the word; you are supposed to figure it out from the context. Also, be careful—it probably isn't the most common definition of the word.

The SAT is tricky. Always look at the word in context, even if you think you know what it "usually" means.

Treat these vocabulary-in-context questions as you would sentence completion. It might help to plug all the answer choices into the sentence from the passage and see which one best replaces the given word or phrase.

Type 6: Comparison (Only on the Double Passage)

1. Which statement from Passage 1 does not have a parallel idea in Passage 2?

2. How would the author of Passage 1 respond to the idea of the "crazy spoons" in Passage 2?
3. Which statement is best supported by the two passages?

Think back to whether the passages are generally agreeing or disagreeing, and think about how their main ideas relate to each other. Chances are, the specifics follow the general trends.

Note about outside knowledge: Critical reading questions refer to what is "stated or implied in the passage." You aren't supposed to use any outside information. So if the passage is about the history of celery and you happen to be an expert on that subject, you still have to read the passage. However, the passages almost never contradict accepted outside knowledge. You won't ever see a passage that claims that the earth is flat. So never choose an answer that you know is making a false statement. On the other hand, never assume that you know the right answer just because you know that a statement is true. There might be other true statements among the choices that are more applicable to the passage.

A Serious Sample Long Reading Passage

Now it's time to attempt a sample long reading passage. Following the passage are examples of the different types of questions and the answer choices that would accompany them. The passage is an excerpt from a scientific journal about a recent technological breakthrough.

Modern science has brought us many wonderful inventions—the television, the water bed, and "I Can't Believe It's Not Butter!" Many more marvelous technological breakthroughs loom on the horizon. The latest development in the field of applied science is no exception. Today, scientists have invented a process through which deceased family pets can be freeze-dried and saved for millennia.

Every pet owner knows that pets are integral parts of the household. When they have been around for so long and have had such an influence on family members, it's hard to let them go when they pass on. Now, through freeze-drying, Fido or Fluffy can remain a household member forever.

When your pet dies, its lovable body is kept intact. You can keep it on the mantel and take it down to pet it at your leisure—and a dehydrated pet does not require feeding, walking, or litter boxes. It emits much less of an odor than regular dead pets, and it looks much better, too.

The projected uses for freeze-dried pets are numerous. If Spot happens to have died in a crouched pose, he can be placed on your lawn as a security device. Snookums can be used as a decorative centerpiece. Market analysts predict a boom in gerbil paperweights, goldfish refrigerator magnets, and poodle hood ornaments. They could even become collectors' items: You could trade them like baseball cards.

Detractors claim, however, that the dehydration wears off after several years, as moisture from the air enters the animal corpse and causes decomposition. This, it is feared, would attract bacteria into the home. Another flaw in the freeze-drying process is that the pet becomes brittle and breaks easily. For a young child, finding Fluffy shattered on the living room floor could be extremely traumatic. Finally, it is feared that people who dislike their pets will have them freeze-dried before they actually die.

Although there are problems with the procedure, the concept of freeze-dried pets is a valuable one. If the method is perfected, it will allow a pet to remain an everyday part of the lives of its loved ones and, indeed, it will permit pets to be passed from generation to generation as family heirlooms.

If Spot happens to have died in a crouched pose, he can be placed on your lawn and used as a security device.

If seeing freeze-dried Fluffy wasn't creepy already...

—Ada

1. This passage is primarily
   (A) a scientific description of the freeze-drying process
   (B) an essay on the religious and moral questions associated with the freeze-drying process
   (C) a general discussion intended to acquaint the reader with the subject of freeze-drying pets
   (D) an expression of someone's opinion
   (E) an advertisement pushing the freeze-drying process
   (Hint: Type 1, General)

Key phrase alert!

—Ada

2. The first paragraph is best described as
    (A) descriptive
    (B) introductory
    (C) irrelevant
    (D) sophomoric
    (E) existential
    (Hint: Type 4, Author's Logic / Type 1, General)

3. The word "detractors" in the fifth paragraph most nearly means
    (A) farm implements
    (B) critics
    (C) supporters
    (D) pet owners
    (E) scientific experts
    (Hint: Type 5, Vocabulary-in-Context)

4. According to the passage, one of the most specific problems associated with the process is
    (A) a freeze-dried pet attracts viruses
    (B) cost is high
    (C) the lack of qualified individuals to perform the task
    (D) freeze-dried pets are not shatterproof
    (E) the fear that freeze-dried pets will stick to the wallpaper
    (Hint: Type 2, Explicit)

5. The author seems to believe that
    (A) freeze-drying is a worthless process when applied to animals
    (B) the difficulties of freeze-drying outweigh the benefits
    (C) it would be easier to freeze-dry an armadillo than a pinecone
    (D) if you give a man a fish, he'll eat for a day; if you give a man two fishes, he'll eat for two days
    (E) the goals of freeze-drying are worth striving for
    (Hint: Type 4, Author's Logic)

Answers: 1. (C) 2. (B) 3. (B) 4. (D) 5. (E)

Now you have an idea of what the critical reading passages are all about. However, most passages won't be that interesting, that short, or that easy. (We couldn't help it; we're also interesting, short, and easy.) For practice, do the reading passages in *The Official SAT Study Guide*. The SAT booklets available at your high school guidance office will also have some reading passages.

The Short Reading Passages

Just because they're short doesn't mean that they're easier! Don't let the ETS catch you off guard.

These passages will show up on the new SAT in place of the long-gone analogies. To tell you the truth, it's a good trade. Instead of memorizing tons of vocabulary, most of which is so specific you will never *ever* use it again in your life (you still have to memorize vocabulary, by the way, but there will be fewer direct questions about it), you get short, perky little passages with two or three questions after them.

The topics and strategies for tackling the short passages are essentially the same as those for the long passages. But these are friendlier than the long passages. For one thing, if it is talking about the growth cycle of celery, at least it's only going to be five lines long. It's really hard to make someone fall asleep during a 100-word passage (although we suspect that the Evil Testing Serpent is going to try).

Here's an example of a short passage:

Don't worry, this book will help you avoid this cruel fate.
—Ada

Among young college students, a trend is emerging. Today, more than ever, these hardworking people are being saddled with skyrocketing tuition, book fees, and boarding costs. So it is not surprising that many of them are taking desperate measures in order to pay the bills. There have been reports of 19-year-olds selling their souls on eBay, blackmailing their siblings with grainy photos of tattoos that Mom and Dad don't know about, and hunting for change on the ground under roller coasters. And, in a show of extreme anguish, some of these young people have even looked for work.

1. In line 4, the word "measures" is used to mean
   (A) events
   (B) quantities
   (C) actions
   (D) calculations
   (E) weights
   (Hint: Type 5, Vocabulary-in-Context)

2. According to the passage, the desperation many
   students feel is the result of
   (A) the impossibility of staying in college
   (B) the ever-increasing bills they have to pay
   (C) the poor relationships they are fostering
      with their brothers and sisters
   (D) the necessity of taking jobs
   (E) seeing that their souls are worth only
      $4.28 on eBay
   (Hint: Type 2, Explicit)

Answers: 1. (C) 2. (B)

See? It wasn't that difficult at all. Again, not every SAT passage is going to be this exciting, but not every SAT passage is written by brilliant and resourceful teenagers.

ABOUT SAT WORDS

Learning the Words You Need to Rock the Verbal Section

hypogyrrationalrhombocuboids
diffeomorphism
supermartingale
myelomeningocele
dacryocystorhinoscopy
floccinaucinihilipilification

Y ou probably don't know what any of the above words mean. You probably don't care what they mean. Once you have finished this book, you still won't know what they mean.

These words may be interesting and useful. But who cares? They were put here simply to intimidate you. They will not be on the SAT. This is because the SAT tests you on the type of words that a college student would be likely to run into. A college student who ran into any of these words would suffer a concussion.

There is a certain type of word that just *is* an SAT word. It is impossible to define precisely what makes a word an SAT word, but by the time you have finished our word lists you will know what we mean. For the most part, they are words that you look at and say, "Man, I should know what that word means, but I don't. It's right here on the tip of my tongue but I can't quite . . ." Another characteristic of an SAT word is that it isn't particularly controversial. It won't have much to do with sex or violence or religion or anything that could offend someone. In all probability, you know more "offensive" words than the ETS does.

Type 1: Almost-Normal Words

Words that you would encounter in the course of doing your homework, listening to articulate people, or watching TV.

Example: If you saw the movie *The Wizard of Oz*, you heard the word *pusillanimous*. However, you probably didn't whip out your pocket dictionary and look it up. (If you did, consider a career with the ETS.) Now that you are in training for the SAT, you will have to start looking up any and all words you encounter. Start now. Do you know what *amalgam* means?

Type 2: Decodable Words

Unusual words that they don't expect you to know offhand but that you can figure out if you are clever.

Example: The word *decodable* is a *decodable* word. You could decode it like this:

"de" = take out; reverse
"code" = words or symbols with secret meanings
+ "able" = capable of being
_____

decodable = capable of being taken out of its secret meaning

Circle and look up every word that you are not 100 percent sure about on practice tests. You want to be positive on the big day.

Don't complain too much—20 years ago you would have had to use a real, printed dictionary.

—Ada

Here's a list of prefixes that are handy to know.

Prefix	Meaning	Example
a	without	amoral
ante	before	antecedent
anti	against	antibody
auto	self	autobiography
bene	good	beneficial
bi	two	bicycle
circum	around	circumnavigate
contra	against	contradict
di	two	dichotomy
dict	speak	diction
dis	apart	disparity
homo	same	homogeneous
hyper	above	hyperactive
hypo	below	hypothermia
inter	between	interstate
mal	bad	malevolent
micro	small	microscope
mis	wrong	mispronounce
multi	many	multiple
neo	new	neophyte
poly	many	polytheism
pro	for	protagonist
re	again	redo
retro	back	retroactive
sanct	holy	sanctify

MEMORIZING SAT WORDS

Larry's Memoirs

When I started studying for the SAT, I had a feeble memory. I would spend a lot of time on the word lists, but nothing seemed to sink in. My feeble memory also affected other aspects of life. One day I met this gorgeous girl and she said, as girls are always saying to me, "I have an unquenchable desire to talk to you. My name is Jenny and my number is 867-5309." I was going to go home and give her a ring, but I couldn't remember her info. I knew then it was time to do something about my memory problem.

So I read some stuff about how to improve my memory. Most of what I read sounded extremely dopey, but I gave it a try anyway. And, as they say in the world of laundry detergent, "It worked! It really worked!"

The moral of my story is that if you have a bad memory, it's not because there is something wrong with your brain, it's just that you haven't learned how to memorize. We will teach you how in this chapter. The techniques we present are more than cute little tricks. They will tremendously improve your ability to remember vocabulary words and may even change your life. You don't have to use them if you don't want to, but if you don't use them, it will take you much, much longer to learn the words.

The most important concept in memorizing things like vocabulary words is the mnemonic ("nuh-mahn-eck") device. A mnemonic device is any technique, other than pure repetition, that helps you memorize something. So for each word in the list that you don't know, close your eyes for 12 seconds and think of a mnemonic device.

Research has demonstrated that the most successful mnemonic devices are visual. If you can associate a word with a picture, you will be more likely to remember the word. For example, if you are trying to memorize the word *opulence* (luxury, great wealth), you could visualize a giant mansion surrounded by manicured lawns and lavish gardens. Above the gold-leaf front door, the word *opulence* would be spelled out in precious gems. Within, you might imagine well-groomed fat gentlemen, the word *opulence* stitched in diamonds across their chests, eating huge amounts of caviar molded into the shape of the word *opulence*. If you make your mental pictures extreme in some way,

they will be more memorable. So make your pictures extremely bizarre, extremely gross, extremely obscene, extremely comical, or extremely whatever you are likely to remember. (Detail is important in mental images like this one. The more details you are able to dream up, the more likely you are to remember the word.)

Move on to the other senses. *Hear* the chorus of castrati in the ballroom singing the word *opulence* over the gentle strains of Chopin played by an 80-piece symphony. *Feel* the silks the ladies and gentlemen wear sliding through your fingers as you trace the word *opulence* with champagne over your desktop. *Smell* the delicate and costly perfumes. And, of course, *taste* the exquisitely fine wines enjoyed by *opulent* society.

After you have seen, heard, felt, smelled, and tasted the word, you can open your eyes. You're still not done, though. Research has also shown that the more you do with a word, the more likely it will stay in your brain. So first read the word and its definition, then write the word and its definition, then sing the word and its definition, then make up a story about the word, then use the word in a conversation, then tattoo the word and its definition on your elbow, then staple the word and its definition to your goldfish.

Clinical tests have also proven that the pun is a very helpful memory technique. We have used puns to illustrate many of the words in the vocabulary list. (Note: Since we want to make sure that no one misses our subtlety, we have <u>pun</u>derlined each one.)

If none of these techniques works, there is one foolproof method. Neurologists say that if the word and its definition are repeated over and over during sexual activity, they will never be forgotten. There is no scientific explanation for this, but it is a widely accepted fact. Of course, we wouldn't know.

Another phenomenon you should be aware of is the *serial position effect.* Suppose you have a long list of words to memorize and you spend the same amount of time studying each word. According to the serial position effect, you will remember the words at the beginning of the list best, the words at the end of the list next best, and the middle words the worst. Therefore, spend the most time on the middle of the list.

Your chances of memorizing something improve if you

Research has shown that the more you do with a word, the more likely it will stay in your brain. So read, write, sing, and say the word and its definition. Tattoo it onto your elbow and staple it onto your goldfish.

We're obvious.
Accept it.
  —Ada

study it right before you go to bed. While you sleep, your brain sorts out what occurred during the day. The last thought that goes into your brain right before you go to sleep gets special attention while your brain is doing its nightly sorting.

Finally, nobody studies better with music. Experiments have been done with people who swear that they study better with Rihanna playing in the background. But chances are this will only lead to you daydreaming about her umbrella.

Two Essential Tools: Flash Cards and an Audio Recorder

Need an audio recorder? Browse the "tools" on your phone or computer.
—Ada

You must keep flash cards and an audio recorder by your side while you study. When you come to a word you don't know, look it up and devote 12 seconds to thinking up a mnemonic device, be it a sentence, a quick drawing, or a bit of song lyric—whatever works for you. Then write the word on one side of a 3" × 5" card and its definition and your mnemonic device on the other.

Carry your flash cards with you everywhere. Study them during the ride to school, while you wait at the dentist's office, and during particularly boring classes. Every night before you go to sleep, test yourself on your words. Put the cards you know in one pile and the ones you don't know in another pile. Every night you should be able to add five cards to the pile of cards you know.

Do a similar thing with the recorder. When you come to a word that you want to remember, record the word, its definition, and either the example sentence that we give you or one that you make up. Then you can listen to the recording while you are in the shower or brushing your teeth. If you can rap or sing some of your words and definitions, it's more fun to listen to. If your friends ask you what you're listening to, respond casually, "It's Gretchen and the Vocab Lists—they're new out of Seattle." If your friends ask to listen, say, "The record company asked me not to play it for anyone until it's been officially released."

Also, you may want to take a pocket notebook around with you to write down any unfamiliar words you come across. This will not only improve your vocabulary, it will also help your social life tremendously.

Then, after you've aced the SAT, you can sell your recording, flash cards, and notebook to your younger sibling.

THE WORD LIST

Don't be intimidated; there are only about 600 words here, and you probably know some of them already.

This is not a complete list of SAT words, but some of these *will* be on the test you take. Also, some of the words on this list could appear in another form. You therefore should learn to recognize various forms of a word, like *refute* and *refutation*. The sentences and illustrations that follow the definitions are examples of the memorization techniques we described. Enjoy, and may you be blessed by the almighty vocabulary god until you get to "zyzzyva."

A

aardvark

Aardvark is the first real word in the dictionary, so we figured that we should start with it even though it has never been and probably never will be on the SAT.

abase

lower; humiliate
"I will not <u>abase</u> myself by admitting that I don't even have <u>a basic</u> knowledge of vocabulary," said Paul.

abash

to embarrass
Arthur was <u>abashed</u> at <u>a bash</u> when he ate too much and tossed his cookies into the trash.

abate

to lessen
Abigail's sister screamed, "<u>Ab ate</u> all the cookies!" Later, of course, her anger <u>abated</u>.

abominate

to loathe; hate
The terrorist <u>abominated</u> his enemy Nate so much that he put <u>a bomb in Nate's</u> boxer shorts.

abstruse

profound; difficult to understand
When Abraham Lincoln wrote a confusing peace agreement to end the Civil War, people commented that <u>Abe's truce</u> was <u>abstruse</u>.

accentuate
to stress; emphasize
An <u>accent</u> mark <u>accentuates</u> a syllable.
While in New York, it was rude of you to <u>accentuate</u> the fact that Brooklyn people speak with an <u>accent you hate</u>.

acclivity
sharp incline of a hill
<u>A cliff</u> is an example of an <u>acclivity</u>.

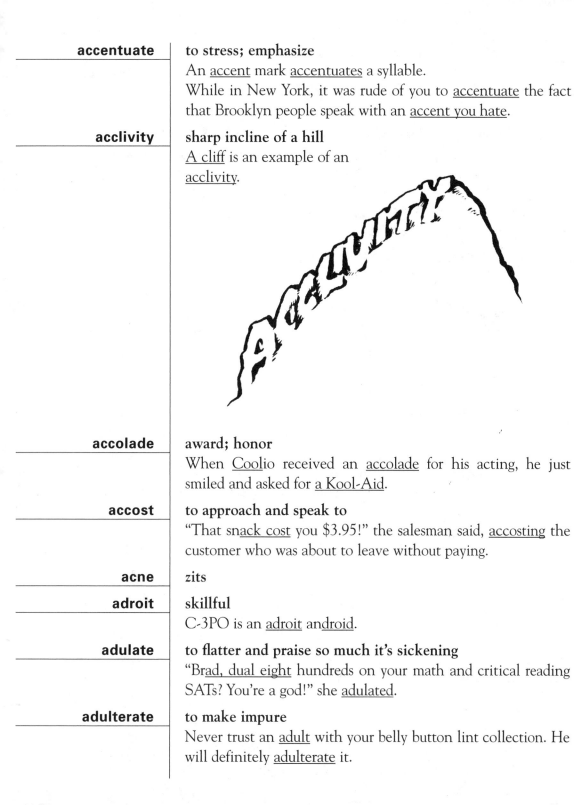

accolade
award; honor
When <u>Coolio</u> received an <u>accolade</u> for his acting, he just smiled and asked for <u>a Kool-Aid</u>.

accost
to approach and speak to
"That sn<u>ack cost</u> you $3.95!" the salesman said, <u>accosting</u> the customer who was about to leave without paying.

acne
zits

adroit
skillful
C-3PO is an <u>adroit</u> an<u>droid</u>.

adulate
to flatter and praise so much it's sickening
"B<u>rad, dual eight</u> hundreds on your math and critical reading SATs? You're a god!" she <u>adulated</u>.

adulterate
to make impure
Never trust an <u>adult</u> with your belly button lint collection. He will definitely <u>adulterate</u> it.

adumbrate | to foreshadow by disclosing only partially
The economic indicators <u>adumbrated</u> that the price of gas would rise to <u>a dumb rate</u>.

adverse | hostile; opposed; unfavorable (see AVERSE)
"It's tough writing a national anthem during a British attack," complained Francis Scott Key. "The only light you have is the rockets' red glare. You have to <u>add verses</u> under <u>adverse</u> conditions."

advocate | to urge; recommend
<u>Ad</u>vertisements <u>advocate</u> products.

aesthetic | artistic; pertaining to a sense of what is beautiful
<u>As the tick</u> was sucking blood from my arm I squashed it. The dead insect smeared on my arm was not <u>aesthetic</u>ally pleasing.

affected | fake (think: a-FAKE-ted)
His <u>affected</u> personality negatively <u>affected</u> our <u>affect</u>ion.

affinity | attraction
There was a natural <u>affinity</u> between him and his new <u>Infiniti</u>.

affluent | rich
<u>A flu went</u> around the <u>affluent</u> passengers of the yacht; their diamond tiaras and Rolexes sparkled when they sneezed.

affray | public brawl
The frog was <u>afraid</u> to enter the <u>affray</u>.

agape | open-mouthed
If you stand <u>agape</u>, there is <u>a gap</u> in your mouth.

aghast | horrified
We were <u>aghast</u> when he "passed <u>gas</u>." (See EUPHEMISM. *Passed gas* is an example of a euphemism.)

agile	able to move in a quick and easy fashion <u>Age'll</u> make you less <u>agile</u>.
alacrity	cheerful promptness The empty auditorium was the result of <u>a lack</u> of <u>alacrity</u> among the sleep-deprived students.
alias	a false name "Your real name was <u>all I a</u>sked for; why did you give me an <u>alias</u>?" the reporter said to Jennifer Garner.
alimentary	supplying nourishment When Watson asked, "What's a ten-letter word meaning 'supplying nourishment'?" Sherlock replied, "<u>Alimentary</u>, my dear Watson."
allay	to soothe; to make more bearable (see ALLEVIATE) *Note:* This is one of a countless number of SAT words with this meaning. He <u>allayed</u> his parents' fears by getting <u>all As</u> on his report card.
alleged	stated without proof It was <u>alleged</u> that he died by falling off <u>a ledge</u>.
alleviate	to make more bearable (see APPEASE) *Note:* think of Aleve, the pain med. <u>A leaf he ate</u> failed to <u>alleviate</u> his hunger.
allude **allusion**	to refer indirectly a reference to something <u>A lewd</u> person <u>alludes</u> to salacious behavior (see SALACIOUS).
altercation	a violent dispute An <u>altercation</u> broke out when, at the <u>altar, Kate</u> said to her groom, "I don't."

amass	to collect; to get a bunch of By publishing this book, we hope to <u>amass</u> <u>a mass</u> of perfect scores for our readers.
ambulatory	able to walk After he was run over by the <u>ambul</u>ance, he was no longer <u>ambulatory</u>.
ameliorate	to improve a bad situation <u>Amelia rated</u> her social life as having been <u>ameliorated</u> since last year.
amity	peaceful relations; friendship *Note:* The root "ami-" means "friend," as in "amiable." There was <u>amity</u> between the students at <u>M.I.T.</u> and their math professors.
amnesia	loss of memory We forgot our sentence for this word because we have <u>amnesia</u>. (See, after this long wild night of vicious partying, combined with excessive exposure to the sun, we became so fried that we lost our ability to recall things and to function normally in society, and . . . what word are we on?)
amok	freaked out and violently pissed off The sch<u>muck</u> in the <u>muck</u> got st<u>uck</u>, ran <u>amok</u>, and guess what word he screamed? (Answer: Sh<u>ucks</u>.)
amorphous	shapeless *Note:* This word is decodable if you know all the pieces: "a" = not (see ATYPICAL) "morph" = shape, form + "ous" = having the qualities of amorphous = not having the qualities of shape If you take too much <u>morph</u>ine, you'll feel like an <u>amorphous</u> blob.

anthropoid	humanlike *Note:* The root "anthropo-" means "human." C-3PO is an anthropoid dr<u>oid</u>. SAT proctors try to appear as <u>anthropoid</u> as possible, but we know better.

antipathy	**hatred; aversion; dislike**
	Note: This word is also decodable:
	   "anti" = against
	  + "pathy" = feeling
	  ―――――――――――――――
	   antipathy = feeling against
	By this time you should be developing a strong <u>antipathy</u> to studying these words and their ridiculous definitions. Take a break. Put the book down, get a soda, or drink a bottle of vitamin-enhanced water. Then return to your work refreshed and ready to continue.

apathetic
 	
apathy
	indifferent; showing lack of interest
	indifference; lack of interest
	Note: Another decodable word:
	   "a"= not
	  + "pathy" = feeling
	  ―――――――――――――――
	   apathy = not feeling
	It's <u>a pathetic</u> thing to be <u>apathetic</u>.
	"They found the cure for <u>apathy</u>, but no one showed any interest in it."—George Carlin

apex	**tip; peak; summit; way up there** *Note:* This word is likely to be found in the analogy section. Its opposites are words such as *nadir* and *bottom.* The <u>ape ex</u>ercised by jumping off the <u>apex</u> of the monkey house in the zoo.
appease	**to soothe; placate (think: apeace; see ASSUAGE)** He <u>appeased</u> his parents by eating <u>a piece</u> of slimy okra.
fishhead	**the head of a fish** Just checking to see if you're still awake.
arbitrary	**chosen at random or without apparent reason** If a college rejects you, its admissions process must be <u>arbitrary</u>.

ardor	heat; passion; zeal With <u>ardor</u> my prom date shouted, "Come in! And if you have to, break down <u>our door</u>."
askew	crooked; off to one side Don't tell us our type is a^{sk}ew. Did we <u>ask you</u>?
assuage	to ease; pacify (see APPEASE) Buying <u>a suede</u> fringed jacket might <u>assuage</u> Donna's compulsive desire to shop.
astute	shrewd; wise; observing <u>A stud</u>ent must be <u>astute</u> to outwit the Evil Testing Serpent.
attribute	**(n.) a characteristic, usually a good one** **(v.) to explain by indicating a cause** In her article on Pamela Anderson, the mean-spirited reporter <u>attributed</u> the actress's most prominent <u>attribute</u> to plastic surgery.
atypical	not typical *Note:* The prefix "a-" usually means "not." For example, amoral means "not moral," asexual means "not sexual," apolitical means "not into politics," and, as we have seen, amorphous means "not shaped." Lady Gaga's face, voice, clothing, and habits are <u>atypical</u> for an earthling.
audacity	boldness Their <u>audacity</u> was evident when they published their <u>odd SAT</u> book.

Who's that running away with *Ardor*?

Ardor

august | majestic; awe-inspiring
When Cleopatra saw <u>Augus</u>tus in all his finery, she said, "<u>Aw, Gus</u>, you look <u>august</u>."

austerity | severity; strictness
His <u>austerity</u> is actually a rarity; sev<u>erity</u> is not his specialty.

averse | opposed; unwilling
I was <u>averse</u> to writing <u>a verse</u>
So at the teacher I did curse
And put mounds of coleslaw in her purse.
My verse started well but then got worse
As I ran out of things that rhymed with -erse.
Note: <u>Averse</u> is a lot like <u>adverse</u>. It probably wouldn't matter if you got the two confused on the SAT, but for the record, you use <u>averse</u> when you want to say that a person or thing is opposed to something else. For example: Eggbert was <u>averse</u> to eating Frisbees. (Note that *to* usually follows <u>averse</u>.)

<u>Adverse</u>, on the other hand, is used when you want to say that something else is opposed to a person or thing. For example: Eggbert received <u>adverse</u> criticism for not eating Frisbees; Eggbert had to eat the Frisbee under <u>adverse</u> conditions.

In the first example Eggbert is <u>averse</u> to eating, whereas in the second and third examples the criticism and the conditions are <u>adverse</u> to Eggbert.

avuncular | a funky word meaning "like an uncle"
This word does not deserve a sentence because only your <u>avuncular</u> <u>Uncle</u> Herbert would ever use it.

awry | twisted; crooked; out of whack; askew; wrong
"Waiter, there is something <u>awry</u> in my bread," she complained. "That thing?" he replied. "Why, that's just <u>a rye</u> seed."

It is helpful to make up a story using as many of the vocabulary words as possible from the list you have just learned. We have written some sample stories, but you should write your own, too. Here is the first one.

An Adventurous Aardvark

The <u>audacious</u> <u>aardvark</u> was rooting around in the grass for some lunch with which to <u>assuage</u> his hunger when his <u>adroit</u> friend Bob the baboon waddled up with <u>alacrity</u> and <u>accosted</u> him. "Hey man," Bob said, beginning an <u>altercation</u>. "Why do you <u>abase</u> yourself in that <u>atypical</u> way? I <u>advocate</u> the <u>agile</u> use of a knife and fork."

"You are a moron," the <u>aardvark</u> replied politely. "It would be more <u>aesthetically</u> pleasing were I to eat that way, but the use of utensils would be too <u>affected</u> for a simple <u>aardvark</u>. In addition, I am <u>averse</u> to such an idea because it might <u>alleviate</u> my <u>acne</u>, which looks good on me."

"That has to be the <u>apex</u> of stupidity," Bob said, <u>aghast</u>. "And while we're on the subject of your appearance, I must ask why you are so <u>apathetic</u> about your hygiene. At least you could <u>ameliorate</u> your looks and odor by taking a bath."

"Never <u>allude</u> to my <u>alleged</u> <u>antipathy</u> to cleanliness again," the <u>aardvark</u> said with <u>austerity</u>. "May I remind you that even with your nearly <u>anthropoid</u> form, you still pick lice out of strangers' hair."

Sensing that the conversation had gone <u>awry</u> and feeling <u>abashed</u>, Bob's <u>audacity</u> <u>abated</u> and he too began to <u>amass</u> a pile of grubs from the grass.

Note: The characters in this story are entirely fictitious. Any resemblance to real people, alive or dead, is entirely coincidental.

Say "hello"
to assonance!

—Ada

B

bacchanalian	orgiastic; like wild drunken revelry

Bacchus was the Roman god of wine, and the Bacchanalia was the festival devoted to him.

He gave a <u>bacchanalian</u> party to welcome <u>back an alien</u>.

baleful **baneful**	*Note:* These words are similar in meaning but not entirely synonymous. Baleful refers to something that exerts an evil influence or foreshadows evil. Baneful refers to something that really is poisonous or deadly. (To remember this: Baneful rhymes with painful—which deadly things tend to be.) We could see from the proctor's baleful look that he was going to do something baneful to us.
barrister	lawyer What do barristers and sperm have in common? Both have a one in a million chance of turning out human. (Sorry, but we had to have a lawyer joke in here somewhere. Please don't sue us.)
bawdy	obscene; coarse; humorous (see LEWD) Many bawdy jokes have to do with certain parts of the body.
beatific	displaying or imparting joy "Be terrific," said the Hare Krishna with a beatific smile.
begrudge	to envy, to resent To be holding a grudge for so long against me means that you must begrudge my happy life.
beguile	trick "The [Evil Testing] Serpent beguiled me and I did eat the apple." (Genesis 3:13)
belated	delayed; late We sent a belated birthday present and in return got a month-old piece of ice-cream cake.
bellicose	violent; warlike You'll know you're sitting next to a bellicose person if during the test his sharpened number 2 pencil into your belly goes.

benevolent

kind

Superman may be the <u>benevolent</u> protector of the world, but have you ever noticed that he wears his underpants outside his tights?

berate

to scold severely

If you don't get into college, your parents will <u>berate</u> you. If you don't do A work, your teachers will <u>berate</u> (<u>B-rate</u>) you.

bereft

lacking something needed

He felt sad and <u>bereft</u> just thinking about how she didn't love him; now he would <u>be left</u> without her.

BEREFT

betroth

to become engaged

She discovered that he wasn't wearing a tuxedo—she really was <u>betrothed</u> to a penguin.

biennial

every two years

Note: This word is decodable:

"bi" = two

+ "ennial" = annual

biennial = two years

My social life has been reduced to <u>biennial</u> parties.

bland

not stimulating; dull

Note: Remember, <u>bland</u> starts with <u>bla</u>.

I found the movie about the politics of cauliflower rather <u>bland</u>.

blandishment

flattery

The sycophants obsequiously lavished me with <u>blandishments</u>. (Yes, you should look up each of these words.)

blighted	ruined; destroyed; withered When much of California was <u>blighted</u> by fires, the former governor tried to drown his feelings of hopelessness in <u>Bud Light</u>.
boisterous	rowdy We have male cheerleaders at our school. When they get in front of the crowd, those <u>boys stir us</u> up until we're <u>boisterous</u>.
bombastic	**grandiloquent (wordy, pompous) in speech or writing** At the end of his long, boring, <u>bombastic</u> speech, the self-satisfied tyrant received a <u>bomb basket</u> as a farewell gift.
braggadocio	cockiness; a braggart <u>Braggadocios</u> tend to do a lot of empty <u>bragging</u>.
brevity	briefness When Janet had a 20-page paper due, but wanted to go out, her friends suggested, "You can write your paper with great <u>brevity</u> and <u>brave a D</u>."
brusque	**brief; curt; gruff; discourteous** The people who take tickets at the movies are always <u>brusque</u>, as though they're not genuinely interested in every single person who walks by them.
bucolic	**pastoral; typical of farms and rural life** The scene was <u>bucolic</u> So we started to fr<u>olic</u> In our feet so bare, Whoops! The cow chips were there!

bumptious	self-assertive The <u>bumptious</u> people <u>bumped us</u> out of line, so we gave them all fierce head-butts.
burgeon	to grow; sprout; flourish Madonna's career <u>burgeoned</u> as soon as she changed the title of her unsuccessful song "Like a <u>Burgeon</u>."
burnish	to polish One of the housekeeper's jobs was <u>burnishing</u> the furnishings.

It's story time again, boys and girls:

A Bolivian Bacchanal

With a <u>bawdy</u> exclamation, the burly buccaneers brutishly threw us out of the helicopter <u>bereft</u> of any parachute, and the <u>brevity</u> of our flight and <u>brusqueness</u> of our landing were not the <u>bucolic</u> experiences described in our blonde travel agent's <u>bland</u> brochure.

We found ourselves in a jungle with all sorts of <u>baneful</u> beasties crawling around our feet and <u>baleful</u> animal noises echoing around us.

"Yo," said my <u>bumptious</u> companion with <u>braggadocio</u>, as he <u>burnished</u> his machete. "What say we bust our way out of this place?"

But before I could respond, we were captured by a <u>bellicose</u> and <u>boisterous</u> tribe of natives about to perform its <u>belated</u> <u>biennial</u> human sacrifice to the fish goddess. We called a <u>barrister</u>, who offered <u>beatific</u> <u>blandishments</u>. But in order to save our skins we both had to be <u>betrothed</u> to the chief's daughter Brunnehilde.

"Yo," said my companion. "This is a bit of a bummer. I should <u>berate</u> you for <u>bombastically</u> <u>beguiling</u> me into going on this <u>blighted</u> vacation."

Then the axe fell and the <u>bacchanalian</u> rituals honoring the <u>benevolent</u> fish goddess began.

C

cache	hiding place (pronounced "cash") The thieves <u>stashed</u> the <u>cash</u> in the <u>cache</u>.
cacophonous	sounding discordant; terrible and generally unpleasant to listen to; the opposite of euphonious As Dracula arose from his <u>coffin</u>, the werewolves let out a <u>cacophonous</u> wail.
cadaver	corpse The medical students named their <u>cadaver</u> Ernie so that they could be "working in dead Ernest."
cajole	to coax "Yes, you <u>can, Joel</u>," they <u>cajoled</u> him. "You can become a professional thumb whistler if you set your mind to it."
callous	unfeeling; unsympathetic Brian complained of the <u>callus</u> on his big toe, but Meg remained <u>callous</u>. If you don't like that sentence, don't <u>call us</u>, we're <u>callous</u>.
calumniate	to slander *Note:* This is one of a bunch of SAT words with this meaning—see page 155.
calumny	slander; defamation It was <u>calumny</u> when I wrote in a <u>column</u> in *The New York Times* that you enjoy poisoning Arctic wombats. I hated you, so I <u>calumniated</u> you.
candor	frankness; candidness "Speaking with complete <u>candor</u>, Hansel," said the wicked witch, "I have chopped Gretel up and <u>canned her</u>."

cantankerous | ill-natured; quarrelsome
"Bloody screaming sea dogs, I can't anchor us!" the cantankerous captain cried.

capacious | spacious
I wonder why they put such   capacious   spaces around this word.

capitulate | to surrender (see RECAPITULATE, which does not mean resurrender)
Olivia Pope never capitulates on *Scandal*.

capricious | unpredictable; following whim
The album charts were capricious; one week Kanye West was on top—but as soon as we had catalogued all the swear words, Taylor Swift took over.

captious | fault-finding
"What?! You're only in the Cs? And your room's still messy, and you haven't cooked us dinner," said the captious review-book authors.

carrion | rotting flesh
The lion tore a hefty chunk of flesh out of the zebra's neck. Later, the jackals came by and pulled more entrails out of the carrion. After the jackals left, the vultures remained to carry on with devouring it.

castigate | to punish
Castration is a severe form of castigation.

cathartic | cleansing; allowing a release of tension or emotion
Manek's method of preparing for the SAT is cathartic (see page 15).

caustic	**burning; characterized by a bitter wit** When she saw the ugly necklace that her boyfriend had bought her, she said to him <u>caustically</u>, "How much did that <u>cost? Ick</u>!" *Note:* Being sar<u>castic</u> and being <u>caustic</u> often go hand in hand, so relate them in your memory via the nonword sar<u>caustic</u>.
cauterize	**to burn tissue (usually because a wound isn't clotting)** When the bleeding <u>caught her eyes</u>, the doctor knew that she would have to <u>cauterize</u> the patient's skin.
cavil	**to raise unnecessary or trivial objections** When I told the vet that I feed my cow Diet Coke, he <u>caviled</u> about how it would make my <u>calf ill</u>.
celerity	**swiftness, speed** When the light turned green, the chauffeur floored the gas pedal with <u>celerity</u> and we suddenly ac<u>celer</u>ated. I nearly spilled my <u>celery tea</u>.
celibacy	**condition of being celibate**
celibate	**without sex; unmarried** The nun declared, "I think being <u>celibate</u> is really something to <u>celebr</u>ate."
censor	**(v.) to remove inappropriate stuff** **(n.) someone who censors things** Fabio <u>sensed her</u> longing and with his rough hands caressed her voluptuous, heaving CENSORED
censure	**to criticize; blame** When someone starts to criticize you, you can <u>sense you're</u> being <u>censured</u>.
cerebration	**thought** The guests at Einstein's birthday <u>celebration</u> were all deep in <u>cerebration</u>.

chagrin	embarrassment <u>She grin</u>ned and blushed with <u>chagrin</u>.
chaos	state of utter confusion "We don't want to cause <u>chaos</u>," we told the customs official. "So just o<u>kay us</u> for passage!"

charlatan	quack; someone who pretends he's someone he's not <u>Charlotte in</u> *Charlotte's Web* was not a <u>charlatan</u>; she really could spell.
chaste	pure; unspoiled; virginal The virgin <u>chased</u> away the men so that she could remain <u>chaste</u>.
chicanery	trickery When I found the sneezing powder in my <u>Chicken</u> McNuggets, I knew you were up to some <u>chicanery</u>.
chimerical	far out; bizarre; really heady *Note:* Think of the mythical creature, the chimera. His dreams were so <u>chimerical</u> that it would ta<u>ke a miracle</u> for them to come true.
choleric	hot-tempered; easily made "hot under the <u>collar</u>" The <u>choleric</u> pit bull did not enjoy it when his owner made him wear the electrified <u>collar</u>.

churlish	boorish; rude Someone who is girlish is probably not <u>churlish</u>.
ciliated	having tiny hairs "Oh Juliet, I love your deep blue eyes." "Oh Romeo, I love the <u>ciliated</u> lining of your nostrils."
circumspect	prudent; cautious *Note:* This is one of those easily decodable words: "circum" = around (as in <u>circ</u>le) "spect" = look (as in in<u>spect</u> and <u>spect</u>acles) circumspect = look around (which suggests being cautious) "<u>Search 'em</u>, in<u>spect</u>or," ordered the <u>circumspect</u> detective.
clemency	mildness of temper—especially leniency toward an enemy or in sentencing a criminal Because Roger <u>Clemens</u> was accused of using steroids, it now remains to be seen if he'll be shown <u>clemency</u> and be voted into the Hall of Fame anyway.

The following three "cog" words all have to do with thinking:

cogent	clear; logical; well-thought-out The two men (<u>co-gents</u>) on the debate team gave a <u>cogent</u> argument.
cogitate	to think about deeply and carefully (see RUMINATE) A good time to <u>cogitate</u> about dairy products is while eating <u>cottage</u> cheese.
cognizant	fully informed and aware; conscious When the factory repairman becomes <u>cognizant</u> that the <u>cog</u> <u>isn't</u> working, he will fix the gear.
comely	attractive; agreeable The more frequently you <u>comb</u> your hair, the more <u>comely</u> you become. Or maybe not.

comestible	food Banana flambé is a <u>comb</u>ustible <u>comestible</u>.
commensurate	equal; proportionate You don't think that this pile of gold is <u>commensurate</u> with that one? Well, <u>come measure it</u>.

commiserate	to sympathize; be miserable together
	Note: Decode:
	   "co" = together
	 + "miserate" = be miserable
	  commiserate = be miserable together
	He <u>commiserated</u> with his friend at Clown College, who also got 200s.

comport	to behave in a particular way *Note:* The root "-port" means "carry," as in the words im<u>port</u> (carry in), ex<u>port</u> (carry out), and trans<u>port</u> (carry across). In this context, <u>comport</u> has to do with how you carry yourself. <u>Comport</u> yourself in a <u>comfort</u>able way.
compunction	strong uneasiness caused by guilt (see REMORSE, CONTRITION) I felt <u>compunction</u> about puncturing your tires with Japanese throwing stars, but I went ahead and did it anyway.

concurrent	at the same time
	Note: This is another decodable word:
	   "con" = together (see CONVOKE)
	 + "current" = at this time
	  concurrent = at a time together
	John Adams's and Thomas Jefferson's deaths were almost <u>concurrent</u>; they both died on July 4, 1826.

congenital	existing at birth *Note:* This is decodable too: "con-" means together and "genital"—well, you figure it out. Unless you've had a sex change, your <u>genitals</u> are <u>congenital</u>.

conjecture	statement made without adequate evidence "Can Jack surely reach that conclusion?" I asked. "Or is it only a conjecture?"
conjugal	pertaining to marriage Unless you can juggle both your careers, you will not have conjugal happiness.
contort	twist; bend We recommend that you contact your local contortionist in order to learn the skills necessary for sitting in an SAT chair.
contrition	remorse; repentance; bitter regret felt owing to wrongdoing When Trish broke the priceless gorilla sculpture, she was overcome with contrition.
controversial	of, relating to, or causing dispute Distributing contraceptives in high school is a controversial issue.
convoke	to call together; to cause to assemble *Note:* Decode: "con" = together + "voc" = call (voice) ——————— convoke = call together The mayor convokes a town meeting so that the citizens can vocalize their grievances.
corp-	a root meaning "body" Example: corpse = dead body
corporal	of the body; bodily Corporal Thomas gave me corporal punishment because I saluted him with my foot instead of my hand.
corpulent	obese; having a fat body The corpulent corporal gave up eating for Lent.

corroborate | to testify in agreement
Do you have any witnesses who can <u>corroborate</u> that this is the restaurant where Bonnie and Clyde <u>(co-robbers) ate</u>?

countermand | to cancel a command
"Work in the stockroom today," the shopkeeper ordered. "No, wait!" he <u>countermanded</u>, "Keep the front <u>counter manned</u>!"

covert | concealed; secret (see OVERT)
When the press finds out about the CIA's <u>covert</u> operations, the CIA tries to <u>cover it</u> up.

cower | to quiver; shrink from fear
The <u>coward</u> <u>cowered</u>.

crass | uncultured
"Is it <u>crass</u> to scratch an <u>ass</u>?" the cow asked the donkey.

credulity | gullibility
His <u>credulity</u> led him to think that the preposterous alibi was <u>cred</u>ible. I found it too in<u>cred</u>ible to believe.

Crestfallen

crestfallen | dejected
"I'm sorry I dropped the toothpaste," he said, <u>crestfallen</u>.

crux | main point; central issue; heart of the matter
Note: <u>Crux</u> is the Latin word for "cross," as you can tell from the word <u>crucifix</u>, and a cross is always made when two lines meet in the center.
"The <u>crux</u> of our work is to <u>crucify</u> <u>crooks</u>," explained the Roman policeman.

cull	to select; weed out
	<u>Coll</u>ege admissions officers <u>cull</u> the best applications from the pile.
cupidity	greed; avarice
	Note: Although Cupid is usually associated with love, he's actually the god of desire, including desire for money.
	Dan is possessed with stupidity as well as <u>cupidity</u>; he stole a lot of money, but then he burned it to get rid of the evidence.

A Mystery

It was one of those steamy nights when the sky is lousy with stars. I was enjoying a <u>cathartic</u> <u>cerebration</u> and <u>culling</u> the blue M&M's from the M&M <u>cache</u> in the office of the Sure-Lock Homes Locksmith and Detective Agency. Suddenly, my <u>cogitations</u> were interrupted by a <u>cacophonous</u> sound and a cataclysmic vibration that reverberated through my <u>capacious</u> office. I stepped with <u>circumspection</u> into the hall because I was afraid someone might be up to some <u>chicanery</u>. I found a <u>chaotic</u> scene: a <u>corpulent</u> man lying <u>contorted</u> at the bottom of the stairs. Blood was gushing through a wound in his side, and I could see the <u>ciliated</u> lining of his small intestine. I decided to take charge.

I asked with <u>compunction</u>, "Golly, are you okay?"

He replied <u>caustically</u>, "Sure, I'm just swell. And how was your day?"

"Peachy," I said.

At that he bellowed <u>cholerically</u>, "You <u>callous</u> piece of <u>carrion</u>! Can't you see I've been shot? Did you think this hole in my gut was a <u>congenital</u> condition? Get me to a hospital with <u>celerity</u>!"

"You don't have to be so <u>captious</u>, <u>cantankerous</u>, and <u>churlish</u>. Let me <u>cogitate</u>!"

"If I don't have this wound <u>cauterized</u>, I'll be a <u>cadaver</u>."

At that moment a <u>comely</u> lady walked into the office. She <u>comported</u> herself calmly. She was voluptuous and yet seemed <u>chaste</u>. I was overcome with thoughts that should be censored. She pointed at the wounded man and said, "We were in my apartment; he got up to answer the door, and suddenly I heard a cacophonous sound and a cataclysmic vibration that must have reverberated in your capacious office."

Just then my assistant, Watt, entered. He said, handing me the phone, "My kid wants to know what sort of tree he should plant in our garden. What do you think, Sure-Lock?"

"A lemon tree, my dear Watt's son," I said.

Then Watt became cognizant of the situation. He cowered and said, "What is that?"

"It's a plant with little yellow fruit and . . ."

He interrupted me, "No, that body on the floor."

"Oh golly, I forgot. We should get him to a hospital. But wait!" I countermanded. "I need to stop for comestibles on the way!"

We all lifted the body concurrently and put it in my car.

When we arrived at the hospital, the doctor informed us that the corpulent man was dead.

"Golly, that's too bad," I said with contrition.

Well, it was time for me to get to the bottom of this heinous crime. Convoking the small crowd, I asked the dame, "Who was that man?"

"My husband," she replied, crestfallen.

"Were your conjugal relations good?"

"Well, no, in fact we had been celibate for a long time."

"Why?"

"Speaking with candor, I chose to be chaste."

"Is it crass to ask why you chose to be chaste?"

"Because it starts with the letter C."

"Aha! Well, let's get to the crux of this situation. Did you kill your husband?"

"How dare you censure me like that. What a calumnious conjecture!"

I repeated, "Did you kill him?"

With chagrin, she capitulated. "Well, only a little, but Watt will corroborate that. He cajoled me into it."

"Watt! What brought you to it? Cupidity? All the time I thought you were on the side of the law and you were really covertly planning this crime. My credulity! You charlatan! I will bring you both to justice without clemency, and I'm sure you will be castigated with a prison sentence and corporal punishment commensurate with the seriousness of the crime."

D

dais	raised platform The nervous speaker whispered, "Da is no way I am going up on the dais!"
daunt **dauntless**	to intimidate; frighten bold, unable to be daunted The dauntless mouse daunted the lion with his .357 Magnum.
dearth	**This word has nothing to do with the word death. It means scarcity (SEE PAUCITY).** When there is nothing but d'earth there is a dearth. Because of Darth Vader, there was a dearth of laughter on the *Death Star*.
debase	to lower in quality or value; adulterate (note the similarity to ABASE) The birds at de base of the statue debased it with excrement.
decoy	a lure or bait The coy duck disguised himself as a wooden decoy, but the hunters shot at him anyway.
defenestration	the act of throwing something out the window *Note:* It's highly unlikely that this word will be on the SAT, but it's the kind of word everyone should know anyway. You could use it if you ever witness the defenestration of a proctor.

delude	to deceive De lewd dude deluded himself into thinking he was deliriously attractive.
demur	to object mildly
demure	reserved; modest The demure poodle demurred at the Saint Bernard's drooling in public.
deplete	to lessen the supply or content of She de-pleated the skirt by ironing it, thus depleting her stock of pleated skirts.
depraved	morally corrupt; debased; perverted As a prank, the depraved criminal de-paved the highway.
deranged	having a severe mental disorder; being insane The deranged cowboy roamed the streets singing wildly, "Rome, Rome on de range."
derogate	to detract; to take away The effect of the spear protruding from Bob's forehead was to derogate from his usually good-looking face.
descry	to discern; to catch sight of something that is difficult to catch sight of Through the mist they could descry the form of the hungry, one-eyed, one-horned, flying purple people eater munching on a bag of purple Skittles.

Hey! What happened to all the folds in these skirts?

Deplete

desultory	aimless; disconnected; rambling; haphazard
	"That's why I love pepper," said Uri, finishing his speech extolling the merits of salt. "<u>De salt, Uri</u>!" yelled his debate teacher.
deter	to prevent or discourage from happening
	Nothing can <u>deter</u> Derek Jeter from hitting a home run for the Yankees.
devastate	to ruin by violent action
	The Blob <u>devastated</u> <u>de vast state</u> of Nevada.
devoid	completely lacking; void; empty; without
	<u>Avoid</u> diving into swimming pools that are <u>devoid</u> of water; you could hurt yourself and that would suck.
dexterous	adroit or skillful in the use of hands or body
	Houdini was <u>dexterous</u>; he could escape from a straitjacket.

Are you remembering to do the mnemonic thing? Picture yourself watching nine acrobats wearing banners across their chests that say *dexterous*. Each contorts into the shape of a letter to spell out the word *dexterous*. They are all named *Dexter*, except for one, who is named *Poindexter*. You lean over to your friend and say, "Wow, are they *dexterous*! I've never seen anyone so *dexterous*. I love *dexterous* people!" Then she looks at you like you're an idiot.

diabolical	fiendish; devilish; nastily scheming
	The <u>diabolical</u> demon devised a deadly dungeon.
diaphanous	translucent; gossamer
	His <u>diaphanous</u> dinner dress caused much discussion.
discern	to detect by the use of the senses
	The watchman <u>dis-earned</u> his pay by not <u>discerning</u> the thieves.
discord	lack of harmony
	"I won't use <u>dis chord</u> 'cause it would create <u>discord</u>," said Mozart.

disparage	to belittle; to reduce in esteem "<u>Dis porridge</u> is too hot," Goldilocks <u>disparaged</u>.
disseminate	**to dispense objects, such as seeds, newspapers; to distribute** While making his stock boy walk the plank, the captain explained, "<u>Dis seaman ate</u> all of the supplies that he was supposed to <u>disseminate</u>."
distraught	**anxious; worried; <u>distressed</u>** Snow White became <u>distraught</u> when the dwarfs drank booze and fought.
divers	several
diverse	**distinct; varied; differing** William Shakespeare's <u>divers verses</u> were about <u>diverse</u> subjects.
doleful	**sad; mournful** You will be <u>Dole-full</u> and sick if you eat 98 cans of pineapple chunks.
drastic	**severe** If your swimsuit strap breaks, you are in <u>drastic</u> need of elastic.
dynamic	**energetic; vigorous; forceful** The <u>dynamic</u> duo fell into the Joker's <u>dynamite</u> trap.

And on to a story:

The Distraught Dogcatcher

Dan was <u>distraught</u>. He knew he'd soon have to go up to the <u>dais</u> and declare his candidacy for dogcatcher. He knew he was <u>devoid</u> of charisma and not a <u>dynamic</u> speaker. He wasn't even <u>dexterous</u> at catching canines. Doubtless, he would <u>debase</u> himself by speaking like a <u>deranged</u> fool.

Trying to appear <u>dauntless</u>, he shambled forward with a <u>dearth</u> of enthusiasm. He tried to picture his audience all in <u>diaphanous</u> gowns, but it did not help his mood at all.

"Ahem," he began, but was <u>deterred</u> from continuing when he <u>descried</u> the <u>diabolical</u> Great Dane that was rapidly <u>depleting</u> his audience by devouring them. Feeling that this <u>devastation</u> might <u>derogate</u> his speech, Dan's thoughts were thrown into sudden <u>discord</u>, and he felt a <u>drastic</u> need to <u>defenestrate</u> himself. Using himself as a <u>decoy</u> to get the beast's attention, he <u>demurred</u>, "Ummm . . . please stop!" People <u>discerned</u> his foolishness.

Later that day, a supporter <u>disparaged</u> Dan's speech. "It was rather <u>desultory</u>. <u>Divers</u> <u>diverse</u> rumors have been <u>disseminated</u> that he is <u>depraved</u>. We'll have trouble <u>deluding</u> the public into believing the contrary."

No, we aren't talking about the swimmers.
—Ada

E

ebullient	**bubbly; overflowing with excitement** The chef took a hefty swig of cooking sherry and then <u>ebulliently</u> tossed <u>bouillon</u> cubes into the soup.
edify	**to enlighten; educate** <u>Ed defied</u> the edict against education by trying to <u>edify</u> his pupils.
educe	**to elicit** He tried to <u>educe</u> as much information as possible from the suspects before he <u>deduced</u> who the murderer was.
efface	**to erase; rub out** Be sure to completely <u>efface</u> any answer circle you wish to change.
effete	**weak; barren; decadent** By the time the authors had finished writing the E word list, they were <u>effete</u>. (Their readers had been <u>effete</u> ever since aardvark.)
effigy	**dummy (mannequin), usually for symbolic torturing** The E words got together to burn <u>F and G</u> in <u>effigy</u>.
elation	**exhilaration; joy** The jolly mountaineers found <u>elation</u> on high <u>elevations</u>.

emaciated	**excessively thin; weak** In May she ate it, but now it's June and she's still emaciated.
emulate	**to imitate closely** When the tornado began, Dorothy called out, "Aunty Em, you late. Emulate Toto and hurry up."
epitaph	**memorial text carved on a tombstone** I read the epitaph, "Here lies a politician and an honest man," and wondered how they could fit two people in one grave.
epitome	**something that perfectly represents an entire class of things; embodiment (pronounced "eh-pit'-oh-me")** "You're the epitome of stupidity," she screeched after I spilled baloney dip all over her dress.
equestrian	**pertaining to horsemanship; on horseback** The equestrian knights went on a quest to Rion, but they were turned away because of a no-horses policy.
equipoise	**equality; balance; equilibrium** *Note:* This is one of those words that isn't often seen in print but might be on the test anyway because it is highly decodable.

$$\begin{array}{r} \text{``equi'' = equal} \\ + \text{``poise'' = balance} \\ \hline \text{equipoise = equally balanced} \end{array}$$

An equipoise of speed and comprehension must be acquired in order to succeed on the critical reading section.

equivocal	**capable of two interpretations; ambiguous** *Note:* This word is decodable, too.

$$\begin{array}{r} \text{``equi'' = equal} \\ + \text{``vocal'' = voice} \\ \hline \text{equivocal = giving equal voice to two sides} \end{array}$$

"A good meal from this cook is a rare treat," is an equivocal statement.

erode	to diminish or destroy by small amounts When a road erodes, there are potholes all over the place.
erudite	scholarly Erudite people say things like, "Ere you diet, would you partake of the torte?" instead of "Want some cake?"
eschew	avoid; shun "Eschew!" he sneezed loudly. "Gesundheit," she replied, while eschewing the globules of his sneeze juice.
esoteric	known only by a few people Now you are one of the few people who knows this esoteric word.
ethereal	not of the material world The lisping child saw the ethereal ghost and asked, "Ith he real?"
eulogy	praiseful speech at a funeral In Santa's eulogy, the priest explained that Santa had died of high cholesterol because of all those Yule logs he ate.
euphemism	nice way of saying something unpleasant "Moved on to the next world" is a euphemism for "keeled over and bought it," which is a euphemism for "died."
exact	**On the SAT, the Serpent will use the secondary definition of this word, which is: to demand** The Stamp Act exacted from the colonists taxes they could not afford to pay. So they "X'd" the act.

exhume | to remove from a grave; disinter (see POSTHUMOUS)
Note: Another one to decode:

"ex" = out of
+ "humus" = earth, dirt

exhume = remove from earth

They <u>exhumed</u> the coffin, but there was no cadaver in it.

exigent | urgent; requiring immediate attention
It is <u>exigent</u> that I find a <u>sexy gent</u> to escort me to the prom.
excessively demanding; excessively exacting
I made <u>exigent</u> demands on my fairy godmother to find me a debonair prom date and a diaphanous dress.

Essay on Eggplant

I want to know which <u>erudite</u> vegetable maker invented eggplant. If he is dead, I will <u>exhume</u> his coffin and <u>efface</u> the <u>epitaph</u> from his tombstone. If he is alive, I will burn him in <u>effigy</u> and ensure he will not be <u>eulogized</u> when he dies. Eggplant is the <u>epitome</u> of bad vegetables and its destruction is <u>exigent</u>. I <u>eschew</u> eating it. Its badness is almost <u>ethereal</u>. I would rather become <u>emaciated</u> than eat eggplant. This is an <u>exacting</u> demand, but would someone please <u>edify</u> me, without being <u>esoteric</u> or <u>equivocal</u>, as to one good thing about eggplant? It is mushy, it has seeds, it makes my tongue itch, it has a dopey name, and it tastes like the droppings that an <u>equestrian</u> slob forgot to clean up. I wish all the soil on the world's eggplant farms would <u>erode</u>. Just thinking about eggplant makes me <u>effete</u>. Oh, and get this—when eggplants fertilize each other, the round ones with lots of seeds are the female ones and the long, narrow ones are the males. (No <u>euphemism</u> can soften this picture.) And they do it <u>ebulliently</u> in public, in front of all the other vegetables. What would happen if humans <u>emulated</u> this behavior?

The end.

F

fabricate — to invent or make up something (often in order to deceive)
When Michael couldn't remove the stain from the <u>fabric</u>, he <u>ate</u> it and <u>fabricated</u> a story that aliens stole it.

facet — side or aspect; face of something (e.g., gemstones)
"<u>Face it</u>! One of the <u>facets</u> of being a jeweler is sometimes selling flawed <u>facets</u>!"

facetious — joking or jesting
She's so <u>facetious</u> that you should not take what she says at <u>face</u> value.

fallacious — false; wrong; incorrect
They used to castigate people who made <u>fallacious</u> statements. (Well, that was a long time ago.)

fastidious — careful about details; impossible to satisfy
Bernie Madoff's <u>fastidious</u> accountant admonished his assistants, "Be careful! Don't shred too <u>fast, idiots</u>."

fatuous — inane; foolish; fatheaded
Eating 30 pounds of chocolate a day is a <u>fatuous</u> idea.

fawning — groveling; overly admiring
The hunter who killed Bambi's mother should have come back and made a <u>fawning</u> plea for forgiveness.

That is an INCREDIBLE outfit!

the hat with the earflaps! VERY "IN"!

and the red checks are so "you"!

Fawning

feasible	workable; plausible; possible Homer's idea of opening a hair salon for bald people was not <u>feasible</u>—who would pay the $30 <u>fee</u>? D'oh!
fecund	fertile "<u>Feh! Couldn</u>'t you do without all this smelly manure?" Slick asked Farmer Brown. "No, we need it to make the soil <u>fecund</u>."
fervor	passion I will fight a ferocious ferret and get its <u>fur for</u> you if it will prove the <u>fervor</u> of my love for you.
fetid	smelly I am proud to have <u>fetid</u> feet that smell of <u>feta</u> cheese.
fictitious	false; not genuine Books of <u>fiction</u> have <u>fictitious</u> plots.
filch	to steal Since they had zilch, they decided to <u>filch</u>.
flagrant	deliberately conspicuous; glaring After the protesters <u>flagrantly</u> burned the Stars and Stripes, the mayor began a <u>flag rant</u>, condemning the rebels.
flaunt	to show off something I flagrantly <u>flaunted</u> my physical <u>flaw</u>lessness to my fawning followers.
fluctuation	irregular variation At the terrifying sight of the nasty sentence completion question, his heartbeat <u>fluctuated</u> wildly.
foible	weakness, flaw The spy's <u>foible</u> was her penchant for attention.

foment	to stir up; agitate; INCITE (think: when you stir something up it <u>foams</u>)
	When your <u>foe</u> warned you not to <u>foment</u> the army against him, your <u>foe meant</u> he was afraid of getting his butt kicked.
forbearance	patience
	He played dead with <u>forbearance</u> until the <u>four bears</u> got <u>antsy</u> and went away.
formication	spontaneous abnormal sensation of ants or other insects running over the skin
	Some people experience this while taking the SAT.
forte	strong point (think: forts are strong. Pronounced "fort" or "for-tay")
	His <u>forte</u> was sneaking into the <u>fort</u> that was just before <u>Fort</u> B.
frenetic	frenzied; frantic; freaked out
	When the pilot and the flight attendants became <u>fren</u>zied, the passengers became <u>frenetic</u>.
froward	stubborn (see OBDURATE)
	The <u>froward</u> guardsmen refused to retreat, so the protesters could not move <u>forward</u>.
frugal	sparing in expense; stingy; miserly
	They told me that I was <u>frugal</u> Because I bought a plastic bugle.
fulminate	to explode; roar; denounce loudly
	After he bombed the SAT, he <u>fulminated</u> for a <u>full minute</u> against the ETS.
futile	completely ineffective
	The one-armed floor layer felt his work was futile because he could lay only a <u>few tiles</u> a day.

Fred the Filcher

Freddy had a <u>flagrant</u> <u>foible</u>. He <u>filched</u> fish, sometimes with <u>fervor</u> and sometimes with <u>forbearance</u>, but he never <u>fluctuated</u> from his <u>forte</u>. One day his mother, returning from the garden (which was <u>fecund</u> with fish remains), said <u>facetiously</u>, "Freddy, is it <u>feasible</u> that you'll <u>foment</u> a <u>fetid</u> <u>fulmination</u> of fish odor if you continue to <u>frenetically</u> <u>flaunt</u> your <u>filching</u> habits?"

<u>Froward</u> Freddy frowned. "That is a <u>fatuous</u> as well as <u>fallacious</u> suggestion." Then he uttered the following <u>fastidiously</u> crafted rationalization. "This <u>facet</u> of my abilities is not <u>futile</u>, as it provides fish for our otherwise <u>frugal</u> dinner. You should <u>fawn</u> over me, not <u>fulminate</u> against me."

The preceding story is <u>fictitious</u>, <u>fabricated</u> by the authors.

G

gainsay — to deny, dispute; <u>say</u> something <u>against</u> what someone else says
The model <u>gainsaid</u> that she'd <u>gained</u> weight, <u>say</u>ing, "The camera always adds 30 pounds."

garbled — screwed up
The <u>garbled</u> message read, "Please spurgle iceberg before rocking breakfast."

garrulous — very talkative; loquacious
Even the Serpent would scare you less
Than talking to someone <u>garrulous</u>.

genre — category
It's hard to place *Up Your Score* in a specific <u>genre</u>. It's an SAT prep book, but also an epic narrative, an investigative report, and a monumental literary work.

germane | relevant; appropriate
"Germany is not <u>germane</u> to our discussion today," said the history professor. "Today we shall discuss last night's rerun of *The Real Housewives of New York*."

gestate | to transform and grow, like a baby inside the womb
Mama Butterfly asked the <u>gestating</u> caterpillar if it wanted something to eat, but it said, "No, I <u>just ate</u>."

But you're a growing boy! Sure you're not hungry?

Naw, I gestate.

Gestate

gesticulation | gesture; signal
Note: Somehow <u>gesticulation</u> seems as though it ought to have obscene connotations, and we would certainly tell you if it did, but it doesn't. You can make up an obscene mnemonic device, if that helps.
Igor <u>gesticulated</u> for Dick to hurry and enter the lab, saying, "<u>Yes, Dick, you're late</u> for your brain transplant."

gibberish | rapid, incomprehensible, or nonsensical speaking; drivel
The Lewis Carroll poem "Jabberwocky," which begins "'Twas brillig, and the slithy toves . . . ," is written in <u>gibberish</u>.

gibe | to heckle or mock; to taunt; to pick on
"Nice <u>jibe</u>," the sailor <u>gibed</u>, after we capsized.

gloaming | twilight
If it weren't for the fireflies <u>gleaming</u> in the <u>gloaming</u>, I'd find it <u>gloomy</u>.

gossamer | light, delicate, or insubstantial
"Let's <u>go somewhere</u> where I can slip into something a little more <u>gossamer</u>," said the Victoria's Secret model.

gourmet	one who appreciates fine food and drink; epicure; connoisseur "After I do a <u>chore, may</u> I have some of that fancy food? I'm practicing to be a <u>gourmet</u>," said Julia's child.
grandiose	excessively impressive; <u>grand</u> Jay Leno has a <u>grandiose</u> chin.
graphic	vivid; explicit In another sequel to his dinosaur movie, Steven Spielberg left out the prehistoric beasts and kept all the violence, titling the film *<u>Graphic</u> Park*.
gratuitous	unnecessary or unwarranted Adding <u>gratuitous</u> sex and violence to this book has been the best thing about writing it.
gregarious	friendly; outgoing; sociable *Note:* The ETS loves this word. My horoscope tells me to be a <u>gregarious</u> Aquarius.
grimace	(n.) a twisted facial expression (v.) to make a twisted facial expression "Things look <u>grim as</u> long as there's a knife at my throat," the victim thought, <u>grimacing</u> with fear.
grisly	gory The bear made a <u>grisly</u> mess of the Cub Scouts.
gruesome	grisly; gory In the <u>gruesome</u> film *The Blob*, the Blob <u>grew some</u> more every second.
gruff	rough or stern in speech or action Arnold Schwarzenegger has made two careers out of acting <u>tough</u> and being <u>gruff</u>.
gullible	believing anything You don't have to know <u>gullible</u> because they took it out of the dictionary. If you believed the above sentence, you sure are <u>gullible</u>.

Lesser-Known Adventures of the Three Billy Goats Gruff

The three Billy Goats <u>Gruff</u> met in the <u>gloaming</u> near the bridge.

"I'm really scared of that <u>gruesome</u> troll," Billy Goat 1 said, <u>gesticulating</u> toward the bridge. "Despite her <u>gossamer</u> gown, she doesn't seem too <u>gregarious</u>."

"I won't <u>gainsay</u> that, and I heard her <u>gourmet</u> appetite includes a <u>grisly</u> taste for goat's hooves!" BG 2 added nervously. "I really don't like <u>gratuitous</u> violence."

"Cowards!" BG 3 <u>gibed</u>. "I don't listen to non<u>germane</u> <u>garbled</u> <u>gibberish</u> that only <u>gullible</u> fools like you would believe. I bet that troll is really a cool gal. Watch me cross that bridge!"

"You have a <u>grandiose</u> opinion of yourself, but you're really pretty dumb. So long, bud," Goat 1 replied with a <u>grimace</u>, anticipating the <u>graphic</u> goat-mutilation horror that soon followed.

H

hackneyed
overused; trite
The plot of the movie *The Texas Chainsaw Massacre* was <u>hackneyed</u>. It was just another horror movie about an axe murderer who <u>hacked knees</u> off.

haggard
unruly; wild; wasted; worn
After a long voyage with the Vikings, <u>Hagar</u> the Horrible looked <u>haggard</u>, kind of like Hagrid from *Harry Potter*.

hallowed
holy; sacred
I was hanging out in the cemetery, but I didn't know I was on hollowed <u>hallowed</u> ground until I fell into a grave.

harangue	mean, nasty, angry speech (think: a speech that is so loud it impairs your <u>hearing</u>) The zookeeper gave us a lengthy <u>harangue</u> about feeding the <u>orangu</u>tan.
harbinger	forerunner; something that signals the approach of something; omen Some words have only one sentence in which they are ever used. The sentence for <u>harbinger</u> is: "The robin is the <u>harbinger</u> of spring."
haughty	proud; vain; arrogant He thinks he's <u>hot. He</u> shouldn't be so <u>haughty</u>.
hedonism **hedonist**	the philosophy of trying to be happy all the time; a funky state of being in which you do your own thing and don't worry about morality one who follows the philosophy of hedonism *Note:* Compare these words to STOICISM and STOIC, which are their respective opposites. You are being a stoic by studying for the SAT so that you can get into college and spend four years being a <u>hedonist</u>.
heinous	grossly wicked; vile; odious The scarecrows said, "Because we have <u>hay in us</u>, it is a <u>heinous</u> crime to invite us to a bonfire."
hierarchy	social pecking order As Heather moved <u>higher</u> up the <u>high</u> school <u>hierarchy</u>, she realized that popularity was not all it's cracked up to be. (This sentence was based on an after-school special.)

Oh great! All the really cool animals get to take the higher ark!

Hierarchy

hirsute	hairy (pronounced "her-suit") He was <u>hirsute</u> in his ape costume, which was really just a <u>hair suit</u>. He borrowed it from his girlfriend Rapunzel; it was <u>her suit</u>.
hoary	**gray or white from age; old** When someone who is hirsute gets old, he is hairy and <u>hoary</u>.
homily	**sermonlike speech** The <u>homely</u> preacher delivered a <u>homily</u>.
homonym	**a word that sounds like another word but has a different meaning** The German word *sechs*, meaning "six," is a <u>homonym</u> of the English word *sex*, meaning "sex."

The Homily

The <u>hirsute</u> young priest was preparing his <u>homily</u>, and he needed advice from the <u>hoary</u> <u>haggard</u> pastor.

"I gotta give a good talk so I can move up in the church <u>hierarchy</u>," he explained. "Can you help me?"

All good advice. —Ada

"You speak on <u>hallowed</u> ground," the pastor began, "so don't <u>harangue</u> and be not <u>haughty</u>. Don't forget to condemn <u>heinous</u> <u>hedonism</u>, though. A good public response to your sermon will be a <u>harbinger</u> of your advancement." The priest worked all night, searching for <u>hackneyed</u> expressions and hip <u>homonyms</u>. But when dawn came he just said, "Oh, the heck with it."

iconoclast	destroyer of tradition When the pope decided that celibacy should no longer be required of the clergy, protesters outside his window yelled "down with the <u>iconoclast</u>" while the pope screamed, "<u>I cannot last</u>."

ignoble	not noble In Orwell's *Animal Farm*, the <u>ignoble</u> <u>pig nobles</u> ruin the barn-yard utopia.
ignominious **ignominy**	characterized by <u>ignominy</u> dishonor; disgrace They suffered an <u>ignominious</u> defeat. He couldn't bear the <u>ignominy</u> of getting a 600 on the SAT.

Two similar words:

imbibe	to drink in; absorb
imbue	to make wet; to saturate; to inspire If you <u>imbibe</u> the meanings of all these words you will be <u>imbued</u> with wisdom.
imminent	about to occur; impending *Note:* Don't confuse imminent with *eminent*, which means "famous." <u>I'm in entertainment and my curtain call is <u>imminent</u>.</u>
immutable	*Note:* The best way to learn this word is to learn the root <u>mut</u>, which means "change." Then you can decode <u>immutable</u> to mean "not changeable." You will also realize that <u>mutable</u> = "changeable," <u>mutation</u> = "a change," and tran<u>smute</u> = "to change from one form to another." "A fat person uses more soap than a skinny person" is one of the <u>immutable</u> laws of physics.
impale	to pierce with a sharp stake or point The <u>imp paled</u> when we took a spike and <u>impaled</u> the mushroom he was sitting on.

impasse	dead end (think: impassable) If you are trying to pick someone up, and none of your <u>passes</u> is working, you have reached an <u>impasse</u>.

impassive	without emotion; expressionless "It looks as if I've reached an <u>impasse</u>," Bart muttered <u>impassively</u> as he slammed into the brick wall on his skateboard.
impeccable	flawless and faultless; not capable of sin Woody is not an <u>impeccable</u> woodpecker; he is always making mistakes.
impending	about to take place (see IMMINENT) The dwarf cowered behind Snow White, sensing <u>imp-ending</u> doom.
imperious	domineering The e<u>mper</u>or was <u>imperious</u>.
impropriety	not <u>proper</u>; not displaying <u>propriety</u> Howard Stern was fined by the FCC for his <u>impropriety</u>.

Here are two words that are sure to confuse you:

impugn	to attack as false; criticize
impunity	<u>immunity</u> from <u>punishment</u>

"You will not have <u>impunity</u> if you <u>impugn</u> my character with such impudence," shouted Michael at Manek when Manek suggested that he was speaking oddly.

incessant	nonstop; ceaseless Her <u>incessant</u> chatter forced me to throw her <u>into</u> a <u>cesspool</u>.
inchoate	incomplete; only partly in existence or operation His plan to trek to Saudi Arabia was <u>inchoate</u>; he was still only <u>in Kuwait</u>.
incite	to arouse; instigate As soon as Drake came back <u>in sight</u>, his groupies' cheering <u>incited</u> the crowd to <u>ignite</u> their lighters and demand an encore.

Impending

incognito	**in disguise so as not to be recognized**
	Note: Remember the root word "cog"? Well, this is another example of it:
	        "in" = not
	   + "cognito" = known
	————————————————
	      incognito = not known
	The president mingled with the people <u>incognito</u> to find out what they really thought.

incommodious	**lacking space; not commodious** His apartment was so <u>incommodious</u> that there was no room for a <u>commode</u>.
incontrovertible	**indisputable** "The evidence is <u>incontrovertible</u>," the lawyer concluded. "The sunburn on your bald head proves that you drive a <u>convertible</u>."
incubus	**nightmare; mental burden** *Note:* <u>Incubus</u> has another meaning that should help you remember it but, as a matter of taste, we chose not to include it. That ought to entice you into looking it up. The SAT is an <u>incubus</u> that hovers in the minds of high school students.
indolence	**laziness** If you study with <u>indolence</u>, they will send you a note of <u>condolence</u> with your score report.
indomitable	**unconquerable; impossible to <u>dominate</u>** He was the best <u>domin</u>oes player around; he was virtually <u>indomitable</u>.
inept	**incompetent** The <u>inept</u> astronomy student thought that unicorns live on <u>Nep</u>tune.
infer	**to conclude based on facts** It can be <u>inferred</u> that people dressed <u>in fur</u> are not animal-rights activists.

ingenious	Two more words that will confuse you: **original; resourceful**
ingenuous	**showing childlike simplicity; innocent**

Remember these words this way: <u>Ingenious</u> has an <u>i</u>, like <u>genius</u>, and it also expresses the main qualities of <u>genius</u>. Baby <u>geniuses</u> frequently discover <u>ingenious</u> ideas in <u>ingenuous</u> ways. (It also helps if you know that <u>disingenuous</u> means <u>crafty</u>, not innocent or straightforward.)

innate	**belonging to someone from birth; inherent (see CONGENITAL)**

The malice <u>in Nate</u> is <u>innate</u>. He's been nasty since birth.

insatiable	**impossible to satisfy**

You must develop an <u>insatiable</u> desire to learn more and more vocabulary words.

inscrutable	**enigmatic; difficult to understand**

The Swedish furniture manufacturer's instructions on how to <u>unscrew</u> the <u>table</u> were <u>inscrutable</u>.

insensate	**unconscious; lacking <u>sensation</u>**

Inhaling too much <u>incense</u> could make you pass out and lie <u>insensate</u> on the floor.

insidious	**working or spreading stealthily; sneaking <u>inside</u> to do something bad**

Note: Do not confuse with INVIDIOUS.
The Evil Testing Serpent uses <u>insidious</u> techniques to torture students.

insipid	**lacking excitement; vapid**

The <u>insipid</u> innkeeper stayed <u>in, sipped</u> wine, and slept.

intangible	**not perceptible to the touch; impalpable**

You can't touch the <u>tangent</u> of $\pi/2$; it's <u>intangible</u>.

invective	**abusive put-down**

If your favorite television show gets taken off the air, you should complain to the producers with <u>inventive</u> <u>invective</u> until they release the series on DVD.

invidious	making people angry; offensive
	The critics of MTV were concerned about the <u>invidious</u> images <u>in videos</u>.
irascible	easily provoked; irritable
	The <u>irascible</u> <u>rascal</u> threw her eraser.

Five Irascible Fools

Ada, Larry, Manek, Michael, and Paul were traveling <u>incognito</u> in the <u>incommodious</u> bus. They had reached an <u>impasse</u> in their <u>indomitable</u> attempts to think of sentences for the I's and were nearly <u>insensate</u> with <u>indolence</u>.

"Hey, Manek, do you have any <u>ingenious</u> ideas for '<u>inscrutable</u>,' you <u>inept</u> fool?" Larry inquired.

Manek's face remained <u>impassive</u>. "You know you're just <u>inciting</u> me to anger with your <u>insipid</u> <u>invective</u>. If you continue this <u>impropriety</u>, this <u>invidious</u> behavior, I'll become <u>irascible</u>."

"Are we to <u>infer</u> that you are questioning Larry's <u>impeccable</u> integrity by implying that he acted in an <u>ignoble</u> manner?" Paul interjected <u>ingenuously</u>. "I'm sure he couldn't stand the <u>ignominy</u>."

"If you all don't shut up, I'll be forced to <u>impale</u> you. Especially since you <u>imbibed</u> my iodine," Ada shouted.

"There seems to be an <u>insidious</u> force at work among us," Larry added. "Our <u>incontrovertibly</u> <u>insatiable</u> desire to help students is failing!"

"But what, ho!" Ada exclaimed. "I believe our destination is <u>imminent</u>."

So the bus stopped and they got off, continuing to argue <u>incessantly</u>.

What can I say? The SAT changes you.

—Ada

J

jaded	wearied, especially by too much of the good life
	They lived out their <u>jaded</u> existence wearing <u>jade</u> jewelry and driving Ferraris.

jingoism	extreme patriotism Francis Scott Key was a <u>jingoistic</u> <u>jingle</u> writer.

These three words all begin with "joc-" and they all mean about the same thing:

jocose	merry; joking
jocular	jolly; joking
jocund	merry; jolly

The <u>jocose</u> jockey did a jig as a <u>joke</u>.
The <u>jocular</u> journalist joined the <u>joker</u>'s club.
The <u>jocund</u> judge joyfully jailed the jolly janitor.

K

ken	range of knowledge "<u>Ken's ken</u> is limited," Barbie complained. "He only knows surfboards."
kiosk	pavilion or small open booth where items are bought or sold The <u>kiosk</u> in Kiev sold cold knishes. (Say this five times fast.)
kismet	fate "<u>Kiss me</u>, baby, it's <u>kismet</u>," slurred the drunk at the singles' bar.
kleptomaniac	compulsive stealer Old <u>kleptomaniacs</u> never die, they just <u>steal</u> away.
knave **knavery**	clever bad guy dishonest, mischievous dealing "<u>Can Avery</u> join the <u>navy</u>?" "<u>Never, he</u> is always up to some kind of <u>knavery</u>."
Crime Doesn't Pay	The <u>jingoist</u> became <u>jaded</u>. He didn't feel as <u>jocose</u>, <u>jocular</u>, or <u>jocund</u> as he once did. Eventually, he turned to <u>knavery</u>, robbing from <u>kiosks</u>. It was <u>kismet</u> that he got caught. It takes little <u>ken</u> to be a <u>kleptomaniac</u>. A lesson for us all.

L

labyrinth   complicated maze or winding series of corridors
You'd be a<u>maze</u>d at how easily the <u>lab</u>oratory rats get lost in the <u>labyrinth</u>.

lacerate   to rip, maul, tear, mutilate, or mangle
A<u>las</u>, when Arth<u>ur ate</u> pickled razor blades, he <u>lacerated</u> his tongue.

lackadaisical   uncaring; <u>lack</u>ing in interest or spirit
The florist exclaimed, "I <u>lack a daisy! Call</u> the flower supplier pronto!" But the <u>lackadaisical</u> stock boy didn't pay any attention.

laconic   not saying much; brief; terse; concise; succinct
This sentence is <u>laconic</u>.
There is a Greek story about the war between Laconia and Athens. The Athenians threatened the Laconians by sending a letter to them that said something like, "If we defeat you we will burn your houses, pillage your villages, maul your women and children, etc. . . ." The <u>Laconi</u>ans sent back the <u>laconic</u> reply, "If."

lambaste   to thrash, maul, beat, whip, or bludgeon with big things and other fun stuff; to scold sharply or rebuke
"<u>Baste</u> that <u>lamb</u> or I'll <u>lambaste</u> you!" the cook yelled to his assistant.

Lambaste

languid	lacking energy; weak
languish	to lose strength; waste away

Note: As you will notice, a lot of L words mean either "lazy and lacking energy" or "lusty."

No doubt learning all this language is giving you so much anguish that you're starting to <u>languish</u>.

languor — languidness; sluggishness

I can't lie here in <u>languor</u> any longer.

larceny — stealing

Stealing from the cartoonist who created *The Far Side* is <u>Larson-y</u>.

lascivious — lusty; lewd

The <u>lascivious</u> lass lusted after Larry.

lassitude — listlessness; a state of exhaustion or weakness

The ship's crew was in such a state of <u>lassitude</u> that they sailed to the wrong <u>latitude</u>.

latent — potential but not yet displayed

He had a <u>latent</u> talent for playing the harmonica, but he didn't discover it until <u>late in</u> his life.

(*Note: Latent* is often used in the phrase *latent talent*, which is a handy memory aid because the two words have the exact same letters.)

laud — (v.) to praise (think: "<u>Praise</u> be the <u>Laud</u>!")
(n.) praise
laudatory — (adj.) praiseful

The students stuck in the <u>loud</u> <u>auditorium</u> did not have any <u>laudatory</u> comments at the end of the pep rally.

lecherous — lewd; lustful; given to sexual activity

The country preacher said to the employees in the brothel, "Yer goin' to Hades 'cause you <u>let yer house</u> be used for <u>lecherous</u> activities." They replied, "Don't <u>lecture us</u>."

lethal | deadly
The lisping landlord said, "If you don't sign the <u>leath, I'll</u> thtab you with my <u>lethal</u> thord!"

lethargy | sluggishness; indifference
Are you overcome by <u>lethargy</u> from all this studying? Well, it's time to wake up, so:

STOP STUDYING!

1. Go to the nearest store.
2. Buy four cups of coffee and a six-pack of 5-hour ENERGY Shots.
3. Rapidly consume everything you just bought.
4. Go back to work (and relax!).

lewd | indecent; obscene
It is <u>rude</u>
To be <u>lewd</u>.

licentious | immoral; morally wild or sexually unrestrained
"I've got my driver's <u>license</u>," Terry proudly exclaimed. "Now we can be <u>licentious</u> in the back seat of my car."

limacine | pertaining to or resembling a slug
This word won't be on the test, but it's a useful insult.

lithe | graceful; supple; limber; moving <u>lightly</u>
When the <u>lithe</u> dancers at the ballet studio spread rumors that the lisping prima ballerina was getting fat, she responded, "<u>Lithe</u>, <u>lithe</u>, they're all <u>lithe</u>!"

loathe | to hate
Note: The last four letters of *loathe* can be reorganized to spell *hate*.
"Pick up some bread at the store, okay?" she asked.
"No, I'll buy tortillas," he replied. "You know I <u>loathe</u> <u>loaves</u>!"

lucubration | hard, scholarly studying (see COGITATE)
Readers of this book won't have to do any <u>lucubration</u>.

lugubrious

mournful or sad

When Lou the undertaker's friends died, he was too <u>lugubrious</u> to bury them. Finally, they got so tired of waiting to be buried that they came back to life and said, "<u>Lou, go bury us</u>."

An Open and Frank Note from the Authors

With such words in this list as <u>lewd</u>, <u>licentious</u>, and <u>lecherous</u>, you're probably looking forward to a great story. Well, you won't find one here, but not because we were too <u>lackadaisical</u> or <u>languid</u>. We actually did write a pretty <u>lascivious</u> one, but instead of <u>lauding</u> it, the editor <u>loathed</u> it. After she read it, she <u>lithely</u> <u>lambasted</u> us with <u>lethal</u> cans of lima beans (we suspect they were obtained through <u>larceny</u>), <u>lacerating</u> our ligaments. This made us a bit <u>lugubrious</u>, but we were willing to <u>lucubrate</u> some more and come up with a new story. But when she <u>laconically</u> called us "<u>limacine</u> idiots," we left, suddenly overcome by our <u>latent</u> <u>lethargy</u>, <u>languor</u>, and <u>lassitude</u>. And so, in protest, we didn't do an L story. Humblest apologies. We hope you'll forgive us.

M

macabre

gross; ghastly; suggestive of horrible death and decay
Note: You will always find this word on the back covers of worthless horror novels.
"This <u>macabre</u> story is about a psychotic farmer who chokes people with corn on the <u>cob</u>."

magnanimous

noble; generous; forgiving; magnificently kind
The <u>magnanimous</u> king allowed the prisoner to live on one condition: that he take the SAT every day for the rest of his life. The prisoner chose death.

Magnanimous, magnificent.
—Ada

The root "mal-" means "bad." The next few words all begin with "mal-":

malaise	a feeling of illness or depression After I ate the jar of <u>mayonnaise</u>, I had a feeling of <u>malaise</u> that made <u>me lazy</u>.
malediction	a spoken curse The male chauvinist's remarks earned him a <u>malediction</u> from the feminists.
malevolent	wishing evil on others; MALICIOUS (the opposite of BENEVOLENT) All year I am <u>malevolent</u>. But I repent for <u>my life during Lent</u>.
malice **malicious**	the desire to do bad to others; spite having malice The Queen of Hearts felt <u>malice</u> toward Alice.
malign	to say bad things about; slander He <u>maligned</u> me by saying that I couldn't remember my lines.
malignancy	a malevolent and malicious act (also, a malignant tumor) In an act of extreme <u>malignancy</u>, the bully was trying to break my leg. Suddenly, the doorbell rang. I said to him, "Get off <u>my leg'n see</u> who's at the door."
malodorous	smelling bad; having a bad <u>odor</u> The air in the testing center will be <u>malodorous</u>.
maneuver	a skillful or clever move The captain used a tricky sailing <u>maneuver</u> to rescue the <u>man overboard</u>. The man thanked him, "<u>Man, you very</u> clever."
maritime	near the sea; concerned with shipping or navigation We had a <u>merry time</u> when we vacationed in a <u>maritime</u> resort.

Mnemonic time again: You're out at sea on the U.S.S. *Maritime*. The crusty old captain, whose facial hair is in the shape of the word *maritime*, orders you to swab the deck. In only two days you will reach the *maritime* resort, where you will party until you pass out on the beach, your body leaving the word *maritime* imprinted in the sand. You will wake to the lulling sound of the waves, *"Maritime, maritime . . ."*

meander | to wander around aimlessly
Me and her meandered down the path.

melancholy | sadness; depression; pensiveness
When he finds out that she can't elope, he'll be melancholy.

Don't be sad, we can still get married.

we just can't elope.

Melancholy

mellifluous | sweet sounding; flowing with honey or sweetness
Mel is fluent in the mellifluous lines of *Hamlet*.

mendacious | untruthful; lying
Men who say they don't fear commitment are probably being mendacious.

mendicant | (n.) a beggar
(adj.) practicing begging
Men dat can't get jobs often become mendicants.
The bum lived a mendicant existence.

meticulous | extremely careful and precise
He was so meticulous that he used the metric system to measure the diameter of his navel lint.

miasma | a poisonous atmosphere or cloud (often in swamps)
Deep in the swamp, Eugene cried, "This miasma is bad for my asthma."

minuscule | very tiny
Minuscule students go to minischools.

misnomer	**an inappropriate or wrong name** "My name is Mrs. Troller!" screamed the teacher. "To call me <u>Miss Gnomer</u> is a <u>misnomer</u>!"
mitigate	**to make less severe** The robber's escape was foiled when he was <u>met</u> at <u>the gate</u> by cops. His sentence was <u>mitigated</u>, however, when he offered the cops donuts.
modicum	**little bit** When Barbra Streisand was just a child, she began to show a <u>modicum</u> of talent, and instead of calling her mother, she would sing "<u>Muduh, come</u>!"

Misnomer

monotonous	**always at the same pitch; boring; repetitious** This word is easy if you break it up into its parts:

> "mono" = the same, one
> "tone" = sound
> + "ous" = having the qualities of

monotonous = having the same sound

The concerto played on the one-keyed piano was <u>monotonous</u>.

moo	**low, deep sound made by a cow** In a low, deep voice the cow said, "<u>Moo</u>."
mordant	**bitingly sarcastic or nasty** She <u>mordantly</u> told him that he needed <u>more dent</u>al adhesive.
morose	**sullen; depressed** If you love learning vocabulary words, you will be <u>morose</u> when you get to the word overt because after it there are no <u>more Os</u>.
myriad	**many; a lot; a very large amount** <u>Mary had</u> only one little lamb, not <u>myriad</u> lambs.

Manek's Problems

In a small <u>maritime</u> village, there lived a <u>morose</u> review book author named Manek. Most of the citizens were <u>magnanimous</u> to him because he was a <u>meticulously</u> clean <u>mendicant</u>, but there was a <u>minuscule</u>-brained <u>malevolent</u> gang in town (led by Michael) who <u>maliciously</u> <u>maligned</u> him. "Hey, Manek," they would yell. "You're more <u>malodorous</u> than a <u>moo</u>-cow. Yeah, Manek is a <u>misnomer</u>: You should be called <u>moo</u>-nek!"

Manek bore the <u>mendacious</u> gang no <u>malice</u>, though he wished he could, through some ingenious <u>maneuver</u>, <u>meander</u> through the town's <u>myriad</u> streets without these <u>monotonous</u>, <u>mordant</u> <u>maledictions</u>. He grew <u>melancholy</u> and suffered from a great <u>malaise</u> as he <u>morosely</u> contemplated their <u>malignancy</u>. He could be found sitting, listening to the <u>mellifluous</u> ocean waves, with a virtual <u>miasma</u> over him, snuffling quietly. There, that story wasn't so <u>macabre</u>, was it?

N

nadir

absolutely lowest point
Note: The word *zenith* is the opposite of nadir. If you ever get these two confused, just remember that no one would name their brand of TV "Nadir."
Nadine knew their relationship had reached its <u>nadir</u> when she asked her husband to watch the Superbowl with her and he said, "<u>Nah, dear</u>."

naive

lacking in worldly wisdom or experience
After God expelled them from Eden, Adam said, "The time is <u>nigh, Eve</u>. We can no longer be <u>naive</u>."

nascent

coming into being; emerging (see RENASCENT)
Your <u>nascent</u> vocabulary will cause <u>an ascent</u> in your verbal score.

nefarious

evil
<u>No fairy is</u> <u>nefarious</u>.

nemesis	vengeful enemy In the book of Genesis, the Serpent is Eve's <u>nemesis</u>.
neologism	**a newly coined word, phrase, or expression** *Note:* Decode this word.

$$\begin{array}{l} \text{``neo''} = \text{new} \\ + \text{``logism''} = \text{idea, word} \\ \hline \text{neologism} = \text{new word} \end{array}$$

Whoever made up the word <u>neologism</u> created a <u>neologism</u>.

neophyte	beginner The <u>neophyte</u> boxer was <u>new</u> to <u>fight</u>ing.
nexus	**bond or link between things** A <u>nexus</u> is a bond that con<u>nects us</u>.
noisome	**offensive; disgusting; filthy; malodorous** *Note:* Don't be fooled; this word has nothing to do with noise. My parents get angry when I don't clean my <u>noisome</u> room. It really an<u>noys 'em</u>.
nonchalant	**appearing casual, cool, indifferent, chilled out** Because the hare considered the race against the tortoise a <u>nonchallenge</u>, he was <u>nonchalant</u> about it and ended up losing.
nonplussed	**perplexed; baffled** She had expected to get an A-<u>plus</u> on the test; when she received an A-minus, she was <u>nonplussed</u>.
notorious	**famous for something bad; infamous** The nefarious noteperson was <u>notorious</u> for leaving nasty <u>notes</u> on people's doors.
novel	On the SAT this won't refer to a literary genre. It will mean **new; unusual; different** Years ago there was <u>no Vel</u>cro. Then someone had the <u>novel</u> idea of inventing it.

novice	beginner; person new to something He was a <u>novice</u> when it came to carpentry—he had <u>no vise</u>.

Novice

noxious	harmful to health or morals In industrial cities, the water can be <u>noxious</u>, and the people ob<u>noxious</u>.
nuance	subtle variation in color, meaning, or some other quality I could tell by the subtle <u>nuance</u> in her voice that my <u>new aunt</u> thought I was being a <u>nuis</u>ance.

A Villain's Death

The <u>nefarious</u> villain had reached the <u>nadir</u> of his <u>notorious</u> career. He had run into his <u>nemesis</u>, Nice Ned, the sheriff, after stealing some counterfeit cash (he often didn't notice the <u>nuances</u> of forged bills). Now he lay dying from two fatal earlobe wounds near a <u>noisome</u> junkyard in the desert.

Looking back, he recalled his <u>nascent</u> life as an outlaw. He had started as a <u>naive</u> <u>novice</u> in New York, but when the <u>noxious</u> city fumes got to him, he headed west, where a <u>novel</u> future awaited him. In later years, no longer a <u>neophyte</u>, his <u>nonchalant</u> attitude had left him <u>nonplussed</u>. Now nearly dead, he wanted to establish a <u>nexus</u> with his lost youth, but it was too late.

O

obdurate	hardened against good influence I can't en<u>dure it</u> when I try to reason with you because you're <u>obdurate</u>.

oblivion	**state of being totally forgotten** Lincoln will never fall into oblivion. No, Abe'll live on in our memories forever.
obsequious	**fawning; too easily compliant** "May I polish your toenails and peel you some grapes?" asked her obsequious attendant.
obsolete	**out of style; outdated** In the age of iPods, the compact disc is becoming obsolete.
obstreperous	**unruly; defiant; boisterous** High school librarians always say things like, "Let's keep the noise level to a minimum," "Cut the chatter," and "Don't be obstreperous in the library."
obtrude	**to force oneself or one's ideas on others; to extrude; to stick out** You gotta be some kinda social slob t' rudely obtrude your opinions on others.
obtuse	You may remember that in math an angle is called obtuse if it is greater than 90 degrees. However, the meaning that would be on the SAT is **stupid, thick-headed (think: an obtuse angle is "thick" and so is an obtuse person).** *Note:* An acute angle is less than 90 degrees and an acute person is sharp-minded—the opposite of obtuse. The obtuse man could not draw an obtuse angle.
occult	**pertaining to supernatural phenomena** A cult holds occult rituals.
odious	**offensive; hateful** The drug dealer was odious—he was trying to "O.D." us.
officious	**obnoxious and pushy in giving opinions** "Swimming in the lake is prohibited!" yelled the lifeguard to the drowning people. To which they replied, "Oh, fish us out and don't be officious!"

ogle	to stare at The skier <u>ogles</u> through her <u>goggles</u> all the cute ski instructors who whiz by.
olfactory	pertaining to the sense of smell The stench of that <u>ol' factory</u> was offensive to the <u>olfactory</u> sense.
omnipotent	all-powerful *Note:* This word is totally decodable: "omni" = all + "potent" = powerful omnipotent = all-powerful Lex Luthor desires to be the <u>omnipotent</u> ruler of the Earth, but Superman always defeats him.
omniscient	all-knowing *Note:* Also decodable: "omni" = all + "scient" = knowledge, knowing omniscient = all-knowing He read every old issue of <u>Omni</u> science magazine in the hope that he would become <u>omniscient</u>.
onerous	burdensome Would you <u>honor us</u> by helping us carry this <u>onerous</u> box of lead?
opulent	rich <u>Opulent</u> Oprah always wore <u>opals</u>—and diamonds and rubies and emeralds and . . .
orifice	small hole, opening, or vent "I've had a hard day at the <u>orifice</u>," said the dentist.

HARD DAY AT THE
Orifice

oscillate	to swing back and forth "His behavior <u>oscillated</u>," the babysitter reported. "He would be d<u>ocile eight</u> hours and then go crazy!"
ostensible	apparent; seeming (but usually not really) The <u>ostensible</u> reason that <u>Austin is able</u> to bench-press 300 pounds is his daily workout routine. The real reason is anabolic steroids. (This could also account for his breasts.)
ostentatious	showy; pretentious Glittering Emerald City is <u>Oz-tentatious</u>.
ostracize	to banish or exclude The <u>ostracized ost</u>rich stuck its head in the sand.
overt	open and observable, not hidden (see COVERT) Meg <u>overtly</u> knocked <u>over</u> Teddy's crystal toothbrush holder in order to attract attention.

A Fairy Tale

I went to the king, seeking to marry his daughter, but he was <u>obdurate</u> in his refusal. I was <u>obsequious</u>, but he was an <u>odious</u> and <u>obstreperous</u> man who kicked me out of the <u>opulent</u> palace because I was not pleasing to his <u>olfactory</u> sense. I went away, determined to <u>obtrude</u> my marital aspirations on him by raising an army and assaulting his <u>omnipotent</u> forces. However, my own forces were blown to <u>oblivion</u>.

I then went to see <u>Omniscient</u> Olga, an old one-eyed witch who dealt in the <u>occult</u> and <u>oscillated</u> between sanity and insanity. When I arrived at the <u>orifice</u> that led to her cave, she <u>ogled</u> me with her one eye as though I was <u>obtuse</u> to visit her. She advised me to go and be of service to the king, to offer to carry out every <u>onerous</u> task, <u>ostensibly</u> out of the kindness of my heart, but really to penetrate the castle and elope with the princess.

I made my way to the <u>ostentatious</u> royal city. As I <u>overtly</u> approached the gate, however, an <u>officious</u> guard informed me that I had been <u>ostracized</u> from the kingdom. Heartbroken, I left and went to seek my fortune selling doorknobs to nomads.

P

palatable	**acceptable to the taste; sufficiently good to be edible (think: plate-able)** The cannibal found his pal edible and quite palatable.
palliate	**to moderate the severity of, abate** "He looks pale; he ate something poisonous," the doctor said. "We'll have to palliate the poison with an antidote."
pallid	**having an extremely pale complexion** He was so pallid that even his eyes had pale lids.
palpable	**capable of being touched or felt (see TANGIBLE); real** I pinched my pal Pablo to see if he was palpable.
paragon	**model or example of perfection** Batman and Robin were a pair of goners, but Robin, that paragon of digital dexterity, managed to reach his utility belt and foil the Riddler's evil trap.
parch	**to make very dry, especially by heating** When things heat up playing board games, my throat sure parches easy, and I have to get a drink. (If you don't get the joke in this sentence, consult your local board game dealer.)
parsimonious	**stingy** The man was so parsimonious that he would not share his persimmon with us.
pathos	**quality in something that makes you pity it; feeling of sympathy or pity (remember "pathy" = feeling)** Feel pathos for me as I wander down this path oh so pitiful.
paucity	**smallness in number; scarcity (see DEARTH)** Remember, never name your pet store "Paw City." The poor city has a paucity of rich people.

pecuniary relating to money
"Lacking pecuniary support" is a euphemism for "being broke."

pedagogue schoolteacher or educator; boring, dry teacher
The teacher was such a pedagogue that Peter gagged at the thought of listening to another one of her boring lectures.

pedant **boring person who knows a lot but has little practical experience; dweeb**
Melvin, the six-year-old pedant, brought his pet ant to show-and-tell and droned on about it until all the kids fell asleep.

pedestrian You already know that this means a person traveling on foot. However, when it's used on the SAT it means **commonplace; ordinary.**
Compared to being a neurosurgeon, being a pediatrician is pedestrian.

penchant **strong liking; inclination**
Baseball teams have a penchant for pennants.

pensive **engaged in deep, often sad, thought**
After much deep, often sad, thought, William Penn decided to call his new state Pensiveania.

Don't get the next two words confused. They have the same first five letters and they both have to do with money, which you can remember because of the word penny. However, penurious has two very different definitions, and only one of them relates to penury.

WELCOME TO PENSIVE~ANIA

Pensive

penurious	parsimonious; stingy Scrooge was <u>penurious</u>. **extremely poor** Tiny Tim was <u>penurious</u>.
penury	**poverty; destitution** Tiny Tim lived a life of <u>penury</u>. <u>Penury</u> is a poor word that doesn't have as many letters as <u>penurious</u>. <u>Penurious</u> is a stingy word with lots of letters but it won't give any of its letters to <u>penury</u>.
perfidious	**dishonest (with an evil connotation)** "Step into my parlor," said the <u>perfidious</u> spider to the fly.
perfunctory	**done routinely, carelessly, and listlessly** If you are studying in a <u>perfunctory</u> manner, it's time for a break. Put on some funk music and let it permeate your room. But you can't do that, because you don't know what permeate means yet. So you'd better forget the break and continue studying.
permeable **permeate**	capable of being <u>permeated</u> **to spread or flow through** Your hair must be <u>permeable</u> to Ogilvie if you want a <u>perm</u>.
perspicacious	**perceptive; understanding** If you look at things from all <u>perspec</u>tives, you are <u>perspicacious</u>.
petulant	**unreasonably irritable or ill-tempered** That <u>pet you lent</u> me barked and snapped and was generally <u>petulant</u>. I'm giving it back.
philanthropy	**improvement of the world through charity; love of humanity in general** We did not write this book out of a penchant for pecuniary matters, as that would have been parsimonious and penurious of us. Instead, <u>philanthropy</u> was our motive.
pillage	**to rob violently** SATilla the Hun <u>pillaged</u> the village.

pithy | concise and meaningful
Pythagoras approached this triangle from the right angle, when he came up with his pithy Pythagorean theorem: $a^2 + b^2 = c^2$.

Note: The root "plac-" in the next two words means "calm."

placate | to appease, pacify, or calm
7 tried to placate gossip-starved 8 by telling her that 9 had 6 with 5, but instead of appeasing her, the news seemed to plague 8.

placid | calm; composed; undisturbed
"Pla!" Sid said, spitting out a mouthful of water. "This lake is calm and placid, but it tastes disgusting."

plaintive | sad; MELANCHOLY (think: complain)
When she realized that Judge Judy was going to rule against her, the plaintiff became plaintive.

plethora | superabundance; plenty; excess (opposite of DEARTH)
In case you haven't noticed yet, there is a plethora of terrible puns in this book.

plunder | to rob (usually violently); to PILLAGE
SATilla the Hun rode in like thunder to plunder our village. I escaped because I hid under my mattress.

politic | shrewd; clever
Politicians must be politic in order to win votes.

posthumous | continuing or done after one's death
Note: Decode:
"post" = after
+ "humus" = earth

posthumous = after earth

Suppose the five of us died of "pun"icillin poisoning. Our book would have to be published posthumously.

pragmatic	practical (think: "pragtical") The Craftmatic adjustable bed is pragmatic because it is <u>prac</u>tically auto<u>matic</u>.
precipice	cliff; steep overhang The <u>precipi</u>tation, combined with the ice, was responsible for his driving off the <u>precipice</u>.
precocious	**characterized by unusually early development** The high school basketball coach hoped that there would be some <u>precocious</u> basketball players in our elementary school, so he <u>precoached us</u>.

You mean, you have to type in all your commands? What about the "mouse"?

This is before all that.

Precursor

precursor	**predecessor; what came before** Although Mickey might disagree, many would say that the <u>precursor</u> to the mouse was the computer keyboard.

presage	**to give an indication or warning of something that will happen in the future**
	  "pre" = before
	 + "sage" = a smart person who tells people things
	   presage = tell before
	
	When the economists <u>presaged</u> that the economy was going to get worse, Michelle watched the <u>prez age</u>.

prevalent	**commonly occurring or existing** Before knights were <u>prevalent</u>, the world was in its <u>pre-valiant</u> period.
prevaricate	Prevaricate means to, ah—it's from the French *prévaricat*—it means to, um, to win the lottery. Yeah, that's it—win the lottery. We <u>prevaricated</u> in the above definition. *Prevaricate* really means **to avoid the truth; equivocate; lie.**

proboscis	long, hollow snout The bumblebee's <u>proboscis prob</u>ed for nectar in the flower.
profuse	abundant; overflowing Our <u>prof use</u>d <u>profuse</u> amounts of <u>prof</u>ane language. Then he was fired.
proliferate	to increase or spread rapidly The <u>pro-life</u> movement <u>proliferated</u> in the fundamentalist part of the state.
prolific	producing lots of offspring or fruit; fertile; producing lots of work or results The guy who writes *CliffsNotes* is <u>pro-Cliff-ic</u>; he's got hundreds of titles in print.
prosaic	lacking excitement or imagination; dull The sad artist thought her art-work was <u>prosaic</u>. She took some <u>Prozac</u>, but she still thought her <u>mosaic</u> of giant artichokes was lacking.
puissant	powerful, mighty Even though it's a compliment, you shouldn't call the school bully "<u>puissant</u>" because he might think you called him something else.
pulverize	to grind to bits If I asked nicely, could I <u>pulverize</u> your gerbil?
pusillanimous	timid; cowardly; wimpy The lion in *The Wizard of Oz* was <u>pussyllanimous</u>.
putrid	decomposed; foul-smelling (pukey) <u>P.U.!</u> <u>Try</u> disinfecting this <u>putrid</u> sneaker.

WHAT'D you call me?

Uh... puissant..?

Puissant

Petulant Peanuts

Philip DePance and his coworker, Peanuts Burnes, were on a lunch break from the philanthropic firm of "Paucity to Plethora" when Phil suddenly asked, "Peanuts, what are we going to do?"

"I guess you should start by changing your name. Have you noticed that it sounds pitiful whether you say Philip DePance, Phil DePance, or P. DePance?" she replied.

"No, it's just a pedestrian name! But what I meant was what are we going to do about the company's pecuniary state? We're on a precipice as it is, and if that porcine pedant of a boss continues his practices, we'll be living in penury for sure!"

"Well, maybe we could frame him for pillaging the company's bank account! Rumors are already permeating the office that he has a penchant for plundering."

"Hmm . . . I'm a little pensive. But I suppose it is the most politic, pragmatic, and perspicacious plan we could think of," said Phil. "I'm parched. Let's start this meal!"

They ordered fruit after the waiter told them that the banana trees were prolific at this time of year, and they were brought spotted bananas that seemed palatable enough.

But soon Phil turned pallid. "My proboscis is detecting something putrid," he said.

"Eww!" Peanuts added. "And it's not palliating! It's the bananas! I knew those spots presaged something."

"Waiter," Phil called. "We are petulant already because of pecuniary problems and, to make a long story pithy, are too pusillanimous to pulverize these bananas properly. You seem puissant enough; do the job before the odor proliferates!"

"I don't smell anything," the waiter replied.

"Oh, don't prevaricate. We will not be placated until we have palpable proof that the prevalent filth is gone!" said Peanuts in the fashion of a true pedagogue.

Plaintively, full of pathos, the waiter smashed the bananas and took them away. "Even posthumously, my precursor still perfunctorily makes me look like the paragon of poor service! These bananas were planted by him!" he muttered as he walked off.

"Well, I feel better, Peanuts. We could work here!" Phil said, once again placid.

A plethora of p-words! —Ada

Q

"The world would be a better place if there were more Q words."
—ANONYMOUS

quagmire
Literally, a **swamp.** However, the definition that would be used on the SAT is, **difficult situation that's hard to get out of,** a figurative use of the first definition.
Batman was in a <u>quagmire</u> when Poison Ivy tried to drown him in swamp muck, but he escaped by using the anti-<u>quagmire</u> Bat-spray.

quail
to draw back in fear
Dan Quayle <u>quailed</u> when he saw Dick Cheney coming at him with a shotgun.

qualm
doubt; uneasiness; sudden pang of sickness or faintness
Tyra had some <u>qualms</u> when the photographer asked her to pose atop a volcano in Guam.

qualitative
quantitative
having to do with a <u>quality</u>
capable of being expressed as, or having to do with, a number or <u>quantity</u>
"I did really well on my history exam" is a <u>qualitative</u> description of how you did on the history exam.
"I got a 96 on my history exam" is a <u>quantitative</u> description of how you did on the history exam.

But, what if I rain and no one's even planned a picnic?

THE **Qualm** BEFORE THE STORM

quandary
state of uncertainty; dilemma
He was in a <u>quandary</u> about whether to do his laundry; he liked the grunge look, but his clothes were beginning to smell.

quarantine	isolate because of a disease

We had to ⟨ quarantine ⟩ this word so that it wouldn't infect its neighbors and make them queasy.

queasy	nauseated; uneasy

Uneasy and queasy rhyme. So does the following poem:
When on the boat it got breezy,
I began to feel queasy.
Drug dealers are sleazy.
(A public service message from the authors.)

querulous	complaining; peevish

In private, the girls on *America's Next Top Model* are querulous. They complain about each other endlessly.

quip	snappy response

Note: Quip = *qui*ck + *p*oint. A quip is a quick and witty point made during a conversation.
I said to him, "Be careful with those detergents." He quipped, "Yeah, I know what you mean. I put some spot remover on my dog the other day and he disappeared." (From comedian Steven Wright.)

quixotic	**having the same foolish, impractical, romantic idealism as Don Quixote (Really, this isn't a pun.)**

Nestlé's CEO had the quixotic notion of making Quik exotic by offering flavors like sun-dried tomato.

quorum	**minimum number of people that have to be at a meeting in order for the meeting to be official**

(It sounds like a video game, doesn't it?)
Before the council can begin the boredom, it's required that they have a quorum.

A Quick Meeting of Minds

"Quorum, quorum, we must have a quorum!" shouted the leader.

"Why?" asked an idiot. "Qualitatively speaking, it's quicker to quantify the quarks in a quarter."

"Ahh, we are indeed in a quagmire. We need a quantitative estimate of how many quacks are here."

"Yes, it is a bit of a quandary," spoke another idiot. "I know, why don't we vote on whether or not to begin the meeting?"

"I have qualms about doing that," said the first idiot.

"Quiet, you idiots, or you'll be quarantined!" quoth the leader.

They quailed before his wrath, and both felt a bit queasy.

"Now then," said the leader, "don't be querulous. I have a plan. You may think me somewhat quixotic, but I truly believe that if we burst forth with enough clever quips, we might be recognized as not being quite so stupid as we really are. And with that thought in mind, I'd like to close this meeting of the village idiots."

R

rampage — (n.) course of wild behavior
(v.) to move wildly
The guy who was supposed to bring us a male sheep went on a rampage, then moved to Hawaii.
Grandma said, "No one at Gramp's age should rampage."

rampant — unrestrained
The ram panted after it ran rampant around the field for two days.

rant — to rave; to speak wildly
My parents always rant and rave like the tyrants they are when I don't wear socks. So I will buy bright orange socks to appease them.

rapacious	plundering; ravenous; greedy

The <u>rapacious</u> velociraptor attacked the children while they were still on their bikes; it ate the fat kids first.

Are you still remembering to do the mnemonic thing? Okay, we'll walk you through it one more time. Picture the velociraptor deep in the jungle, wearing a sweatshirt that says *rapacious*. It opens its frightening mouth and exhales its foul-smelling breath, and you see that its teeth spell out *rapacious*. Hear the wild shrieks (*"rapacious! rapacious!"*) as it pounces on the kids on their bikes, using its sharp claws to tear the word *rapacious* into the tender flesh. Blood gushes onto the ground, where it forms the word *rapacious*.

Yes, we know we're sick and twisted. But we also know our vocab words.

rapprochement	reconciliation (think: re-approachment)

Carrying an iPad as a peace offering, Julie <u>approached</u> her estranged little brother, but her attempt at <u>rapprochement</u> ended when he shot her with his squirt gun.

ratiocination	logical, methodical thinking

Through a process of <u>ratiocination</u>, you could have figured out this word because it sounds like <u>rational</u>.

rationalize	to make rational; justify

It is impossible to <u>rationalize</u> the senseless crime of cat juggling.

ravage	plunder

SATilla the Hun <u>ravaged</u> the countryside.

ravenous	hungry

The <u>raven</u> was so <u>ravenous</u> that he ate his own wing.

raze	to tear down; demolish The striking cereal workers used an enormous <u>razor</u> to <u>raze</u> the <u>raisin</u> bran factory.
realm	kingdom The king promised me half his <u>realm</u> if I would take the critical reading section for him, but I knew he was lying.
recalcitrant	stubborn I adamantly and obdurately refuse to admit that I am <u>recalcitrant</u>.

Raze

recapitulate	**to repeat, or state again, in a form that is more laconic and much briefer than the manner in which it was initially stated** Now we are going to <u>recapitulate</u> the above definition: to repeat concisely. Think: When a sportscaster <u>recaps</u> the game, she gives a brief summary of what has happened.
reciprocal	**mutual** We have a <u>reciprocal</u> agreement not to spit watermelon seeds at each other.
recondite	**abstruse; profound** If this story weren't so <u>recondite</u>, I <u>reckon I'd</u> understand it. **concealed; hidden from sight** He kept his pet condor <u>recondite</u> for fear that his environmentalist sister would set it free.
rectify	**to cor<u>rect</u>; set right** Tim had to visit the proctologist to <u>rectify</u> <u>recur</u>rent <u>rect</u>al problems.

recumbent	lying down

With both legs broken and his th<u>umb bent</u>, he spent most of the day <u>recumbent</u>.

redolent	fragrant

I use Pep<u>sodent</u> because it's so <u>redolent</u> of peppermint.

redoubtable	frighteningly awe-inspiring; formidable

Un<u>doubtedly</u>, the prospect of serving 100 hungry murderers a Thanksgiving dinner with<u>out a table</u> is <u>redoubtable</u>, but we think you can do it.

redress	to set right, remedy, compensate

When Cinderella arrived at the ball wearing only a slip and glass slippers, the prince suggested it was time to <u>redress</u> the situation.

redundant	repetitious; done over and over many times; repeatedly repetitive

The above definition is <u>redundant</u>.

refractory	disobedient; stubborn

The <u>refractory</u> prism refused to <u>refract</u> the light rays, so it was sent back to the factory.

refulgent	shining; radiant

"It's time to <u>refuel, gents</u>," said the driver, who loved gas stations, with a <u>refulgent</u> smile.

refute	to disprove

"<u>Ref, you'd</u> better listen up while I <u>refute</u> your call," said the irate player. "That ball was in."

reiterate	**to repeat**
	Note: Iterate also means repeat.
	I would like to reiterate my accusation—you are a noodlehead.
relevant	**having significant importance**
	Peanuts are relevant to an elephant's development.
remorse	**bitter regret; guilt**
remorseless	**having no remorse**
	When the remorseless spy catcher took away our telegraph machine for the second time, we were re-Morse-less.
renascent	**coming into being again (see NASCENT)**
	During the Renaissance, classical culture was renascent.
reticent	**silent; restrained in behavior**
	Scarlett said to Rhett, "Why are you so reticent?" He did not respond. "Is it because I didn't write you a letter?" she asked. He nodded. "But Rhett, I sent you a postcard."
retrograde	**moving backward to an earlier, usually inferior, position**

Decodable alert!
—Ada

After receiving an A grade in history first semester, Michael's B grade second semester was retrograde.

I can't believe I've slipped back down to a C-

REPORT CARD

Retrograde

Retsyn	We're not sure what this is, but there's a glistening drop of it in every little Cert.
rhubarb	This won't be on the test, but try repeating it five times quickly out loud.
rob	**to filch, pilfer, loot, purloin, peculate**
	You know that rob means "steal," but do you know all the words in the definition? Each is a different kind of stealing. Go filch a dictionary and look up the different connotations of each word.

ruddy	having a healthy, reddish color (<u>ruddy</u> rhymes with bloody) When you get a facial, the beautician makes your face muddy so that it will be <u>ruddy</u>.
ruminate	**to chew cud (this definition won't be on the SAT)** **to think a lot about; cogitate** *Note:* The definitions are related. "To think a lot about something" is kind of like "chewing something over in your mind." Also, when cows are chewing their cud, they look like they're thinking. The physicist went into the laboratory <u>room 'n' ate</u> cupcakes while <u>ruminating</u> about how to put the filling inside Twinkies.
A Romance	He was <u>recumbent</u> on his bed, <u>ruminating</u> on his <u>renascent</u> affair with the countess. She had left him and then <u>redressed</u> their relationship by returning, and they had reached a <u>rapprochement</u>. Now that she was <u>reciprocating</u> his love, he was once again the happiest man in the <u>realm</u>. Or was he? There was a rap on the door and the air was suddenly <u>redolent</u> of her perfume. "Darling," she said, opening the door, her face <u>refulgent</u> with rapture. He frowned as she kissed him, and she laughed. "Really. Don't be such a <u>recalcitrant</u> child. You're being altogether too <u>reticent</u>." She kissed him again. He remained <u>refractory</u> and refused to smile. She came over and reclined next to him. "I'm sorry I left you. I had to. I needed room . . ." She began <u>recapitulating</u> the <u>relevant</u> parts of the <u>recondite</u> explanation she had given when she left. He did not respond. Suddenly, there was an explosion on the street below. Riotous sounds reverberated through the air. The countess strode swiftly to the window. "It's the Roman army. They've been threatening to <u>raze</u> the city and now they're on a <u>rampage</u>." A group of soldiers began to batter the front door. "Our only recourse is to run to the roof as rapidly as we can," she <u>ratiocinated</u>. She climbed to the roof and crept over to the neighboring building. He hesitated

at the gap between the buildings, momentarily paralyzed by the <u>redoubtable</u> distance to the ground. Then he leapt across, and they raced over the roofs, with the <u>rapacious</u> soldiers running <u>rampant</u> through the streets below, <u>ravaging</u> the city. "<u>Remorseless</u> rogues," she muttered. "They'll change their tune later when they have to <u>rectify</u> all the damage they're doing."

"Undoubtedly, they've <u>rationalized</u> their behavior by saying it was the only route left open for them," he replied.

They rested a moment, trying to recover from the exertion. Their faces were <u>ruddy</u>.

"You're wonderfully quick," he remarked.

"I can't <u>refute</u> that. I'm also <u>ravenous</u>. We'll have to risk a reappearance."

The outskirts of town were quiet. They slipped into a restaurant. They were led to a table and gratefully sat down. "Now listen here," he scolded, sipping his red wine. "I want some assurance that you won't run off again and leave me rueing the day I met you."

"Whatever are you <u>ranting</u> about?" she retorted.

He <u>reiterated</u> his request, becoming riled.

She laughed. "Darling, you're being ridiculous as well as <u>redundant</u>. It's such a bore, really. Waiter, there's a drop of <u>Retsyn</u> in my <u>rhubarb</u> soup. Please be good enough to remove it." She turned to him again. "Relax. I'm here now, and so is our repast, at last."

S

| saga | long adventure story |

Titanic is the <u>soggy saga</u> of a boatload of beautiful people hitting a really big ice cube.

| sagacious | wise |

As age makes people more <u>sagacious</u>, parts of their body begin to <u>sag</u>.

salacious	lecherous; erotically stimulating "Ooooo, that's <u>so luscious</u>," he said, licking his plump red lips <u>salaciously</u>.
sanguine	reddish, blood-colored The fierce black bull's hopes <u>sank when</u> he saw his <u>sanguine</u> wound. **optimistic; cheerful** "I'm so glad to be an arctic bird," <u>sang Gwen</u> the <u>sanguine</u> penguin.
scanty	insufficient; small (often used in expressions like **"The <u>scantily</u> clad models were displaying the fall line of underwear.")** Food is <u>scanty</u> in the <u>shanty's</u> pantry.
scrutiny	inspection; study; careful searching An inspection of Canadian police is a <u>scrutiny</u> of the Mounties.
sedate **sedative**	to soothe, calm, or tranquilize **something, usually a drug, that <u>sedates</u>** In *One Flew Over the Cuckoo's Nest*, <u>sedatives</u> are given to <u>sedate</u> Jack Nicholson.
sedition	conduct or language inciting rebellion against authority Karl Marx's publisher rejected Marx's first manuscript of *The Communist Manifesto*, saying, "Thi<u>s edition</u> does not contain enough <u>sedition</u>."
sequester	to separate, set apart, isolate Tired of having his SAT studies interrupted, Larry hired a boat and went on a <u>sea quest</u> for a desert island where he could <u>sequester</u> himself for a semester.
servile	humbly yielding; submissive The <u>serv</u>ants were <u>vile</u> and <u>servile</u>.

shiftless

lazy; showing lack of motivation; incompetent
The shiftless secretary couldn't type capital letters. (Get it?)

simultaneous

happening at the same time
I will now attempt to rub cheese on my chest while simultaneously drinking salsa through a straw and juggling ostrich eggs.

sinister

foreboding of evil
Note: Sinister means "left" in Latin. In ancient times the left side was considered unlucky—the side from which evil would approach. This notion survives today in phrases such as *right-hand man* and *left-handed compliment*. Six sinister sisters scared seven silly senators. (Say this ten times fast.)

skeptical

doubting; disbelieving
You think you can escape tickle torture? I'm skeptical.

sloth

indolence; inactivity
"I'm at a loss to explain my sloth," confessed the lazy, two-toed furry animal hanging languidly in the tree.

slovenly

messy; characteristic of a slob
Remember: Whenever "love" gets in the middle of anything, it gets messy.
Unless you're Rachael Ray, your oven may look slovenly after you make Sweet and Tasty 800 Bars (see page 319).

SLOVENLY

somber	dark; dull; gloomy The remorseful b<u>omber</u> was <u>somber</u> when he realized what he had done.
soporific	sleep-inducing The other SAT books are <u>soporific</u>; ours is sophomoric.
sparse	thinly spread or distributed; not crowded I was still hungry after eating at the fancy restaurant. The food was arranged <u>sparsely</u> and the gaps on the plate were filled with <u>parsley</u>.
stagnant **stagnate**	not moving or flowing; motionless, <u>stationary</u> to be <u>stagnant</u> The air in SAT testing halls is often <u>stagnant</u>, which perhaps explains why the proctors look stale and crusty.
static	On the SAT, this probably would not refer to the fuzzy noise you hear when you get too far away from a radio station's signal nor to the effect produced when you rub a balloon across your head. Instead, it will probably mean **having no motion; at rest; stationary.** The contents of our <u>attic</u> are <u>static</u>; they haven't changed in years.
steadfast	fixed or unchanging No matter how many times we tried to fix the clock, it <u>stayed fast</u>. It was <u>steadfast</u>. faithful One must be <u>steadfast</u> on Yom Kippur, and not eat. In<u>stead, fast</u>.
stinkhorn	Look up this word in an *American Heritage Dictionary*, New College Edition (the first edition). The picture is the most phallic image you will ever see in a venerable reference book.
stolid	showing little emotion or pain; emotionally <u>solid</u> Even though I loved my pet <u>stinkhorn</u>, I tried to be <u>stolid</u> when they <u>stole it</u>.

submission	**the act of yielding to the authority of another** The submarine captain demanded the <u>submission</u> of the sailors on the <u>sub</u> <u>mission</u>.
subvert	**to overthrow or undermine the power of** The prizewinning poet was accused of trying to <u>subvert</u> his poetry when he started writing his verses on submarine sandwiches.
succulent	**juicy; interesting** Eve <u>sucked</u> on the <u>succulent</u> forbidden fruit.
suffrage	**right to vote; franchise** Before 1920, women <u>suffered</u> from a lack of <u>suffrage</u>. But the <u>suffragettes</u> changed all that and now women can rock the vote along with men.
summon	**to call forth; to call together** The king <u>summoned</u> his advisor. When his advisor's footsteps could be heard in the hall, the king's submissive assistant exclaimed, "<u>S</u>omeone's c<u>omin'</u>."
	Following are four superior words beginning with "super-."
supercilious	**haughty; conceited; disdainful** The <u>supercilious</u> person said, "I am perfect, but you are a <u>super silly ass</u>."
superfluous	**beyond what's necessary; extra** <u>Super</u>man once <u>flew us</u> home without his cape. This suggests that his cape is just a <u>superfluous</u> item and not something he needs in order to fly.
superlative	**most; of the highest order; surpassing all others** We're going to be <u>super late if</u> the car breaks down, and Mom is going to be <u>superlatively</u> pissed off.

supersede | to take the place of
After Farmer Clark planted the new tomato super seed, it completely superseded the regular seeds.

surreptitious | done clandestinely (secretly) or by stealth
Afraid that the public might see, Daniel stroked the cow's udder surreptitiously.

sweat gland | small secretory gland in the skin that excretes water and body salts
Are you awake?

swindle | to cheat or defraud
This airplane doesn't really work, but this wind'll keep it up in the air long enough for me to swindle the customer into buying it.

sycophant | servile person who follows and flatters another person in the hope of winning favor
After the concert, Miley Cyrus was surrounded by sycophants. Suddenly she screamed, "I'm sick of fans. You guys are crazy. You're nothing more than a bunch of psycho fans."

synthetic | not real; man-made; fabricated
"Synthetic fabric is one thing—I like my polyester and rayon gowns," cried Cruella De Vil, wrapping her white coat with black dots around her. "But synthetic Dalmatian fur? Never!"

A Shocking Courtroom Saga

My sweat glands were working overtime in the stagnant air of the courtroom as I stolidly continued my unscrupulous questioning of the sinister defendant on trial for sedition (related to the surreptitious taking away of suffrage). Although he remained steadfast in proclaiming his innocence, the jury was obviously skeptical. When I superseded him on the courtroom

Boy, did I get left in the dust!

NEW SUPER SEED

OLD REGULAR SEED

Supersede

floor, it was clear that the other lawyer's points were <u>soporific</u> compared to my <u>superlative</u> arguments. His <u>scanty</u> arguments were <u>sparsely</u> filled with <u>synthetic</u>-sounding facts and his words <u>stagnated</u> as he spoke. He was an obvious <u>sycophant</u>, but the judge just sat <u>somberly</u> in the shadows, <u>servile</u>. I was confident. All further speech was <u>superfluous</u>. I know you'll think me <u>shiftless</u>, but I thought I could afford to be <u>slothful</u> and not <u>summon</u> any more witnesses. So, <u>superciliously</u>, I said, "The State rests, Your Honor." I ran out to lunch, and the jury was <u>sequestered</u>.

Two hours later the jury was <u>summoned</u>, and I waited, drooling <u>salaciously</u>, expecting the <u>succulent</u> word "guilty." So I was surprised when I heard the word "not" as well. "I've been <u>subverted</u> and <u>swindled</u>!" I yelled. Then the bailiff hit me over the head and I <u>submissively</u> accepted a <u>sedative</u>.

Now I cultivate <u>sanguine</u> <u>stinkhorns</u> and lead a much quieter, <u>static</u> life.

"Shiftless" and "listless" are pretty similar!

–Ada

T

table	The SAT would not refer to the four-legged household object. Rather, the SAT definition would be **to remove from consideration.** The legislature <u>tabled</u> the amendment that would have made everyone eat their vege<u>tables</u>.
taciturn	untalkative; uncommunicative The normally chatty billionaire was <u>taciturn</u> when the IRS asked what his <u>assets earn</u>.
tact	skill in dealing with people in difficult situations (think: good social <u>tactics</u>) When at a funeral, it is not <u>tactful</u> to say, "Darn, she owed me money."

tangible

existing materially; palpable; able to be touched

Compare with in<u>tangible</u>: Love, fear, and hope are in<u>tangible</u>. <u>T</u>angerines, antelopes, and pencils are <u>tangible</u>.

tedious

boring; tiresome; trivial

The other team scored so many touchdowns that it became <u>tedious</u> to watch them <u>TD us</u>.

temerity

recklessness; wild craziness; lack of regard for danger

"Boromir's <u>temerity</u> in facing the Orcs was nothing compared to ours facing the ETS," boasted the brash review-book authors.

temperance

the quality of being temperate

temperate

showing self-restraint by not doing things to excess; moderate

She was <u>temperate</u>: She rarely lost her <u>temper</u> and never <u>ate</u> too much.

tempestuous

stormy; turbulent; like a tempest (violent windstorm)

When we lose our <u>temper</u>s, <u>eschew us</u> because we behave <u>tempestuously</u>. (If you've forgotten what *eschew* means, we "<u>sugg-eschew</u>" go look it up.)

tenacity

persistence; tending to hold on firmly

The student took <u>ten SATs</u> with <u>tenacity</u> until she got a perfect score. It took her so many tries because she hadn't read *Up Your Score*.

tenet

principle or doctrine

The Ten Commandments are <u>ten eternal</u> <u>tenets</u>.

tepid

lukewarm; somewhat warm

(Did you ever try the one where you put a sleeping person's hand in <u>tepid</u> water and . . .)

Tom's tea was <u>tepid</u>, so he nuked it in the microwave.

terrestrial	**of the earth** Often when I gaze celestial, I forget all things <u>terrestrial</u>. Problem is, when I look at space, I always fall flat on my face.
terse	**concise; free of superfluous words** This <u>verse</u> is <u>terse</u>.
thwart	**to prevent from taking place; challenge** "We must <u>thwart</u> <u>the wart</u>," the dermatologist decided.
tirade	**long and vehement speech** The dean gave the sorority girls a <u>tirade</u> for responding to the fraternity's panty raid with a <u>tie raid</u>.
torrid	**parched by the sun; hot; burning** I plan <u>to rid</u> myself of this <u>torrid</u> climate by moving to Alaska. **passionate** Soap opera previews always talk about "<u>torrid</u> love affairs."
treachery	**betrayal of trust; traitorousness** When <u>Treach</u> left his rap group Naughty by Nature to embark on a solo career, the group called him <u>treacherous</u>.
trepidation	**fear; state of anxiety or fear that makes you <u>tremble</u>** We couldn't think of a good sentence so we made up a bunch of bogus words: prepidation—fear of clothes from Abercrombie & Fitch strepidation—fear of getting a sore throat stripidation—fear of taking off your clothes trapidation—fear of getting stuck tripidation—fear of vacations, stumbling, and drugs troopidation—fear of getting drafted or of watching *Flags of Our Fathers* This should be enough to remind you that <u>trepidation</u> means "fear."

tribute | **gift expressing gratitude or respect**
Elton John's <u>tribute</u> to Princess Diana at her funeral was described by French critics as "<u>très beautiful</u>."

triskaidekaphobia | **fear of the number 13**
If you have <u>triskaidekaphobia</u>, you'll always skip questions numbered 13 on the SAT. (This word won't be on the test, but you should use it as much as possible.)

truncate | **to shorten by chopping off the end**
The elephant's <u>trunk</u> was <u>truncated</u> when his friend <u>ate</u> his <u>trunk</u>.

Like I needed it shorter.

kind of rubbery

BURP

Truncate

U

ubiquitous | **being or seeming to be everywhere at the same time; omnipresent**
The Evil Testing Serpent is <u>ubiquitous</u>. He tortures students all over the nation at the same time.
Take five yellow Post-it notes and write <u>ubiquitous</u> on each one. Then stick them all over your house. The stickers will then be <u>ubiquitous</u>.

There are a lot of SAT words that start with "un-." However, since "un-" usually means "not," most of these words just mean the opposite of what they mean without the "un-." For example: unabashed = not abashed.

However, some "un-" words aren't direct opposites. Others aren't even words without the "un-" (for example, *uncle*).

unassuming	not pretentious; modest Although they were rich enough to pay off the federal deficit, they were <u>unassuming</u> and lived in a tent.
unawares	This word doesn't mean <u>not aware</u>; it means **by surprise; unexpectedly** (*Note:* it's an adverb); compare UNWITTING. We came up behind him <u>unawares</u> and saw him in his <u>underwear</u>.
uncouth	crude; unrefined; awkward (think: uncool) The <u>uncouth</u> <u>youth</u> hit people in the <u>tooth</u> (then scratched his hairy pits and grunted).
unruly	difficult to govern; impossible to discipline They were used to living without <u>rules</u>, so they were <u>unruly</u>.
unscrupulous	unprincipled; lacking ethical values After the church robbery, the minister lamented, "It takes an <u>unscrupulous</u> criminal to <u>unscrew</u> the seats and leave us <u>pewless</u>."
unwitting	unaware; not knowing The Evil Testing Serpent fiendishly devours <u>unwitting</u> students.
upshot	outcome; result *Note:* This word was originally an archery term. The last shot of an archery tournament was called the <u>upshot</u>, and it often determined the result or outcome of the tournament. Bart was hit in the rear by an <u>upshot</u> at the archery tournament. The <u>upshot</u> of this was that he had to take the SAT standing <u>up</u>.
usurp	to illegally seize the power or rights from another Yusef <u>usurped</u> Boris's position by staging a coup.

usury	**lending of money at outrageously high interest; loan sharking** When the 250-pound loan shark practiced <u>usury</u>, his creditors <u>usually</u> paid him back pretty quickly.

Tutu Story

"Don't be <u>taciturn</u>!" urged the talkative twerp wearing a tutu. "Look at me—I have great <u>tact</u>, and no one could accuse me of <u>trepidation</u>," he continued. "In fact, it's often been said that my <u>temerity</u> pays <u>tribute</u> to my <u>torrid</u> soul."

His <u>temperate</u> companion held <u>tenaciously</u> to her <u>tenets</u> and tried to tune out her <u>tempestuous</u> tutued friend's <u>tirade</u>. She muttered, "He must not be <u>terrestrial</u>."

The situation was entirely too <u>tedious</u>, so I turned to someone else at my table and asked, "Do you think Congress will <u>table</u> the discussion about the new chairs?"

There was an almost <u>tangible</u> silence. Then a sandaled young man put an ice cube in his <u>tepid</u> tea and said, "That's a touchy subject here. We're all upset about our senator's <u>unscrupulous</u> <u>treachery</u> in supporting the bill."

"We're going to try to <u>thwart</u> him," said the <u>temperate</u> companion <u>tersely</u>. "If that bill passes, I'll <u>truncate</u> his term with allegations of <u>usury</u>, and the <u>upshot</u> of this will be that I will <u>usurp</u> his power."

Her words caught me <u>unawares</u>. The girl had seemed to me to be polite and <u>unassuming</u>, but instead she was an <u>uncouth</u> and <u>unruly</u> youth.

Craziness was <u>ubiquitous</u>.

V

vacillate	**to waver from one side to the other; oscillate** While the skier <u>vacillated</u> about whether to use Vaseline or ChapStick, his lips got chapped.

vacuity	emptiness; vacuum The scientists were amazed by the utter <u>vacuity</u> in the proctor's brain—there was not a trace of brain matter anywhere.
vainglorious	<u>vain</u>; boastful <u>Vainglorious</u> <u>Gloria</u> boasted about her vocabulary in <u>vain</u>—she got a 210 on the critical reading section.
valor	courage; bravery <u>Val</u>erie showed <u>valor</u> when she fought off the Evil Testing Serpent and got a perfect score on her SAT.
vehement	with ardor; energetically or violently forceful They fed the sedatives to the <u>vehement</u> protesters <u>via mints</u>.
ver-	**The motto of Harvard is "Veritas" and the motto of Yale is "Lux et veritas." These two schools may be knocking down your door once you get your 2400, so you might as well know that *veritas* is Latin for "truth." (*Lux* means "light.") When you see the root "ver-" in an SAT word, that word probably has something to do with truth.** Examples: veracity—truthfulness; accuracy verification—proof that something is true verisimilar—appearing to be true or possible verisimilitude—quality of being verisimilar veritable—unquestionable; actual; true verity—statement or belief considered to be the permanent truth vermicide—anything used to kill worms (Well, it doesn't always work.)
verbose	excessively wordy *Note:* This word has nothing to do with truth. They wrote and transcribed and copied down on paper and composed and thought of and typed a sentence that would be <u>verbose</u> because it had excessive <u>verbs</u>.

Or, "la verdad"
means "the truth"
for those of us
in Spanish classes.
¡Vamos!
— Ada

vex	to irritate or bother
vexation	the act of vexing

His <u>vexing</u> habit of reciting vocabulary words during sexual activity ruined his sex life.

vilify	to slander; defame (think: make vile)

Senator Joe McCarthy's <u>vill</u>ainous lies <u>vilified</u> many innocent people.

Although the next two words have the same first six letters and are related, they are not at all synonymous.

vindicate	to clear of blame or suspicion

The lawyers will <u>vindicate</u> their client by displaying evidence they ha<u>ve, indicating</u> that he didn't mean to steal the adult diapers from the grocery store.

vindictive	vengeful

The <u>vindictive</u> Wicked Witch of the West wanted to kill Dorothy to avenge the death of the Wicked Witch of the East.

vivacious	animated; full of energy

Sleepy the Dwarf took some <u>Viva</u>rin and became <u>vivacious</u>.

vocabulary	what you need to be successful in life, according to the ETS; the bane of our existence, according to anyone who has made it all the way to the Vs

vociferous	obnoxiously loud

The <u>vociferous</u> student demanded in a loud <u>voice</u> that the proctor turn on the lights before handing out the tests.

voluble	fluent in speech (especially in the derogatory sense of someone who talks too much)

The professor was so <u>voluble</u> that we had to take <u>volu</u>mes of notes.

voracious	eager to consume mounds of food We were so <u>voracious</u> that we even ate the Tupperware.

Vulcan	pointy-eared alien, devoid of warmth and emotion, who thinks logically Come on! Don't fall asleep. Only a few more pages to go.
vulnerable	unprotected The Evil Testing Serpent is <u>vulnerable</u> to the tricks in *Up Your Score*.

W

wanton	immoral; unchaste; cruel Blowing up the <u>one-ton</u> truck was an act of <u>wanton</u> destruction. They had a <u>wanton</u> night of passionate entanglement in a vat of <u>wonton</u> soup.
whim	capricious, freakish idea On a <u>whim</u>, the tournament directors decided to let the <u>wimp</u> play at <u>Wim</u>bledon.
wily	crafty <u>Wile E</u>. Coyote uses <u>wily</u> methods of sneaking up on the Road Runner <u>while he</u> isn't looking.
wistful	yearning; <u>wishful</u> with a hint of sadness As he thought of his lost love, William <u>whistled</u> a <u>wistful</u> melody and drank a bottle of her perfume.

wow | of or pertaining to golly-gee-whillikers

wrath | anger; rage
Elmer Fudd is full of <u>wrath</u> at that <u>wrath</u>cally wabbit that keeps eating his garden.

X

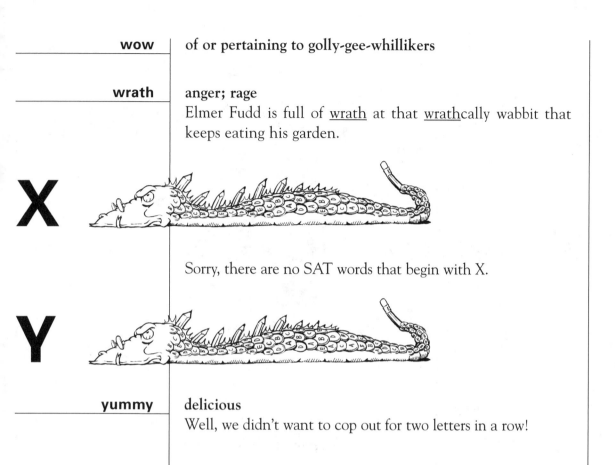

Sorry, there are no SAT words that begin with X.

Y

yummy | delicious
Well, we didn't want to cop out for two letters in a row!

An Avuncular Vendetta (or I'm Hungry, You Vile Worm)

My uncle was <u>valorous</u>, yet he was inclined to be quite <u>voluble</u> when faced with danger. His <u>verbose</u>, <u>vacuous</u> speeches terrified and bored his enemies. Certain <u>vindictive</u> individuals have attempted to <u>vilify</u> his reputation by insisting that he was a <u>vulnerable</u> wimp, but he has always managed to <u>vindicate</u> himself by <u>vehemently</u> <u>verifying</u> the <u>veracity</u> of his claims of courage.

Anyway, one day while my uncle was <u>vacillating</u> over a choice of beverages, the <u>vainglorious</u> Victor Ventura burst in on him, extremely <u>vexed</u>. He voiced his message <u>vociferously</u>: "I consider you a vile swine, and in the future I will not hesitate to spray you with <u>vermicide</u>."

"Pray tell," said my uncle <u>vivaciously</u>, "what is the cause of your <u>vexation</u>?"

"I came here with a <u>voracious</u> appetite," replied Victor, "and on a <u>whim</u> you <u>wantonly</u> denied me any food, you wretched worm."

"<u>Wow</u>," said my <u>wily</u> uncle <u>wistfully</u>, "you may as well spare me your <u>wrath</u>, because I don't have anything <u>yummy</u> to offer you."

Z

zany	crazy; <u>insane</u> The zany antics of the jackasses from *Jackass* earned them their own feature-length movies.
zeal **zealous**	enthusiasm full of zeal The <u>zealous</u> seal spun the ball with <u>zeal</u>.
zenith	peak; summit; acme (see NADIR, <u>zenith</u>'s antonym) If the <u>Zenith</u> company could invent a TV that would change channels automatically whenever a show started getting stupid, that would be the <u>zenith</u> of television technology.
zest	gusto; happy and vivacious enjoyment If you use <u>Zest</u> soap, you will feel full of <u>zest</u> for the rest of the day. You will also feel <u>Zest</u>fully clean.
zyzzyva	any of various tropical weevils of the genus *Zyzzyva,* often destructive to plants Who cares about <u>zyzzyvas</u>? You are done with the word lists. Congratulations! Think of all the words you know now that you didn't know before. Good work. You are going to rock on the critical reading section.

A Final Poem

A <u>zany</u>, <u>zealous</u>
<u>Zyzzyva</u>
<u>Zestfully</u>
Zigzagged up to the
<u>Zenith</u>.

USEFUL SYNONYMS

Following are lists of synonymous SAT words. Actually, they aren't exact synonyms, but they are closely related. When one of these words shows up on the test, it is usually enough to recognize that it's one of the *Slander* words, for example. However, sometimes you have to know the word's specific connotations. Use these lists only as aids; you should know the particular meaning of each word.

Ada says: Mixing up your vocab studying is very important. You want to make sure you don't just know all the "b" words on your list because you've read them in order so many times, but know their meanings if you see them in a different context as well. So shuffle those lists and flash cards!

Steal/Plunder	*Soothe/Make Better*	*Lusty*
depredate	allay	bawdy
filch	alleviate	lascivious
loot	ameliorate	lecherous
peculate	appease	lewd
pilfer	assuage	licentious
pillage	conciliate	salacious
plunder	mitigate	
purloin	mollify	*Stingy*
ravage	palliate	frugal
rob	placate	parsimonious
swindle	sedate	penurious

Lacking Interest or Spirit	*Slander*	*Wealth*
lackadaisical	calumniate	affluence
languid	be captious	opulence
lethargic	denigrate	ostentation
listless	impugn	superfluity
	make innuendo	Bill Gates
	insinuate	
	malign	
	vilify	

Proverb	*Excessively Flattering*	*To Free from Responsibility*
adage	adulatory	absolve
aphorism	fawning	exculpate
axiom	fulsome	exonerate
dictum	laudatory	vindicate
maxim	obsequious	

To Hate/Dislike	*Brief/To the Point*	*Secret/Stealthy*
abhor	concise	clandestine
abominate	laconic	furtive
detest	pithy	surreptitious
execrate	terse	ETS
loathe		
repudiate	*Deceptive Action*	
	ploy	
Without Preparation	ruse	
extemporaneous	stratagem	
impromptu	subterfuge	
improvised		

SIMILAR-LOOKING WORDS

These words make great flash cards!
—Ada

The following is a list of pairs of words that look similar and are easily confused with each other. Make sure you know the difference between them. Trying to confuse you with these pairs is one of the ETS's favorite tricks.

- adulate and adulterate
- adverse and averse
- anachronism and anarchism
- antipathy and apathy
- ascent and assent
- ascetic and aesthetic
- baleful and baneful
- capitulate and recapitulate
- censure and censor
- demure and demur

- discreet and discrete
- disparate and desperate
- divers and diverse
- elicit and illicit
- heterogeneous and homogeneous
- illusion and allusion
- imbibe and imbue
- imminent and eminent
- ingenious and ingenuous
- mendicant and mendacious
- mettle and meddle
- penury and penurious
- peremptory and preemptory
- pestilence and petulance
- qualitative and quantitative
- zyzzyva and aardvark

IMPORTANT LITERARY TERMS

If you're taking the SAT, you might not see any of the following literary terms or you might see all of them (no, not really), but you should probably expect to see at least a few. You're probably familiar with most of these terms since they're pretty standard fare for English class. But in case you had an English teacher who thought *Captain Underpants* was deep reading, we present . . .

*We can do a lot, but we aren't psychologists.
—Ada*

Literary Terms Guaranteed to Enrich Your Life*
(*This statement has not been evaluated by the people who evaluate such things.)

allegory

A story or narrative that is an extended metaphor in which characters and objects have symbolic meanings. An allegory's symbolic message is usually pretty obvious. In other words, you don't have to read *too* deeply to get it. Think: George Orwell's *Animal Farm*.

alliteration	The repetition of sounds, usually consonants or stressed sylla-bles, within a group of words. For example: "Sally sells seashells by the seashore."
allusion	A writer's brief reference to another work, person, place, or event within their own writing, left for the reader to notice and understand. Many literary texts allude to Greek classics (think: *The Odyssey*), canonized texts (think: Shakespeare), and, of course, the Bible.
ambiguity	The use of a word or a phrase to mean two or more different things. For example, if your girlfriend tells you, "I can't stop thinking about you. And believe me I've tried," her meaning is somewhat ambiguous. (Advice: Dump her before she dumps you.)
anecdote	A brief unelaborate story, often interesting and humorous. Something we all wish we could tell.
antagonist	The opposition to the main character (or protagonist). This can be a person, a thing, a feeling, a force. For example, Loki is the antagonist of *The Avengers*, while Moby-Dick is the antagonist in Herman Melville's novel. (Important: The antago-nist is not *always* the bad guy or villain.)
apostrophe	A direct address to an absent person, object, animal, or even a concept. For example, "Twinkle, twinkle little star, how I wonder what you are" is an apostrophe where the speaker addresses an object that can't respond.

autobiography	A book written about the author's own life.
biography	A book written about another person's life. (If you didn't know those two, close this book, lift it above your head, and drop it.)
characterization	How an author establishes a distinctive character in a book.
climax	The high point of the continuing action, usually just before the turning point and ending of the story. (And of other things, too.)
comedy	A genre of writing where stories and plays are amusing and funny (or supposed to be) and usually have happy endings.
conclusion	The outcome or ending of the story.
conflict	Opposition between characters or forces in a story. The three main types of conflicts are (1) person vs. person; (2) person vs. nature; (3) person vs. self.
connotation	An idea or meaning that's implied with a word but has nothing to do with what it actually is. For example, "eagle" connotes liberty and freedom, but these ideas have nothing to do with an actual live eagle.
dialogue	"A dialogue is a written conversation." "Really? No way!" "You betcha."
diction	An author's choice of words and conversational style that helps set the mood of a piece. For example, if your teacher changed her diction and started talking like a drill sergeant, the feel of your classroom would change.

epic	A long, sprawling literary work told in a formal style about the journeys of a hero or divine figure. The fate of a tribe, a nation, or even the entire human race is usually dependent on the result of the hero's journey. A modern example of an epic story is The Lord of the Rings trilogy.
epigraph	A quotation that's put at the beginning of a work.
euphemism	A phrase that replaces a less pleasant one. For example, we say, "Your barn door is open" when we really mean "Your pants are unzipped."
fable	A type of anecdote or short story with a moral lesson, usually on human behavior, at the end. Aesop's . . . er . . . Fables, and Joe Chandler Harris's Uncle Remus stories, are familiar examples.
falling action	Events that happen after the climax.
farce	A comedy in which impossible plots, slapstick humor, and exaggerated characters are used. *The Hangover* and *Bridesmaids* are farces.
figurative language	Language that uses figures of speech to convey a point. A speaker or writer using figurative language doesn't mean *exactly* the words they say. For example, if you say, "I ran faster than the wind to get here," you simply mean, "I ran very fast to get here," not that you *actually* ran faster than the wind.
flashback	A reference to an event that took place in a previous part of the story, or before the story even began.
foil	Someone who serves as a sharp contrast to another person. For example, the characters Darth Vader and Yoda in *Star Wars* are foils of each other. Characters that are foils don't have to be enemies, although many times they are.

genre	Different types of literature, such as satire, comedy, mystery, tragedy, or science fiction, each having its own qualities.
hyperbole	A gross overstatement or exaggeration. For example, "I was so embarrassed I wanted to die."
imagery	Using words that appeal to the senses in order to create a vivid description.
inference	A conclusion reached by evaluating the given facts. For example, if your friend is running at you with a red face, steam pouring out of his ears, and a raised baseball bat, you can *infer* that he is probably very angry at you. (You could also infer that the best thing for you to do is to start running.)

irony

The incongruity between what might be expected to happen and what actually happens. There are many different types of irony but the two most commonly used are dramatic irony and verbal irony. Dramatic irony involves a situation where a character performs an action that results in the exact reverse effect desired. For example, when Shakespeare's Juliet drinks a potion to appear dead so that she can run away and marry Romeo, it's dramatic irony when Romeo believes she is really dead and commits suicide. Verbal irony is when someone says something but really means the exact opposite. When your mom says, "Oh, you sure cleaned up your room!" she's using verbal irony.

metaphor	A comparison between two unlike things without using the words *like* or *as*. For example, the Katy Perry song "Firework" uses metaphor to tell listeners that they are fireworks, meaning they're strong and colorful.
mood	A feeling or emotional ambience created in a work, such as suspense, hope, fear, patriotism, or contentment.
myth	A traditional story meant to explain why the world is the way it is. Many ancient cultures, for example, used myths to explain natural events they did not yet understand, like why the sun sets and rises.
onomatopoeia	A word that makes the sound that it describes. For example, *pow, zip, splash,* and *bam!* Think of the old Batman comics.

oxymoron	A combination of words that are opposites. For example, *deafening silence, jumbo shrimp, genuine imitation, act naturally,* or *military intelligence.*
parable	A simple story illustrating a moral or religious lesson. Many religious texts are full of 'em, especially the Bible.
paradox	Something that seems to contradict itself, but actually reveals a truth. For example, "Youth is wasted on the young."

parallel structure	A series of sentences that uses the same basic structure. For example, Martin Luther King Jr.'s "I Have a Dream" speech has parallel structure.
parody	Something that humorously imitates another serious piece of work. Weird Al Yankovic parodies the songs that he rewrites, and *Scary Movie* and its sequels all parody different horror flicks.
pastoral	A literary piece nostalgic for the simplicity of rural life and natural settings.
personification	A figure of speech in which animals or objects are given human or living characteristics. For example, "The engine growled" is personifying the noise of the engine.
plot	The story. What actually happens. Hopefully the story has one.
point of view	The perspective from which the story is being told. It could be in the first person—"I"—or in the third person—"he/she." The second person point of view—"you"—is rarely used, but a good example is the Choose Your Own Adventure books you remember reading when you were in second grade.
protagonist	The central character (doesn't necessarily have to be "the good guy").
pun	A play on words that uses different words with similar or identical sounds. Many of the sentences in the *Up Your Score* vocabulary section are puns.
rhyme	A pattern of repeated end syllables. This is most applicable to poetry.

saga	A story of a family told through many generations.
satire	A work that's making fun of its subject, usually to criticize it. For example, in Jonathan Swift's *A Modest Proposal: For Preventing the Children of Poor People in Ireland from Being a Burden to Their Parents or Country, and for Making Them Beneficial to the Public*, Swift makes the satiric suggestion that poor Irish children should be *eaten* in order to cure their hunger and decrease the number of starving people. Through this outlandish suggestion, Swift criticizes the English government's treatment of the Irish poor.
setting	The time and place of a story.
short story	Exactly what it says.
simile	A comparison between two things that uses *like* or *as*. For example, "Life is like a box of chocolates."
soliloquy	When a person talks to him- or herself, either aloud or in their head. For example, Hamlet's famous speech that begins, "To be or not to be . . ."
stereotype	A way of describing people that is overly simplistic and usually based on prejudices. For example, an athletic African American, an Asian American computer genius, a blonde bimbo, a lonesome cowboy, and a redneck southerner are all stereotypes.
suspense	Expectation and excitement in anticipation of an uncertain outcome, like waiting for your SAT scores.
symbolism	When an object or a person describes an idea. For example, Enron now symbolizes corporate scandal for most Americans.

theme

The general concept of the story. For example, the theme of Rebecca Black's "Friday" is the joy of the end of the school week (or whatever you got out of it). Beware: The theme of a story is not necessarily what happened. A book could be about a girl traveling the world, while its theme is the importance of family.

tone

Tone expresses the speaker's attitude toward his reader or audience. There are as many tones in literature as there are in real-life conversations, such as anger, approval, pride, piety.

tragedy

A literary genre in which many bad things happen to the protagonist, culminating in an unhappy ending.

understatement

Making something seem considerably less significant than it is. The opposite of a hyperbole. For example, if you get a perfect score on the SATs and you say, "I did okay," you are understating your achievements.

THE MATH SECTION

45°

45°

THEORY OF STUDY

Unfortunately, you shouldn't expect jokes on the real SAT.

— Ada

Why was six afraid of seven?

Because seven ate nine.

With this lame joke as an introduction, we welcome you to the wonderful world of SAT math.

As most people know, the most appropriate place for doing math is in the bathroom. First of all, there are many geometric shapes in the bathroom: square tiles, round drains, cylindrical toilet paper rolls. Second, there is generally ample time for even the most freakish discoveries—an ancient Greek calculated pi to 70 digits while relaxing on a pay toilet in fourth-century Ithaca. Einstein himself concluded that space is bent while trying to catch a slippery bar of soap during an excursion in the tub. And everyone knows that Doc Brown from *Back to the Future* came up with the flux capacitor when he fell off the can.

What we mean to say is that when you go to the bathroom, you're not doing anything else useful, so you might as well study math.

This was Larry's idea, by the way.

The math sections of the SAT have standard multiple-choice questions and grid-in questions, both of which will be explained later.

This chapter covers seven main issues—calculator use, fractions/units, word problems, equations (including Algebra II problems), geometry problems, funny symbol problems, and grid-in problems. We do not intend to teach the fundamentals of math—instead we're showing you test-wise problem-solving techniques.

On the next two pages is a list of topics covered by the math section of the SAT. If you have trouble with very basic things, or if you need additional help with any of these topics, go talk to your math teacher. Direct contact with a good teacher is far more useful than anything we could tell you, but be sure to use rubber gloves.

*Ada says:
If you are in
precalculus or
higher in school,
a lot of the math
on the SAT will
not be fresh in
your mind. Even if
you're a certified
Math Whiz, set
aside time to
review the basics.*

Arithmetic

- Averages (including mean, median, and mode)
- Percent
- Prime numbers
- Properties of odd and even numbers
- Ratio and proportion
- Sequences involving exponential growth
- Sets (elements, union, intersection)

Algebra

- Factoring
- Linear equations and inequalities
- Positive integer exponents
- Sequences
- Quadratic equations
- Word problems
- Simplifying algebraic expressions
- Substitution
- Absolute value
- Rational equations and inequalities
- Radical equations
- Integer and rational exponents
- Direct and inverse variation
- Function notation
- Concepts of domain and range
- Functions as models
- Linear functions: equations and graphs
- Quadratic functions: equations and graphs

Geometry

- Area and perimeter of a polygon
- Area and circumference of a circle
- Volume of a box, cube, and cylinder
- Pythagorean Theorem, including special properties of isosceles, equilateral, and right triangles
- Geometric notation for length, segments, lines, rays, and congruence
- Problems in which trigonometry may be used as an alternative method of solution
- Properties of tangent lines
- Higher-level coordinate geometry

Geometry (*continued*)

- 30°-60°-90° and 45°-45°-90° triangles
- Properties of parallel and perpendicular lines
- Coordinate geometry
- Geometric visualization
- Slope
- Similarity
- Qualitative behavior of graphs and functions
- Transformations and their effect on graphs of function

Other

- Logical reasoning
- Newly defined symbols based on commonly used operations ("funny symbol problems")
- Probability/Combinations
- Data interpretation, scatterplots, and matrices
- Geometric probability

Sometimes in this chapter, we discuss some relatively advanced subjects. If you are shooting for a good math score, we recommend that you learn the material in these sections. Even if your math experience is limited to Sudoku puzzles, you should still read all of the advanced sections anyway, just to see where you are at. If you can follow along, great. Otherwise, if you are not shooting for a particularly high math score, don't sweat it.

One thing to look out for when you're taking the math section is the vocabulary. "What?!" you say. "*More* vocab?" Yup. Sorry.

Expect the SAT to use some technical terms that are intended to throw you off by putting in a term that sounds, well, math-y. Don't laugh. It actually worked. When the ETS inserted one little term into a math question, the number of students who got it right went from 68 percent to 21 percent. So know your math vocabulary. Do you know what the union of two sets is? What about their intersection? Yes, it sucks to have to learn math vocabulary in addition to your regular vocabulary list, but it will take just a few additional brain cells and a little extra time.

Overall Strategies: Quick and accurate are the operational words for the math section. If you run out of time, you lose points. And if you do certain things wrong, you lose points. Either way, your grandmother won't be able to brag about your scores (and you wouldn't want that, would you?).

Something to bear in mind as you do the math section is that the Serpent's roar is often worse than his bite. His specialty is what we like to call "shock and awe questions": problems that look really hard—big equations with fancy variables and exponents—but are actually relatively easy. Faced with an equation that looks like this, $2(n + 5)^2 = 6$, for example, many students panic, thinking they have to solve it, when in fact all the question asks is that they simplify the equation. (The correct answer choice is $2n^2 + 20n + 50 = 6$.) So when you see a problem that's loaded with letters, numbers, and symbols, don't panic. Realize that it's probably noisy and harmless, and look at the answer choices *before* solving it.

A Test-Taking Tip: As on the critical reading section, if you skip a question make a mark in the margin of your test booklet. Put an X next to the questions you don't think you'll be able to figure out. Put a ? next to the ones you think you could figure out with more time. If you do your work on a separate sheet, be sure to keep it as neat and organized as you can. Otherwise, you'll waste time trying to decipher your scribbles.

CALCULATORS

"Wow!" yelled Jimmy. "I get to use a calculator on the SAT! I'm going to ace this test!" Jimmy assumed he could get by on the math section of the SAT with only a calculator, blew off all his math classes, and didn't bother to study at all. When test time came, Jimmy realized that there was a lot more to the test than calculators. Jimmy now walks the streets wearing only a garbage bag and bowling shoes.

What is the moral of this sad tale? Don't put too much faith in your calculator. The ETS says that students who use them do slightly better than those who don't, but no problem can be completed solely by knowing how to push buttons, and

The fatal mistake of our generation...

—Ada

every math problem can be answered *without* using a calculator. While we're not going to discourage the use of a calculator, if you're good at arithmetic, you'll do fine without it. The trick is knowing when to use it. In addition, make sure you:

1. Know how to use your calculator.

You're going to feel pretty stupid if halfway through the test you realize you don't know where the equal sign button is. This is especially true for those of you who have a graphing calculator. Our recommendation: Unless you are totally comfortable using a graphing calculator, bring a regular four-function or scientific calculator instead. The College Board recommends using at least a scientific calculator because of the higher-level math involved. We disagree. Although a graphing calculator can be useful, you could make lots of mistakes if you don't know the subtleties in entering even a basic problem into the calculator. Even if you're comfortable with your grapher, you should bring a simpler calculator with you as well to use for basic arithmetic.

Here's a story: You're sitting at the testing center. It's 20 minutes into the first math section and you are finally on the last problem. You read it, realize that you know how to figure it out, and congratulate yourself on your brilliance. You reach for your calculator and . . . it dies. The moral of this story is, always, always, bring a spare calculator or, at least, extra batteries. Janet, a past guest author, brought three calculators. Paranoid? Yes. But she also got an 800 on the math section.

2. Know your arithmetic.

The main thing your calculator will be able to help you with is arithmetic: adding, subtracting, multiplying, and dividing. But most of the math problems will not involve complex calculations, and it may be quicker to do them in your head than to use your calculator. For instance, if a problem calls for you to add 21 and 13, your head will move a lot quicker than your fingers to tell you the sum is 34. If you find yourself trying to multiply 3,425 by 9,461, you're probably doing the problem wrong. Make sure you know the order of the operations—the order in which to plug the numbers into your calculator. First

Ada says: If you find yourself trying to multiply 3,425 by 9,461, you're probably doing the problem wrong.

are all parentheses, then all exponents, then multiplications and divisions, then additions and subtractions. Helpful acronym: PEMDAS. Mnemonic: Please Excuse My Dear Aunt Sally. (Sorry, it was made up by math teachers.) Remember it.

$$\frac{(\text{PLEASE})^{\text{EXCUSE}} \cdot \text{MY}}{\text{DEAR}} \quad +\text{AUNT} -\text{SALLY}$$

Some problems will ask you to decide if something is a factor. Knowing your dividing rules will help a lot. Here's a chart.

It's divisible by	If	Example
1	It is an integer.	Do you really need one?
2	It's an even number.	Hmm . . .
3	Its digits add up to a multiple of 3.	186. $1 + 8 + 6 = 15$ $15 = (3 \times 5)$
4	Its last two digits form (not "add up to") a number divisible by 4.	103,424. 24 is divisible by 4 $(24 \div 4 = 6)$
5	It ends in 5 or 0.	5,746,893,765
6	It is divisible by 2 *and* 3.	522
7	There's a rule, but it's more complicated than it's worth.	
8	Its last three digits form a multiple of 8.	10,496,832 $(832 \div 8 = 104)$
9	Its digits add up to a multiple of 9.	34,164. $3 + 4 + 1 + 6 + 4 = 18 = (2 \times 9)$
10	It ends in 0.	1,600

We tried the following problem using these rules and then again using a calculator. We got the answer faster the first time.

> What is the *least* positive integer divisible by the numbers 2, 3, 4, and 5?
> (A) 30
> (B) 40
> (C) 60
> (D) 90
> (E) 120

You can immediately tell that they're all divisible by 2 and 5 because they end in 0. You can use the 3 rule to cross out (B) and the 4 rule to cross out (A) and (D). That leaves (C) and (E), and since we want the smallest number, (C) is the answer. That wasn't that bad, was it?

Here's another arithmetic trick that might come in handy: Check the last digits. If you're multiplying two numbers together, you can figure out what the last digit of the answer is without multiplying them completely. Multiply the end numbers together and take the last digit of this product.

Example: $23 \times 257 =$ (A) 5,911
(B) 5,312
(C) 4,517
(D) 6,417
(E) 5,118

Without multiplying it out, let's do a last-digit check: 3×7 (the two last numbers) = 21; last digit = 1. Only choice (A) ends in 1, so the answer is (A).

3. Know your squares.

In addition to rules 1 and 2, you should also know your squares and square roots. Questions usually don't directly ask for squares and square roots, but sometimes you can see shortcuts if you know them. Here's a table of the squares of numbers 11 to 20 (plus 25). Learn them so that you can save time on your calculations.

Number	Square	Number	Square
11	121	17	289
12	144	18	324
13	169	19	361
14	196	20	400
15	225	25	625
16	256		

If you see one of these squares in a problem, chances are you'll have to take the square root.

4. Calculators and fractions don't mix well.

If a problem has fractions in both the question and the answer, don't use your calculator (unless it's a graphing calculator). Changing fractions to decimals can be confusing, and there's no need for it.

5. A word on graphing calculators.

Never use a complicated calculator for the first time on the SAT, but if you have experience with a graphing calculator—if you've used it for more than three months—you can save yourself a bundle of time on the math section.

Say you have to determine when two equations are equal to each other. Often the easiest way is to enter each equation into the graphing window of your calculator, then find where the intercept point is. (Some calculators can even directly solve equations. Check yours to see if it has this function.) They can also be programmed. For instance, you can write simple programs to find the area or volume of any geometric shape or solid. Because you have to know the concepts beforehand, the calculator is only useful as a time-saving device—*not* a machine that does the work for you.

As you may already know, some calculators are also mini-computers that can store information, such as vocab definitions. But if you were planning to use these to cheat, don't count on it. No handheld computers or anything else with a lettered keyboard are allowed for the test. (And, yes, the proctor will check.) Also, you can't keep your calculator on your desk during the critical reading and writing sections.

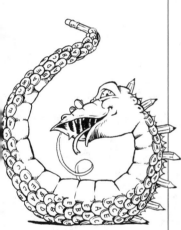

Either bring an extra calculator or extra batteries; it isn't worth the risk.

—Ada

FRACTIONS/ UNITS

You've done a lot of fractions in math class, so you know, more or less, how to work with them. But do you know what a fraction means? Do you completely understand that ⅗ not only means *three-fifths*, it also means 3 *divided by* 5? Also, do you completely understand that miles/hour means *miles divided by hours*? If not, read this section extra carefully. Fractions and units are the most important things to master for the math SAT.

The Meaning of a Fraction

The following problem will illustrate why *three-fifths* and 3 *divided by* 5 are the same thing.

The Quiche Problem

Arnold Schwarzenegger, Russell Crowe, Matt Damon, Bruce Willis, and Hugh Jackman are having dinner together. They order 3 quiches, which they plan to divide equally. How much quiche does each person get?

Step 1: Cut the first quiche into 5 equal pieces (i.e., into fifths) and give 1 piece to each person.

Step 2: Do the same thing to the second quiche.

Step 3: Do the same thing to the third quiche.

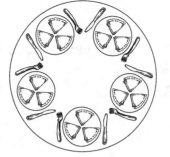

Now, as you can see, everyone has 3 slices of quiche. Each slice is a fifth of a quiche, so everyone has three-fifths (⅗) of a quiche. So, 3 quiches were divided equally among 5 people to give each person ⅗ of a quiche.

This is what this problem was designed to demonstrate—that 3 divided by 5 and ⅗ are the same thing: 3 quiches divided by 5 people = ⅗ of a quiche per person. Read this paragraph over and over again until you understand it. Then go eat some quiche.

Complex Fractions

The Serpent loves testing your ability to work with fractions by creating problems that contain complex fractions. A complex fraction is a regular fraction divided by another regular fraction. Here are some examples of complex fractions:

$$\frac{\dfrac{3}{5}}{\dfrac{7}{13}} \quad \text{or} \quad \frac{\dfrac{a}{b}}{\dfrac{c}{d}} \quad \text{or} \quad \frac{\dfrac{\text{hours}}{\text{mile}}}{\dfrac{\text{wombat}}{\text{person}}}$$

Since complex fractions are a pain in the neck, you want to make them into regular fractions. There is a simple rule for simplifying complex fractions.

Simple Rule: Flip the bottom fraction and multiply it by the top fraction.

Simple? Well, actually it is. You just have to recognize each individual fraction. Label the complex fraction like this:

$$\text{upper } \left\{ \frac{\dfrac{\text{top of the upper}}{\text{bottom of the upper}}}{\dfrac{\text{top of the lower}}{\text{bottom of the lower}}} \right. \text{lower}$$

What the Simple Rule says is that you can simplify any complex fraction by flipping the bottom fraction and multiplying it by the top fraction. It works because division is really multiplying by the reciprocal ("reciprocal" means "what ever it was, only flipped over"). This is what the Simple Rule looks like:

$$\frac{\dfrac{a}{b}}{\dfrac{c}{d}} = \frac{a}{b} \times \frac{d}{c} = \frac{ad}{bc}$$

You may want to draw arrows: $\dfrac{\dfrac{a}{b}}{\dfrac{c}{d}}$

Another way to think of this is: $\dfrac{\dfrac{a}{b}}{\dfrac{c}{d}} = \dfrac{a}{b} \times \dfrac{1}{\dfrac{c}{d}}$

Using real numbers: $\dfrac{\dfrac{2}{3}}{\dfrac{7}{6}} = \dfrac{2}{3} \times \dfrac{1}{\dfrac{7}{6}} = \dfrac{2}{3} \times \dfrac{6}{7} = \dfrac{12}{21}$

Here are some problems. Make each complex fraction into a simple (regular) fraction. Practice the Simple Rule.

1.
$$\frac{\frac{3}{5}}{\frac{4}{7}} = \quad ?$$

You should immediately rewrite this as:

$$\frac{3 \times 7}{5 \times 4}$$

2.
$$\frac{\frac{kumquats}{person}}{\frac{brains}{oat\ bran}}$$

You should immediately rewrite this as:

$$\frac{kumquats \times oat\ bran}{person \times brains}$$

The SAT will probably use numbers. Don't worry. —Ada

Word Fractions

Miles per hour is a way we measure speed. You've probably seen miles per hour written as a fraction: miles/hour. Using the quiche problem, we just confirmed that *fractions* mean "division." So *miles per hour* must mean "miles divided by hours." But what does that mean? How do you divide a mile by an hour? What does it mean to travel 400 miles divided by 8 hours? The following problem will attempt to answer all these questions.

The Frozen Yogurt Problem

After our quiche eaters finish eating, they get into the car to go to an ice cream shop. The ice cream shop is 500 miles away. If it takes them 10 hours to get there, what was their average speed?

Answer: The key is to realize that if they drive 500 miles in 10 hours then they have 500 miles to divide among 10 hours of driving. (It's just like having 3 quiches to divide among 5 people.) So rewrite it as:

$$\frac{500 \text{ miles}}{10 \text{ hours}} = \frac{50 \text{ miles}}{1 \text{ hour}} = 50 \text{ miles/hour}$$

Now you know why *miles per hour* is the same thing as miles/hour.

Units

Anything you can count or measure has a unit associated with it. *Pounds* are units, *miles* are units, *hours* are units, *miles/hour* are units, even *noodles* can be units if you are counting or measuring with noodles.

Knowing the tricks of working with units can help you do problems faster and can show you how to do problems that you otherwise wouldn't know how to do. The rule for working with units is that you can multiply and divide them just as you would numbers. For example, when you multiply (or divide) fractions containing units you can cancel units in the numerator with units in the denominator:

A fancy math term for this is "dimensional analysis."
—Ada

$$\frac{10 \text{ miles}}{1 \text{ hour}} \times 5 \text{ hours} = 50 \text{ miles}$$

$$\frac{10 \text{ pizzas}}{3 \text{ people}} \times 7 \text{ people} = \frac{70}{3} \text{ pizzas}$$

And you can divide using the Simple Rule:

$$\frac{\dfrac{5 \text{ pounds}}{\text{chicken}}}{\dfrac{3 \text{ chickens}}{10 \text{ McNuggets}}} = \frac{50 \text{ (pounds} \times \text{McNuggets)}}{3 \text{ (chickens)}^2}$$

After some practice, multiplying and dividing units will

be as simple and as natural to you as multiplying and dividing numbers.

We will now do a few practice problems from real SATs that show the procedure for doing units problems.

> A gasoline tank on a certain tractor holds 16 gallons. If the tractor requires 7 gallons to plow 3 acres, how many acres can the tractor plow with a tankful of gasoline?
> (A) $6\frac{6}{7}$ (B) $7\frac{1}{6}$ (C) $7\frac{1}{3}$ (D) $10\frac{2}{3}$ (E) $37\frac{1}{3}$

There are two steps to all units problems:

1. Figure out what information is given.
2. Pick, from only three options, what to do with that information in order to get the correct unit in the answer.

Step 1: Figure out the information given.

    a. "7 gallons to plow 3 acres" $= \dfrac{7 \text{ gallons}}{3 \text{ acres}}$

    b. "A gasoline tank holds 16 gallons" = 16 gallons
    c. "How many acres?" means . . . answer in *acres*.

Step 2: Do the right thing with the information given.

In all units problems, you have three options for what to do with the given information:

1. Multiply the first thing × the second thing.
2. Divide the first thing/the second thing.
3. Divide the second thing/the first thing.

The great thing about units problems is that it is not necessary to understand what's going on in order to know which of the three options to use. You automatically know which one to choose because only one of the options will give you the answer in acres (the unit you want). Look at the three options:

1. $\dfrac{7 \text{ gallons}}{3 \text{ acres}} \times 16 \text{ gallons} = \dfrac{(16 \times 7) \text{ gallons}^2}{3 \text{ acres}}$

Nope! The answer has to be in terms of acres, not in terms of $\dfrac{\text{gallons}^2}{\text{acres}}$.

2. $\dfrac{\dfrac{7 \text{ gallons}}{3 \text{ acres}}}{16 \text{ gallons}} = \dfrac{7 \text{ gallons}}{3 \text{ acres} \times 16 \text{ gallons}}$

Nope! We want acres in the numerator.

3. $\dfrac{16 \text{ gallons}}{\dfrac{7 \text{ gallons}}{3 \text{ acres}}} = \dfrac{16 \text{ gallons} \times 3 \text{ acres}}{7 \text{ gallons}} = 6\dfrac{6}{7} \text{ acres}$

Yes! This is the right answer. Notice that we didn't even have to figure out what the problem was all about; we just manipulated the information so that the answer would be in the correct unit.

Let's do another one:

A mechanic can install carburetors in 3 cars every 4 hours. At that rate, how long will it take the mechanic to install carburetors in 5 cars?
(A) 6 hrs. 20 min.
(B) 6 hrs. 40 min.
(C) 7 hrs. 15 min.
(D) 7 hrs. 30 min.
(E) 7 hrs. 45 min.

Step 1: Figure out the information given.

$$\text{“3 cars every 4 hours”} = \dfrac{3 \text{ cars}}{4 \text{ hours}}$$

$$\text{“install in 5 cars”} = 5 \text{ cars}$$

Because the answer choices are in terms of hours and minutes and because the question asks, "How long will it take?" the answer will be in terms of hours and minutes.

Step 2: Do the right thing with the information given.

Try the three options. Remember, all we care about is that the answer be in terms of the unit "hours."

1. $$\dfrac{3 \text{ cars}}{4 \text{ hours}} \times 5 \text{ cars}$$

Nope. Gives answer in cars²/hour.

2. $$\dfrac{\dfrac{3 \text{ cars}}{4 \text{ hours}}}{5 \text{ cars}}$$

Nope. Gives answer in $\dfrac{1}{\text{hours}}$. We want the hours in the numerator.

3. $$\dfrac{\dfrac{5 \text{ cars}}{3 \text{ hours}}}{4 \text{ cars}} = \dfrac{5 \text{ cars} \times 4 \text{ hours}}{3 \text{ cars}} = \dfrac{20}{3} \text{ hours} =$$

6 hrs. 40 min. (B)

Sure enough, the third option works.

Sometimes units problems require more than one operation. For example, if you want to calculate how many seconds there are in a day, you would do the following set of operations:

$$\dfrac{60 \text{ sec}}{1 \text{ min}} \times \dfrac{60 \text{ min}}{1 \text{ hour}} \times \dfrac{24 \text{ hours}}{1 \text{ day}} = \dfrac{60 \times 60 \times 24 \text{ sec}}{\text{day}}$$

Note that even if you hadn't known that the right way to do this problem was to multiply these quantities together, you could have figured it out by trying all the possibilities of dividing and multiplying. Only one of those possibilities would have given an answer in terms of seconds/day.

Note: Don't be tempted to bring mechanical pencils to the test. The College Board forbids them.

WORD PROBLEMS

And now we break for a commercial . . .
Don't you hate it when rabid elephants attack you and steal your pencils? I do. On the crucial day of my test, I was carrying no fewer than four number 2 pencils, and this tremendous elephant, foaming at the mouth, lunged out of the test center and grabbed my writing implements. I was ticked off.

But then I decided to try new improved Oxford Anti-Elephant soap. It not only cleans and softens my skin but also keeps those pesky pachyderms away. Now I can carry as many pencils with me as I like, and it's improved my whole life.

Well, some of my life. Actually, the point of this message is to remind you to have enough number 2 pencils around when you take your test. Also, we wanted to give you a break from reading about math—after all, math is not the most exciting material available for perusal.

Now, get back to work!

You really don't need to know much more than the basics of math to get through the word problems—but you do need to know how to think. It turns out that a lot of the math questions deal more with words than with straight math. Often the hard part is translating the words into math. You see,

$$\frac{(378,614 \times 2) + 4}{136,319} = y$$

looks like a hell of a problem. But it isn't that bad because it's just numbers and you can do it knowing only how to add, multiply, and divide. You don't really have to think—you just have to apply the skills you've (supposedly) known since second grade. In fact, you could solve it on your calculator effortlessly.

The really hateful questions are the word problems:

> Bill has four apples and is 18 years old. Sue has 25% more apples than Bill and is ⅓ as old. Alex had twice as many apples as Sue (and is ³⁄₂ as old), but he gave one of his

apples to Bill (and that's why Bill has four instead of three).

> For which individual is the ratio of apples/age the greatest?

Not only do you need to know about ratios and percentage and addition, but you also need to know how to translate the words into math. (The answer is Alex, by the way.)

So let's start with words—okay? (Put the Doritos away and pay attention.)

Key Words

Following are a bunch of rules for how to change confusing words into easy-to-understand numbers and mathematical symbols.

Rule 1: *Of* usually means multiply. For example, "½ of y" means multiplying ½ times y.

Rule 2: *Exceeds by* or *is greater than by* means subtract (or add).
Examples:

x exceeds y by 7	means $x - y = 7$ or $y + 7 = x$
x is greater than y by 7	means $x - y = 7$ or $y + 7 = x$

Rule 3: *Percent* (%) usually goes with *of*.
Remember that *percent* means *per hundred*, so a percent problem is really just a problem with fractions. They tell you the numerator and give you the "%" sign, which you translate into meaning "over one hundred." For example, 25% is really $^{25}/_{100}$, which is a fraction.

25% of y becomes $^{25}/_{100}$ of y (remember *of* means multiply), so it's $^{25}/_{100} \times y$ or, if you're using a calculator, .25 × y.

Do the same thing for percentages greater than 100%. For instance, 250% means $^{250}/_{100}$, or 2.5.

Rule 4: But wait, there's *more*. Percent can be made trickier with the word *more*.

If Sue has 25% *more* apples than Bill, then she has *as many* apples as Bill *plus* 25% more. So the word *more* can be broken down into "*as many —— plus ——.*"

But we can do better than apples:

> Bill has exactly 8 pairs of underwear, all of which are sexy. Sue has 50% more pairs of underwear than Bill. 75% of Sue's total collection of underwear is sexy.
>
> Who has more sexy underwear? (Don't get distracted.)

Here's the answer:

By Rule 4, Sue has *as many* pairs as Bill *plus* 50%.
So, Sue has 8 pairs + $^{50}/_{100}$ of 8.
Sue has 8 + 4 = 12 pairs of underwear.
75% of her 12 total pairs of underwear is sexy.
Using Rule 3, this becomes $^{75}/_{100}$ of 12.
And finally, using Rule 1, this becomes $^{75}/_{100} \times 12 = 9$.

Sue has 9 pairs of sexy underwear and Bill has 8, so Sue has more. But they both have about as much fun.

This is what your sexy underwear looks like... right?
—Ada

Rule 5: There's even more. *Percent increase or decrease* means subtract or add.

> Jim has $50, which he invests wisely; it increases by 10%. How much money does he now have?

Percent means per hundred, so a 10 percent increase means that you add 10% of the original number. 10% of $50 is $5, so $50 + $5 = $55. The same holds true for percent decrease.

Alternatively, you can multiply the original number by the increase (fraction) plus one. In this example, that would be 1.10 x $50 = $55.

Rule 6: *Ratio*—okay, so what's a ratio? A ratio is just a comparison.

If you say $y > x$ then you're comparing y and x and finding out that y is larger than x. (And, you might ask, who really cares?)

But $y > x$ is not a ratio. Ratios involve "division comparisons":

"the ratio of y to x is 5" means $y/x = 5$

Here, y is being compared to x. Again y is bigger—but now we know that y is five times bigger. (Wow. Excitement.) This expression could also be written:

"y is to x as 5 is to 1" or $y:x$ as $5:1$

Okay, well, how *is* 5 to 1? 5 *is* five times as big as 1 (obviously). So y is five times x, get it?

It's probably easiest to think of this as a fraction:

$$\frac{y}{x} = \frac{5}{1}$$

Rule 7: *Chance or probability* is a type of ratio.

When a problem asks what the chance or probability is that a particular thing will happen, all it's really asking you to do is to set up a ratio like this:

$$\frac{\text{number of times the particular thing could happen}}{\text{number of times any of the things could happen}}$$

Here's an example going back to the sexy underwear:

> If there are 12 pairs of sexy underwear and 36 pairs of not-so-sexy underwear in a huge laundry bag, what is the probability that, at random, Bill will grab a pair of sexy underwear?

Number of times Bill could grab any pair of underwear = 12 pairs of sexy underwear + 36 pairs of not-so-sexy underwear = 48 total pairs of underwear.

$12/48 = .25$

Bill has a 25% chance of grabbing a pair of sexy underwear. Good luck, Bill!

Rule 8: *Average*—an average is a number that summarizes or represents all the numbers in a group.

There are three types of averages: mean, median, and mode.

Arithmetic mean is the most commonly used average, and if you are asked to simply find the average, you should find the mean.

Arithmetic mean = $(a + b + c + d \ldots)/n$ where a, b, c, d . . . are the numbers and n is the number of numbers being averaged. For example, the mean of 3, 5, 6, 7 is

$$(3 + 5 + 6 + 7) / 4 = 5¼$$

Notice that $n = 4$ because there are four numbers in the group. Sometimes figuring out what n is can be tricky. Here's an example of such a problem:

> Larry's average for the first three tests was 90%; his average for the next two was 80%. What was his overall average?

To find n in this problem you have to notice that there are *five* test scores to average: the first three can be thought of as 90s, the next two as 80s, and the average becomes

$$\text{Mean} = \frac{(90 + 90 + 90 + 80 + 80)}{5} = 86\%$$

If you tried to do this by averaging 80% and 90% you'd be wrong. And Larry would be upset because you'd give him an 85% instead of an 86%.

Median is the middle value of a group. It's the number that would be right in the middle of the list if you arranged the numbers from smallest to largest. The median of

$$1, 4, 56, 59, 342, 697, 3{,}455$$

is 59. If the number of values are even (which would mean there are two "middles"), then the median is the mean of these two middle values. The median of

$$3, 8, 45, 67, 107, 156, 223, 1{,}032$$

is the mean of 67 and 107, or 87. (If you are given a list of numbers that is not in numerical order, put it in order before looking for the median.)

Mode is the value or values that appears the greatest number of times. The mode of

$$3, 24, 95, 24, 56, 74, 61, 74, 74$$

is 74. The modes of

$$34, 46, 27, 1, 83, 46, 90, 1, 63$$

are 1 and 46.

Sample Problems

1. The ratio of tattoos to nose rings in this room is 3 to 1. The number of nose rings is 12. How many tattoos are there in total, and what can we do to curb society's fascination with bodily mutilation?

Sorry, but we can only help you on the first part of the question. Let's set it up like a *math* problem:

a. By Rule 6 (ratio): $\dfrac{\text{tattoos}}{\text{nose rings}} = \dfrac{3}{1}$

b. Number of nose rings = 12

c. Replace the words *nose rings* in the first step with the number 12: $\dfrac{\text{tattoos}}{12} = \dfrac{3}{1}$

Now, solve for tattoos. Tattoos = 36.
Why? Because $\dfrac{36}{12} = \dfrac{3}{1}$, right? Or 36:12 = 3:1.

2. 5 is what percent of 10?

"Wait—I haven't done this!" you moan. Just relax—you can do it with what you already know. Change the question around to read

What percent of 10 is 5?

Of means multiply—so something *times* 10 is 5. You should be able to figure out that the something is ½. (Right? ½ × 10 is 5, isn't it?) And ½ is 50%, so that's the answer: 5 is 50% of 10.

Another way to set this up is using a ratio:

5 is to 10 as *x* is to 100

5 : 10 :: *x* : 100

$$\frac{5}{10} = \frac{x}{100}$$

Solve for *x* by multiplying both sides by 100:

$$\frac{5}{10} \times 100 = x = 50$$

3. On a map, if 1 inch represents 30 miles, then how many inches represent 75 miles?

This is a thinly disguised ratio problem—the key word here is *represent.* The problem can be translated to look like this:

1 inch : 30 miles :: *x* inches : 75 miles

$$\frac{1}{30} = \frac{x}{75}$$

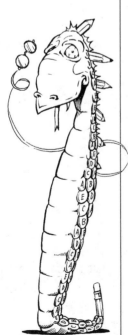

Solving for *x* gives us *x* = 2½ inches.

It might be easier if you just think in your head, "Okay, the problem is asking how many times 30 goes into 75. That's easy! 2½! God, I'm smart!" Sometimes problems are easier than they look.

4. Mary's average salary for her first 6 years of work was $15,000; her average salary for the next 2 years was $16,000. What was her average salary over the entire 8 years?

Notice that *n* for this problem is 8; the average is

$$A = \frac{(6 \times 15,000 + 2 \times 16,000)}{8}$$

$$= \frac{(90,000 + 32,000)}{8}$$

$$= \$15,250$$

5. If Paul ate 300% more pizza than Manek ate, and Manek ate an entire pizza, then how many pizzas did Paul eat?

Paul ate *as many* pizzas as Manek *plus* 300%.

So Paul ate ONE pizza PLUS 300% of one.

So Paul ate FOUR PIZZAS! (Paul, you glutton.)

6. Suppose Ada took the SAT 8 times and her combined scores each time were 2230, 2230, 2280, 2300, 2340, 2400, 2400, 2400. What was her median score? What was the mode of her score?

Well, 2300 and 2340 are the 2 in the middle, so average them and you'll see that the median equals 2320. And since 2400 shows up the most times, 2400 is the mode. Also, by the way, Ada didn't really take the SAT 8 times. She has a *way* cooler life than that.

Another thing to watch out for in word problems is common sense. Make sure you don't pick an answer that says that Chris travels 200 miles an hour on his bike or that Amy ate 3,000 cookies in one day. The SAT isn't creative enough to have outlandish answers.

Advanced Math for Word Problems

The Moving People Problem

These questions are famous. They have no relevance to anything, really, but they involve people making work for themselves by going places and coming back again for no apparent reason.

Example:

> A man in a bus travels 4 miles in 3 minutes. Then he gets out of the bus and walks back to his starting point, taking $\frac{9}{20}$ hour. What was his average speed for the whole trip?

Answer: 16 miles/hour

The best way to deal with this type of word problem is to plot it out, with distances and times:

> 4 miles in 3 min by bus + 4 miles in 27 min walking
> = 8 miles in 30 minutes total

Remember:
$$D = rt$$
−Ada

Get it? Add up total miles, divide by total time, and you'll, like, totally get the answer. (Remember to convert 30 minutes to $\frac{1}{2}$ hour in order to get the answer in miles/hour.)

Example:

> A boat travels 3 miles north, 4 miles east, and then sinks. If it sank to a depth of 1 mile, then how far is it from its starting point?

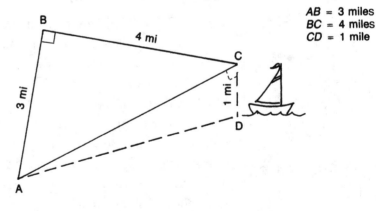

AB = 3 miles
BC = 4 miles
CD = 1 mile

Use the Pythagorean Theorem and a picture to get the answer. Point A is where the boat began. It sailed 3 miles north to point B, then 4 miles east to point C. It then sank 1 mile, to point D. The distance of the boat from its starting point is AD. So you must solve for AD, but first you must figure the distance of the hypotenuse, AC, of the triangle ABC.

$$AC^2 = AB^2 + BC^2$$
$$AC^2 = 3^2mi + 4^2mi$$
$$AC^2 = 25mi$$
$$\sqrt{AC^2} = \sqrt{25}mi$$
$$AC = 5 \text{ mi}$$

Now you're ready to solve for AD, the hypotenuse of triangle ACD:

$$AD^2 = AC^2 + CD^2$$
$$AD^2 = 5^2mi + 1^2mi$$
$$AD^2 = 26 \text{ mi}$$
$$\sqrt{AD^2} = \sqrt{26} \text{ mi}$$
$$AD = \sqrt{26} \text{ mi}$$

So the distance of the boat from its starting point is $\sqrt{26}$ miles, or 5.1 miles.

Example:

A man's goldfish swims around the edge of its cylindrical fish tank, which has a radius of 1 meter (it's a big fish tank), at a rate of 1 lap per 30 seconds. How long does it take the fish to swim 32π meters, if after every 4 laps the fish takes a 5-second break to eat some McNuggets? (Include the final break.)

(A) 16 minutes
(B) 500 minutes
(C) 8⅓ minutes
(D) 32 minutes
(E) ³⁰⁄₃₂π minutes

*Ada says:
Make a list of key points from the word problems so you don't have to go back and reread the question. Saves time and effort!*

Since the circumference of a circle is π times diameter, then each lap is 2π meters. The fish swims 32π meters, or 16 laps:

$$16 \text{ laps} \times \frac{30 \text{ sec}}{1 \text{ lap}} = 480 \text{ seconds} = 8 \text{ minutes}$$

However, we also need to add the breaks. Since there are 16 laps, the fish must take 4 breaks:

$$4 \times 5 \text{ seconds} = 20 \text{ seconds}$$

Answer: 8 minutes, 20 seconds =
8⅓ minutes = (C)

Enough of this math stuff—the SAT requires fast thinking in difficult situations. So here's a scenario—you have three seconds to come up with the appropriate response.

A psychotic iguana with a bottle of dishwashing detergent is chasing you and gaining every second. The soft grass you're running on barefoot suddenly ends and you're faced with the option of treading on a minefield strewn with broken glass or walking across a river of flowing lava. Which do you choose?

Answer: Neither. What are you, stupid? I'd much rather face an iguana (even a psychotic one with detergent) than deal with a minefield or hot lava. So remember, if you really don't like *any* of your choices, then "it cannot be determined from the information given" may be an option.

EQUATIONS

The rule for equations is *do it to both sides*. We don't care what *it* is, but do it to both sides. That keeps everything nice and equal. So if your lover is your enemy:

(lover = enemy)

and you want to kill your enemy, you must kill your lover, too:

(kill your lover = kill your enemy)

There. Nice and equal. Well, equal, anyway. So if you have

$$x + 36 = 40$$

and you want to solve for *x*, then do it like this. Subtract 36 from the left *and* subtract 36 from the right:

$$x + 36 - 36 = 40 - 36,\text{ which means that }x = 4.$$

Now check it by substituting 4 for *x* in the original expression:

$$4 + 36 = 40$$
$$40 = 40 \quad \text{Bingo!}$$

Examples:

1. $12x = 24$
   Divide both sides by 12 to get $x = 2$.

2. $3x + 4 = 28$
   Subtract 4 from both sides to get $3x = 24$.
   Divide both sides by 3 to get $x = 8$.

3. Solve for fish:

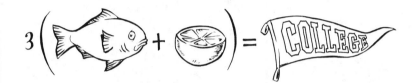

$$3(\text{fish} + \text{grapefruit}) = \text{college}$$
Divide both sides by 3:

$$\text{fish} + \text{grapefruit} = \frac{\text{college}}{3}$$
Subtract grapefruit from both sides:

$$\text{fish} = \frac{\text{college}}{3} - \text{grapefruit}$$

Okay. "Number 3 was a moronic question," you might say to yourself. Yes. It was. But they ask similar questions on the SAT just to see if you know these rules. They use x, y, and z more than they use fish and grapefruit, but it's the same basic idea.

4. $x - y = 17$
   What is $y + 12$?
   (A) x
   (B) $x + 5$
   (C) $x - 5$
   (D) $x - 7$
   (E) It cannot be determined from the
       information given.

Answer: $x - y = 17$
$$x - y + y = 17 + y$$
$$x = y + 17$$
$$x - 5 = y + 17 - 5$$
$$x - 5 = y + 12$$

(C) is correct.

5. $x + 3 - y = 10$

Solve for x in terms of y.

(A) $y + 7$
(B) $y + 3$
(C) $y - 7$
(D) $10 - y$
(E) $13 - y$

Answer: $x + 3 - y = 10$
$$x + 3 - y + y = 10 + y$$
$$x + 3 = 10 + y$$
$$x + 3 - 3 = 10 + y - 3$$
$$x = 7 + y$$

(A) is correct.

Plugging In

When faced with complicated algebraic expressions, test takers can get confused or flustered. While simple problems should be solved algebraically, more complicated problems can be solved in another way. Instead of working through the problem, consider substituting numbers for variables. Choose numbers that are easy to work with, such as 1, 2, or 10. Also try a negative number such as −1 or −2. Zero is useful, too.

Example:

Last year, a town had a population of $2{,}000 + x$. If the population increased by 25 people this year, which of the following expressions represents this year's population?

(A) $2{,}000 + 25x$
(B) $2{,}025 + x$

(C) $5,000 + 25x$
(D) $5,025 + 25x$
(E) $5,250 + x$

While this can and should be solved using pure algebra, substituting the number 1 for x is an easy alternative. By doing this, the population was 2,001 and then increased by 25, becoming 2,026. By substituting 1 for x in the answer choices, you find that choice (B) is correct.

More complicated example:

$4^x + 4^x + 4^x + 4^x =$
(A) 4^{x+1}
(B) 4^{x+2}
(C) 4^{x+4}
(D) 4^{4x}
(E) 4^{x^4}

This problem can be solved algebraically, by saying that $4^x + 4^x + 4^x + 4^x = 4 \cdot 4^x = 4^{x+1}$. If, however, you get stuck or have a difficult time following this method, you can substitute a number for x instead. By saying that $x = 2$, $4^2 + 4^2 + 4^2 + 4^2 = 64 = 4^3$. Substituting 2 for x, we see that $4^{x+1} = 4^{2+1} = 4^3$. Therefore, the answer is 4^{x+1} or (A).

Factoring

Whenever you have to factor, you should always ask yourself these five questions to get the thing factored.

1. *Is there anything in common?*
    Example: In $3x^2 + 6x$, there's a $3x$ that both terms have in common.
    $3x^2 + 6x = 3x(x + 2)$

2. *Is this a difference of two squares?*
    If both terms are perfect squares, they are factorable.
    Example: $x^2 - 36 = (x - 6)(x + 6)$

Or as they call it outside of the States, factorising!

—Ada

3. *Is this a trinominal?*
   Sometimes, an expression with three terms can be factored into two expressions with two terms each. (For an explanation of this, see page 201.)
   Example: $x^2 - x - 12 = (x + 3)(x - 4)$

4. *Is this the sum or difference of two cubes?*
   If both terms are cubes, you can factor them based on these formulas:
   $x^3 + y^3 = (x + y)(x^2 - xy + y^2)$
   $x^3 - y^3 = (x - y)(x^2 + xy + y^2)$
   Example: $8 - y^3 = (2 - y)(4 + 2y + y^2)$

5. *Can I group this?*
   Grouping means to rearrange the terms so that a common factor can be pulled out.
   Example: $3x^2 + 6x + 5xy + 10y = 3x(x + 2) + 5y(x + 2) = (3x + 5y)(x + 2)$

Relations, Functions, and Function Notation

A **relation** is a set of ordered pairs (x, y). The **domain** is the set of all possible x values, while the **range** is the set of all possible y values.

A **function** is a relation where each x has its own y, but each y can correspond with a variety of x's. Confused? Well, just remember that each student (x) in math class gets a grade (y). Each student gets only one grade, but a specific grade can be given to more than one person. You can also just do the **vertical line test.** If you can draw a vertical line through any part of the graph and it touches only one point, then it is a function (e.g., the sine graph). But if it touches more than one point, it is not (e.g., a circle).

Functions are usually defined by $f(x) =$ something. Just remember that for such an equation, $f(x)$ is always equal to the y value.

Function:

Not a Function:

—Ada

Example 1: Let the function f be defined by $f(x) = x^2 + 2$. What does y equal when $x = 3$?

Plug in 3 for x:

$$f(x) = 3^2 + 2.$$
$$y = 9 + 2 = 11$$

The answer is 11.

Example 2: The function f, where $f(x) = (1 + x)^2$, is defined for $-2 \leq x \leq 2$. What is the range of f?

(A) $0 \leq f(x) \leq 4$
(B) $0 \leq f(x) \leq 9$
(C) $1 \leq f(x) \leq 4$
(D) $1 \leq f(x) \leq 5$
(E) $1 \leq f(x) \leq 9$

Since f is only defined for $-2 \leq x \leq 2$, then that is the domain of the function. To get the range, plug in random numbers between -2 and 2. You won't always have to plug in every number, but if it's a small set, it's probably a good idea. No matter what the size of the set, though, it's usually also a good idea to check the end points and the values of x that create zeros.

x	$f(x)$
-2	1
-1	0
0	1
1	4
2	9

Clearly, the lowest number is 0, and the highest is 9. So (B) is the right answer. Notice that if you had plugged in only -2 and 2, you would have gotten (E) as the answer.

You get a function's **inverse** by switching the x's and the y's. If the inverse also turns out to be a function, the original function is called **"one-to-one"** and passes both the vertical and horizontal line tests.

Special Functions

There are five special functions you will probably want to be familiar with:

Function	Looks Like	Notation	Explanation
Linear	Line	$f(x) = mx + b$	m is the slope, b is the y-intercept.
Constant	Horizontal line	$f(x) = k$	The y value is always equal to k.
Absolute value	V, with point at (0,0)	$f(x) = |x|$	Makes all negative values positive, but positive values stay positive.
Quadratic	Parabola	$f(x) = ax^2 + bx + c$	
Polynomial	Could be lots of things	$f(x) = ax^n + bx^{n-1} + \ldots z$	

Combining Functions (or, When Functions Reproduce . . .)

Okay, you can stop quivering at the disturbing imagery.

When you combine functions, all that happens is that you insert whatever x is into the first equation. You could end up with a number or an expression. Then, for the second function, whenever you see x, you insert whatever you ended up with from the first function.

> Example: Let $f(x) = x^2 + 3$ and $g(x) = 3x$. What does $f(g(x))$ equal when $x = 5$?
> Since $g(x)$ gets substituted for x in $f(x)$, that means that you do $g(x)$ first.
> $g(5) = 3 \times 5 = 15$
> So $g(x) = 15$. Plug that in for x in $f(x)$.
> $f(15) = 15^2 + 3 = 228$

If the problem had asked you to find $g(f(x))$, the answer would have been 84. Try it for yourself.

Linear Functions

A linear function is anything that can be graphed as a straight line. They are always in the form $f(x) = mx + b$.

You solve linear equations just like you solve any other kind of equation.

> Example: $7x + 3 = 5x + 6$, $x = ?$
> You have to subtract 3 from both sides (or you can subtract 6, it really doesn't matter, but most people find it easier to work with positive numbers).
> $7x + 3 - 3 = 5x + 6 - 3$
> $7x = 5x + 3$
> Then you subtract $5x$ from both sides (or you can subtract $7x$).
> $7x - 5x = 5x + 3 - 5x$
> $2x = 3$
> Finally, divide both sides by 2, and you're left with $x = \frac{3}{2}$

If you aren't confident and you have time, you can check your answer by plugging in $\frac{3}{2}$ for all the x's in the original equation. If both sides are the same, then you've got yourself an answer.

Solving a Quadratic Equation

Quadratic equations, or equations in the form $ax^2 + bx + c =$ something, can be solved by factoring the trinomial (expression with three terms) into two binomials (expressions with two terms). We factor by using the wise, age-old, foolproof system of . . . trial and error.

Let's look at an example. We have the following three terms: $2x^2 - x - 6 = 0$. In order to solve it, first we should ask, Does it factor? It looks likes it doesn't, because there's nothing that all three terms have in common, and they aren't cubes or squares or anything.

But looks can be deceiving.

Let's see . . .

Remember: linear functions make straight lines.

—Ada

If you want to use the "check your answer by plugging it in for x" strategy on a question, mark it, finish the rest of the section as best you can, and come back to it at the end if you have time.

When trinomials are factored into binomials, they form something like $(ax + b)(cx + d)$. So you write down your trinomial, and the binomials, with blanks for missing numbers:

$2x^2 - x - 6 = 0$

Factors:

$(\_x + \_)(\_x + \_)$

And then you ask yourself, what two numbers multiplied together would give me 2, the first coefficient?

Well, this one's pretty easy. So you fill in the first two numbers:

$(2x + \_)(x + \_)$

And then you take a look at the constant (the last number). What two numbers multiplied would give me 6?

Well, there's 3 and 2, and then there's 6 and 1. So try all four combinations.

$(2x + 6)(x + 1)$
$(2x + 1)(x + 6)$
$(2x + 3)(x + 2)$
$(2x + 2)(x + 3)$

Which one works? To check, FOIL them. You multiply the **F**irst terms of each binomial together, then multiply the **O**utside terms, then the **I**nside terms, and finally the **L**ast terms.

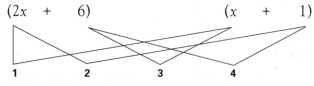

$(2x + 6) \qquad\qquad (x + 1)$

1   2   3   4

$2x^2 + 2x + 6x + 6$

After FOILing all four sets of binomials, you might say, "Oh drat! None of them work."

To which we say, "Hmm, you're right. Guess this method doesn't work."

Just kidding. The thing is, the original trinomial has two negative signs in it. This means its binomial factors have to have a negative somewhere in there, too. So off you go again, this time trying various combinations of negative second terms.

Sooner or later, you'll come up with: $(2x + 3)(x - 2) = 0$.

So now, to solve for x, try setting each of the binomials equal to zero, because if $A \times B = 0$, then either A or B *must* equal zero. In other words, you can separate these binomials into two equations of their own:

$$(2x + 3) = 0 \qquad (x - 2) = 0$$

Now solve each equation for x. You should come up with two solutions: x can be either $-\frac{3}{2}$ or 2.

This might have taken you a minute. It might have taken you twenty. But don't worry about it—the more problems you do, the better you get at seeing the answer without having to do many calculations.

Not all trinomials can be factored like this, but more on that coming up.

Example: The sum of the two roots of a quadratic equation is 5 and their product is –6. Which of the following could be the equation?
(A) $x^2 - 6x + 5 = 0$
(B) $x^2 - 5x - 6 = 0$
(C) $x^2 - 5x + 6 = 0$
(D) $x^2 + 5x - 6 = 0$
(E) $x^2 + 5x + 6 = 0$

First of all, since the product is negative and the sum is positive, you know that one of the numbers is negative and the other is positive. Start with the product (there are fewer possibilities)—how many pairs of numbers would have a product of –6? The answer: –1 and 6, –6 and 1, –3 and 2, –2 and 3. Then look at the sum. Out of all of these pairs, which one has a sum of 5? –1 and 6 satisfy both conditions, so –1 and 6 are the roots.

Next, put those roots down as the answers to a quadratic equation—$(x + 1)(x - 6) = 0$. Then FOIL this out, and you'll get the answer: (B).

A quick tip: In any quadratic equation $ax^2 + bx + c = 0$, the sum of the two roots is equal to $-\frac{b}{a}$ and the product of the two roots is equal to $\frac{c}{a}$. Try it, it works!

The quadratic formula is not given to you on the SAT, so you will have to memorize it.

—Ada

Quadratic Formula

Sooner or later, you'll try to solve a quadratic equation that looks something like this: $5x^2 - 3x - 4 = 0$. Sometime after the thirtieth try, you'll realize that it doesn't factor nicely. That's where the quadratic formula comes in.

With a trinomial in the form $ax^2 + bx + c = 0$

the two roots are $x = \dfrac{-b \pm \sqrt{b^2 - 4ac}}{2a}$

(If you need to convince yourself, try this using a trinomial that you know factors nicely.)

Example: Solve for x if $5x^2 - 3x - 4 = 0$
In this trinomial, a = 5, b = –3, and c = –4.
Plug these into the formula.

$$x = \frac{3 \pm \sqrt{9 - 4(5)(-4)}}{2(5)} = \frac{3 \pm \sqrt{89}}{10}$$

So the two factors are

$$\frac{3 - \sqrt{89}}{10} \text{ and } \frac{3 + \sqrt{89}}{10}.$$

Since the quadratic formula works for every trinomial in the entire universe, it may be much easier for you to do if you don't like the two-binomial thing you tried above.

Systems of Equations

When you get two linear equations, and you're supposed to solve for x and y, there are two ways of tackling them. (Or three, if you have a graphing calculator.) Sometimes the first method is easier, and sometimes the second method is. Know how to use both of them.

Say that you're supposed to solve for this:
$$2x + 3y = 6$$
$$5x + 8y = 11$$

First Method

Keep them stacked up, then multiply or divide the equations to make the coefficients of either the x's or the y's equal. Sometimes they're equal when you start out. But this time we're not so lucky. Let's say we go with the x's. In order to make the coefficients equal, multiply the top equation by 5 and the bottom equation by 2:

$$5(2x + 3y) = (6)5$$
$$2(5x + 8y) = (11)2$$

You end up with:

$$10x + 15y = 30$$
$$10x + 16y = 22$$

Subtract the bottom equation from the top one:

$$10x + 15y = 30$$
$$-10x - 16y = -22$$
$$-y = 8$$
$$y = -8$$

Then take any equation and plug in -8 for y.

$$2x + 3y = 6$$
$$2x + 3(-8) = 6$$
$$x = 15$$

Second Method

Or, you can take the first equation, and solve for y in terms of x (or solve for x in terms of y—it's up to you).

$$2x + 3y = 6$$
$$3y = 6 - 2x$$
$$y = \frac{6 - 2x}{3}$$

Then you plug in the whole thing for the y in the second equation (if you solved for x in terms of y, then just plug in the whole thing for x).

$$5x + 8y = 11$$
$$5x + 8\left(\frac{6 - 2x}{3}\right) = 11$$

Multiply $\left(\dfrac{6-2x}{3}\right)$ by 8

to get: $5x + \left(\dfrac{48-16x}{3}\right) = 11$

Multiply both sides by 3 to get rid of the fraction.

$$3\left(5x + \dfrac{48-16x}{3}\right) = 3\,(11)$$

$15x - 16x + 48 = 33$
Then solve for x.
$x = 15$

Now you can solve for y. We don't want to bore you to death, so trust us, it turns out to be -8.

The Graphing Calculator Way

If you have a graphing calculator, then just plug the equations in to get your answer.

Exponents

The rules of exponents are pretty simple. Know them like the back of your hand.

1. $c^a \times c^b = c^{a+b}$

2. $\dfrac{c^a}{c^b} = c^{a-b}$

3. $(c^a)^b = c^{a \times b}$

4. $c^a \times d^a = (cd)^a$

1. If the cube root of the square root of a number is 3, what is the number?
   (A) 27
   (B) 54
   (C) 243
   (D) 729
   (E) 2,187

The point where the two graphs meet is your answer.

—Ada

First of all, figure out what they're really asking. Make the unknown number x. So, they're saying, if x is square-rooted and then cube-rooted, the answer is 3. What's x?

In mathematical terms, then, it's $3 = \sqrt[3]{\sqrt{x}}$. Since that looks too complicated, try to make it simpler:

$$3 = \sqrt[3]{\sqrt{x}}$$
$$3^3 = \left(\sqrt[3]{\sqrt{x}}\right)^3$$
$$27^2 = \left(\sqrt{x}\right)^2$$
$$729 = x$$

And (D) is the right answer.

You could have also used the four exponent rules to know that $\sqrt[3]{\sqrt{x}}$ is really equal to $\sqrt[6]{x}$, and get the answer by taking 3 to the 6th power.

Negative and Fractional Exponents
$x^{-1}, y^{1/2}, z^{-2/3}$

Are you shuddering? Don't. Negative and fractional exponents look annoyingly complicated, but they're not.

All you have to do for negative exponents to make sense is to make them into a fraction with 1 on top and the exponented number on the bottom (eliminating the negative, of course).

So: $x^{-m} = \dfrac{1}{x^m}$

Example 1: $2x^{-2} = ?$

You should immediately flip it upside down:

$$2x^{-2} = 2 \times \frac{1}{x^2} = \frac{2}{x^2}$$

Fractional exponents are even easier, but it gets really stupid when we explain it with words. Just remember this:

$$x^{p/q} = \sqrt[q]{x^p}$$

An Enlightening Carrot Diagram:

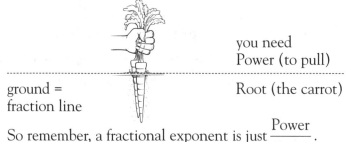

you need
Power (to pull)

ground =
fraction line

Root (the carrot)

So remember, a fractional exponent is just $\dfrac{\text{Power}}{\text{Root}}$.

*If it looks scary,
it probably isn't.
Just relax and
rely on the tricks
you've learned.
You'll be fine.
So don't panic!*

Example 2: $4^{2/3} = ?$

First, you should raise x to the p power, and
then take the q root:

$$4^{2/3} = \sqrt[3]{4^2} = \sqrt[3]{16} = 2.520$$

Also, if you ever see a question that asks you what
1,293,254 to the 0th power is, you can punch it into your calculator, or you can simply remember that *anything (that's not
zero) to the 0th power is equal to 1*. Even if it's $1{,}293{,}254^0$. It's
just 1.

Solving Radical Equations

Radical equations on the SAT will probably consist of x
under a radical. When you see something like $\sqrt{x}$, all you
have to remember is one thing: The plan of attack is to isolate the enemy. Get the radical by itself. The rest is a piece
of cake.

Example: If $\dfrac{1}{2}\sqrt{x} - 4 = 2$, then what is x?

The first thing you do in a problem like this is to
get all the constants on one side, so you would
add 4 to both sides:

$$\frac{1}{2}\sqrt{x} - 4 = 2$$
$$\phantom{\frac{1}{2}\sqrt{x} - 4} + 4 + 4$$
$$\frac{1}{2}\sqrt{x} = 6$$

Then, in order to get the radical by itself, you have to divide both sides by ½ or multiply both sides by two.

$$2\left(\frac{1}{2}\sqrt{x}\right) = (6)2$$

$$\sqrt{x} = 12$$

In this case, since x was just square-rooted, all we would have to do is square both sides and see that *x* equals 144.

Direct and Inverse Variation

When *y* is **directly proportional** to *x*, that means that an equation $y = kx$ can be written (*k* is any constant number). For example, $y = 5x$ and $y = (\frac{1}{5})x$ are directly proportional equations. On the other hand, when *y* is **inversely proportional** to *x*, then the equation is $y = k/x$. The equation $y = 5/x$ is inversely proportional.

Need a visual?

Direct:
$y = kx$

Indirect:
$y = \frac{k}{x}$

—Ada

GEOMETRY

Basic Math for Geometry

Fir022st off, familiarize yourself with the following symbols, definitions, laws, and formulas.

Symbols: ‖ means "is parallel to." $l_1 \parallel l_2$ means line 1 is parallel to line 2.

⊥ means "is perpendicular to." $l_1 \perp l_2$

Congruent angles have equal numbers of degrees. (They fit perfectly over each other.)

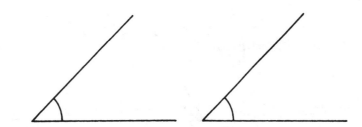

Here's a tip that may help you with geometry problems and possibly with other parts of the math test as well. If the caption for a diagram says "not drawn to scale," then the first thing you should do is make a quick sketch that is to scale. One of the reasons they don't draw things to scale is to obscure the answer. So, if possible, draw it to scale—nothing elaborate, nothing time-consuming, just a quick sketch. Maybe it will reveal the answer immediately.

Complementary angles add up to 90 degrees of arc. (If they look complementary, and it doesn't say "not drawn to scale," they probably are complementary. Don't bother proving it to yourself if you're pressed for time.)

Supplementary angles add up to 180 degrees of arc. (If they look supplementary, they probably are.)

Parallel lines cut by another line: These things are full of congruent and supplementary angles. You could try to memorize which pairs of angles are congruent and which pairs are supplementary, but why bother? The ones that look supplementary are supplementary, and the ones that look congruent are congruent. In some problems, you may need to extend the lines for it to look like this:

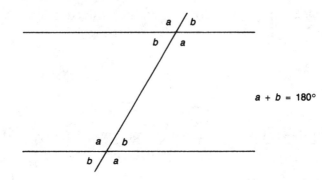

Parallelogram: Opposite sides are parallel. Parallelograms have two pairs of *equal* (or *congruent*) angles and four pairs of *supplementary* angles. In the diagram, the ones that look equal are equal and the ones that look supplementary are supplementary.

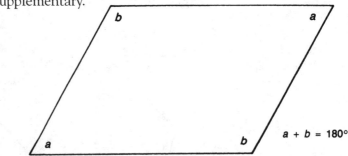

Similar triangles: Well, boys and girls, now it's time to give you some exciting insights into similar triangles. But after extensive research, we've decided that there is nothing exciting about similar triangles. In fact, there's been nothing *new* in similar triangles for something over 2,000 years—but (and this is the incredible part) they're still in fashion with the ETS. So don your toga and get psyched for a bacchanalian triangle party!

What are similar triangles? Similar triangles are two or more triangles with angles of the same measure in different sizes. Here, for example, are two similar triangles:

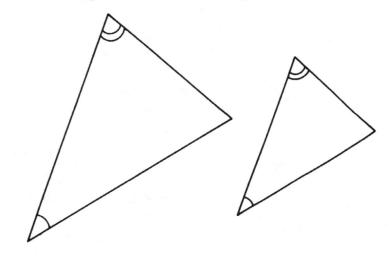

Continuing along this line of thought, here are two similar fish:

For all of
your fish-
sizing needs.
—Ada

Same shape, different sizes (size 6 and size 10).

The technical way to think about similar triangles is that the two triangles have three angles of corresponding measures. And if you think about it, knowing that *two* of the three angles are the same is enough to ensure that *all three* are the same, since the angles of a triangle always add up to 180°.

So, to jump right in here, what is the measure of angle *x* if A and B are similar triangles?

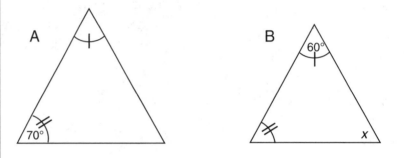

Answer: *x* = 50°. Why? Because both triangles have a 70° angle and a 60° angle. The last angle must be 50° in order to add up to 180°.

Here's another one: If $\overline{AB}\|\overline{CD}$, then what is θ?

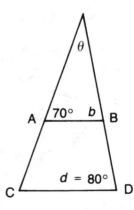

Answer: 30°. The key here is the parallel lines. Remember the congruent angles involved with parallel lines? Sure you do. So think of them when looking at the picture: Angle *b* must be the same as angle *d*, namely 80°. Which brings us to a:

Similar Triangle Rule: The top triangle is similar to the big triangle if their bases are parallel.

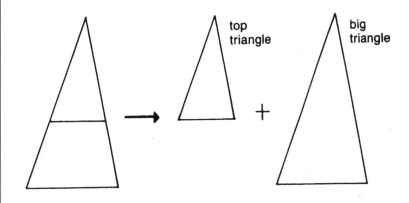

Got it? So if you see a triangle intersected by a line parallel to its base, the two triangles are similar.

Here's some more important information on triangles.
• Pythagorean Theorem for right triangles: $a^2 + b^2 = c^2$

The SAT gives you geometry reference information in the front of each math section, but you can save time if you know it by heart.

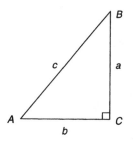

• In a 30°-60°-90° triangle, the ratio of the sides is $1 : \sqrt{3} : 2$.

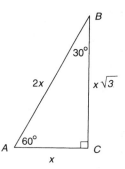

• In a 45°-45°-90° triangle, the ratio is 1: 1: $\sqrt{2}$.

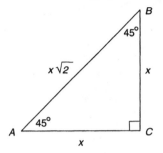

Another important thing to remember about triangles is that the sum of the lengths of any two sides of a triangle must always be larger than the length of the third side.

Circles: Here are some formulas for the components of a circle:

area = $\pi \times r^2$ (r is radius)

circumference = $2 \times \pi \times r$

arc = measure of central angle

arc also = $2 \times$ measure of inscribed angle

Well, what the hell is all this *arc* stuff? Let us show you.

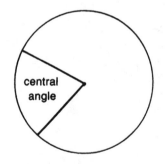

If the central angle = 30°, then the arc would also equal 30°.

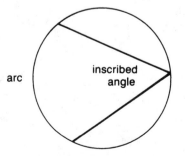

As you can see, an inscribed angle is an angle made by drawing two lines from a point on a circle. The degree of the arc is always 2× that of the angle, so if the angle is 35°, the arc is 70°.

Area: In general, area is a length times a width.

Circle: area = $\pi \times r^2$

Rectangle: area = $b \times h$ (b is base and h is height, or vice versa)

Triangle: area = $\frac{1}{2} \times b \times h$ ($\frac{1}{2}$ comes in because a triangle is $\frac{1}{2}$ as large as a rectangle with the same base and height)

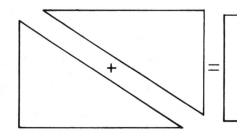

Volume: In general, volume is an area times a height.

Rectangular solid: volume = length × width × height

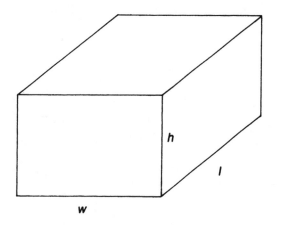

Surface area, or the amount of area on the surface of a solid, is often seen as lots of little areas added up.

Rectangular solid: surface area = $(2 \times l \times w) + (2 \times h \times w) + (2 \times h \times l)$. Why? Because there are three different pairs of sides.

Cylinder: surface area = $(2 \times \pi \times r^2) + (2 \times \pi \times r \times h)$. The $2 \times \pi \times r^2$ are the two ends (circles), and the $2 \times \pi \times r \times h$ is the rectangle you get if you unroll the side.

Important note: Most of the geometrical formulas are actually printed in the SAT exam instructions. So if you draw a blank, scan the instructions for the formula you need.

Now, solve these sample problems.

1. Jennifer wants to build a fence (God knows why people are always building fences in questions like these) to enclose a circle with an area of $144 \times \pi$. How much fencing will she need? (Draw a picture. It usually helps.)

Amount of fence = circumference

Circumference = $2 \times \pi \times r$

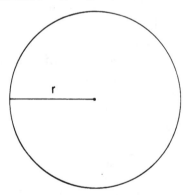

Well, we can't solve it without knowing the radius. So find the radius from the known area ($144 \times \pi$).

$$144 \times \pi = \pi \times r^2$$

$$r^2 = 144$$

$$r = 12$$

Answer: Jennifer needs $2 \times \pi \times r = 2 \times \pi \times 12 = 24 \times \pi$ fence. She also needs a psychoanalyst.

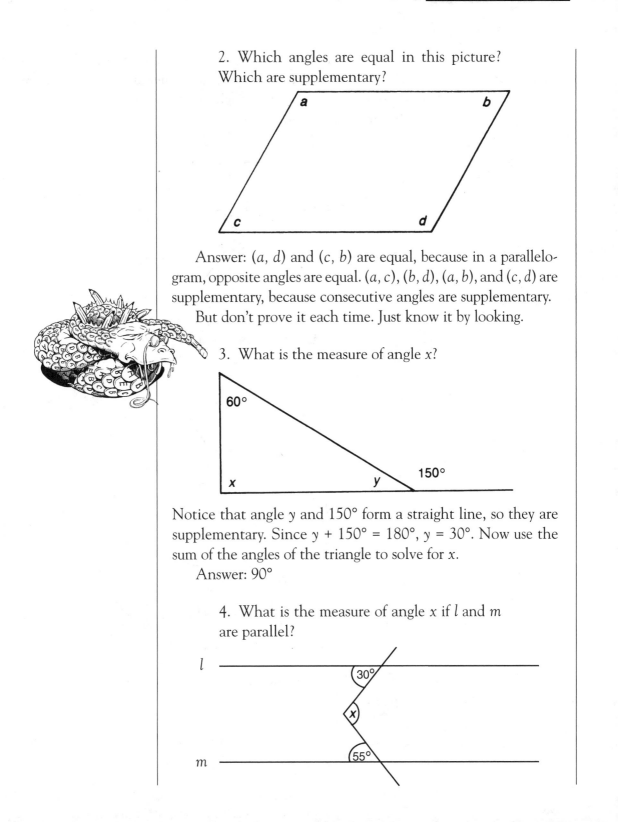

2. Which angles are equal in this picture? Which are supplementary?

Answer: (a, d) and (c, b) are equal, because in a parallelogram, opposite angles are equal. (a, c), (b, d), (a, b), and (c, d) are supplementary, because consecutive angles are supplementary.

But don't prove it each time. Just know it by looking.

3. What is the measure of angle x?

Notice that angle y and 150° form a straight line, so they are supplementary. Since $y + 150° = 180°$, $y = 30°$. Now use the sum of the angles of the triangle to solve for x.

Answer: 90°

4. What is the measure of angle x if l and m are parallel?

Remember those parallel lines cut by another line? The ones that are full of congruent and supplementary angles? Draw a third parallel line right through the middle of angle *x* and fill in the angles you know.

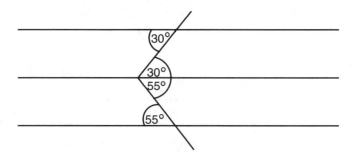

Voilà! The answer: 30° + 55° = 85° = *x*.

5. What is the measure of angle *x*?

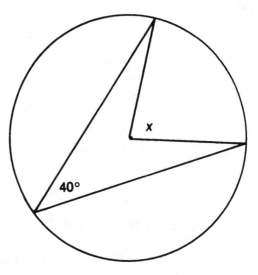

The 40° angle is *inscribed*, so the arc shown is 80°, as is, therefore, central angle *x*.

Answer: 80°

6. What is the measure of angle *x*?

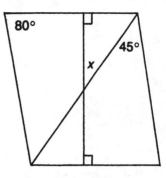

Ada says:
As you can see with this practice problem, sometimes geometry questions are easier if you redraw the diagram in a simpler manner so that you can see what the question is really asking for.

Break down the figure into the following components to find *x*.
First:

The angles in the following figure are supplementary, therefore: $y = 100°$.

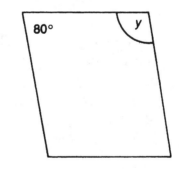

Second:
$z + 45° = y = 100°$
$z = 55°$

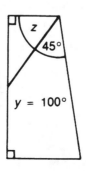

Finally:

$x + 55° + 90° = 180°$

$x = 35°$

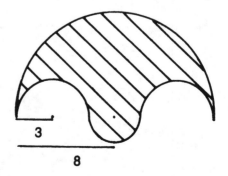

Answer: 35°

Questions 3, 4, 5, and 6 are worded the same, yet they deal with different geometric shapes. It's important that you learn to deal with angle measures in a variety of geometric figures.

Advanced Geometry

Advanced geometry involves a little more thinking and a whole bunch of tricks.

Weird Geometry Questions

Some of the nastier questions involve weird geometry—geometry that is hard to figure out at first from the diagrams but which turns out to be really easy if you look hard enough. The main strategy is to separate the big shape into lots of little shapes, and then solve them one by one.

1. What is the area of the shaded thing?

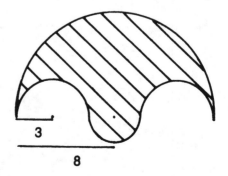

Well, what is that thing? There's no formula for shapes like this, but don't panic.

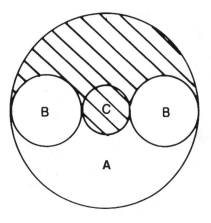

This shape is actually a bunch of circles—the big one (A), two medium ones (B), and the small one (C). You know the formula for the area of a circle ($\pi \times r^2$), so you can solve this problem by subtracting the two medium circles from the big circle, adding the small circle, and dividing everything by 2. Answer: $\frac{1}{2}(64\,\pi - 18\,\pi + 4\,\pi) = 25\,\pi$. Pretty cool, no?

2. Again, find the shaded area.

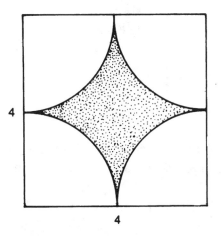

The shaded part is what's left over when you cut quarter circles out of a square. So you can solve for the area of the square

minus 4 × 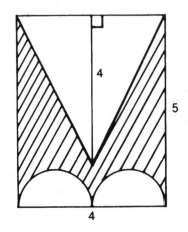. Four quarter circles equal one whole circle, therefore the area of the shaded area equals the area of the square minus the area of a circle with a radius of 2.

Answer: 16 – 4 π

3. Yet again, find the shaded area.

The area of the rectangle is 5 × 4 = 20. The area of the two semicircles = area of one whole circle. Since the whole side of the rectangle = 4, then the radius of the circle is 1, so the area of the circle is π. The triangle can be rearranged into a rectangle whose sides are 2 × 4 = 8.

Answer: 20 – π – 8 = 12 – π

COORDINATE GEOMETRY

Have an extra-grumpy math teacher? I hear they like apples.

—Ada

Usually, there are some problems that require you to know some coordinate geometry (graphs). We'll go over the stuff you need to know, but if this doesn't sound familiar or if you've forgotten it, we recommend you get a brand new pad of graph paper and go visit your math teacher at lunchtime. Math teachers love students who come for help eagerly carrying their own graph paper.

This is the basic graph with some points on it:

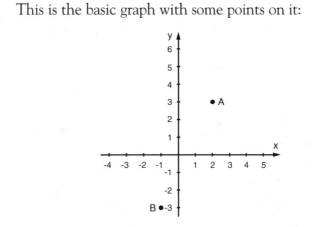

The y-axis goes down-to-up. The x-axis goes left-to-right. The origin is the point where they meet.

Any point on a graph has two coordinates. For example, point A on the graph shown has coordinates (2,4), which means that if you start at the origin and want to get to A, you have to go 2 units to the right and 4 units up. For point A, 2 is called its "x-coordinate" and 4 is called its "y-coordinate." The origin has coordinates (0,0), and point B has coordinates (−1, −3).

Distance Between Two Points

For any two points, say (a,b) and (c,d), the distance between them is given by the following formula, which looks fancier than it is:

$$\text{Distance} = \sqrt{(a-c)^2 + (b-d)^2}$$

For example, to get the distance between point A and point B on the graph above, you would plug them into the formula (it doesn't matter which you call (a,b) and (c,d)) and get

$$\overline{AB} = \sqrt{(2-(-1))^2 + (4-(-3))^2}$$
$$= \sqrt{3^2 + 7^2}$$
$$\text{Answer} = \sqrt{58}$$

(If you care why the distance formula works, just draw a right triangle using AB as the hypotenuse, and you'll see that the formula is just another version of the Pythagorean Theorem.)

Slope

The slope of a line is an indication of how "steep" it is. To figure out the slope of a line that connects two points (a,b) and (c,d), you use the formula

$$\text{Slope} = \frac{\text{change in } y}{\text{change in } x} = \frac{b-d}{a-c}$$

(Note that the slope of a vertical line is undefined because the change in x—the denominator—equals zero.)

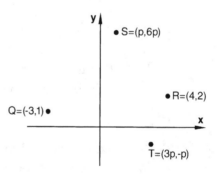

The following two questions relate to this graph.

1. What is the slope of the line that would connect point Q and point R?

Just plug the coordinates of the two points on the line into the formula:

$$\text{Slope} = \frac{\text{change in } y}{\text{change in } x} = \frac{1-2}{(-3)-4} = \frac{-1}{-7} = \frac{1}{7}$$

2. What is the slope of the line that would connect point S and point T?

$$\text{Slope} = \frac{\text{change in } y}{\text{change in } x} = \frac{6p-(-p)}{p-3p} = \frac{7p}{-2p} = \frac{-7}{2}$$

Formula of a Line

Another useful formula for a line is $(y-y_1) = m(x-x_1)$*, where* m *is the slope and* $(x_1\ y_1)$ *is a point the line passes through.*

The formula $y = mx + b$ describes a line with a slope of m and a y-intercept of b. (The *y-intercept* is the y-coordinate of the point where the line hits the y-axis.) This means that for any point on the line, you can figure out the y-coordinate by multiplying the slope by the point's x-coordinate and then adding the y-intercept. Here's an example:

> 3. The equation of a line is $y = 3x + 5$. If the x-coordinate of a point on the line is 1, what is the y-coordinate of that point?

Answer: $y = (3 \times 1) + 5 = 8$

Note: The SAT also has questions involving quadratic equations. It might give you two equations and ask you to compare their graphs.

Bar Graphs and Pie Charts

Since the SAT is big on practical reasoning ability, it usually includes lots of bar graphs and charts of real-world information that you have to interpret. The charts might indicate profits of a company on the y-axis and months on the x-axis, or amount of energy used on the y-axis and five different cities on the x-axis, or any two related things. The questions are usually pretty easy if you know the principles of coordinate geometry we have just reviewed. Start reading the graphs and pie charts in the bottom corner of the front page of *USA Today*. They're incredibly inane, but if you get used to reading them, you'll do fine when you get to questions about similar graphs on the SAT. Common sense. That's all you need.

Geometry Basics

We start off with symbols:

$\overleftarrow{AB}$	a line with A and B as points on the line
$\overrightarrow{AB}$	a ray with point A as an endpoint
$\overline{AB}$	a line with A and B as endpoints
$\triangle ABC \cong CDE$	triangle ABC is congruent (equal) to triangle CDE

Conic Sections

Circles and parabolas (and ellipses and hyperbolas—which you won't see on the test) are called **conic sections** because they can all be formed by cutting a cone with a knife. (Only mathematicians would think of something like this.) Conic sections also go by another name: The Serpent's Next Evil Invention. C'mon, he had to do *something* to replace those darling quantitative comparisons of his from the old SAT.

Circle

A circle looks pretty familiar:

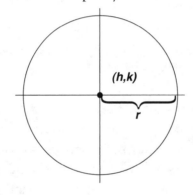

A **circle** is defined as a series of points that are all equal in distance from the center. Its formula is:

$$(x - h)^2 + (y - k)^2 = r^2 \qquad (h,k) = \text{center}, r = \text{radius}$$

Parabola

A parabola looks something like this:

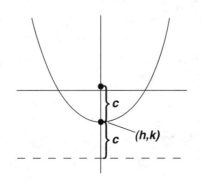

A **parabola** is a set of points that all have the same distance from the focus (the dot) as from the directrix (the dotted line). c is the distance between the vertex (h,k) and the directrix, and is also the distance between the vertex and the focus.

The formula for a parabola is:

if it's opening to the left or right

$(y - k)^2 = 4c(x - h)$ (h,k) = vertex, c = distance from vertex to directrix/focus

or, if it's opening upward or downward

$(x - h)^2 = 4c(y - k)$ (h,k) = vertex, c = distance from vertex to directrix/focus

Perpendicular and Tangent Lines

When two lines are **perpendicular,** they intersect at right angles. You can immediately tell that two lines are perpendicular if their slopes are opposite reciprocals of one another. For example, $y = -2x + 6$ and $y = \frac{x}{2} + 12$ are perpendicular to each other because the slope of the first line is -2 and the slope of the second is ½.

Tangent lines have to do with circles (or any other conic section, for that matter, but the SAT's probably not going to ask about tangents to hyperbolas). Basically, a line is **tangent** to a circle if it makes a right angle with the circle's radius and is outside the circle.

See that? We just went on a tangent about tangents!

—Ada

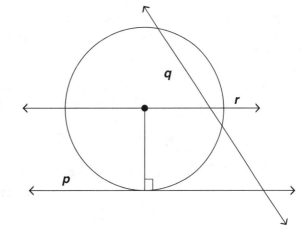

In the circle above, only the line p is a tangent line.

Example 1: A circle of the equation $x^2 + y^2 = 25$ has a tangent line at the point (4,3). What is the equation of the tangent line?

First of all, we have to visualize this circle. Because there's nothing after the x's and the y's, the center of the circle is on the origin (0,0). The radius is the square root of 25, and so it's 5.

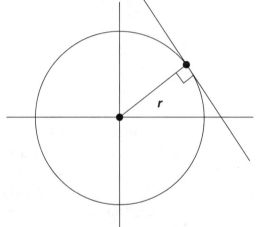

The tangent line is perpendicular to the radius, so we have to figure out what the equation for the radius is at this point. We know the center is (0,0), and the point is (4,3), so:

$$\text{slope} = \frac{\Delta y}{\Delta x} = \frac{3 - 0}{4 - 0} = \frac{3}{4}$$

So now we know that the slope of the radius is ¾. We're trying to get the tangent line, so we need the perpendicular slope, which is –⁴⁄₃.

Now all we have to do is plug everything into an equation:

$$(y - k) = (x - h)$$

$$(y - 3) = \frac{-4}{3}(x - 4)$$

And we have our tangent line.

Note that this also could have been written as

$$y = \frac{-4}{3}x + \frac{25}{3}$$

Trigonometry

The College Board says there are problems on the SAT that can be solved using trigonometry. Unless you're already comfortable with it, though, we suggest you just memorize the properties of the similar triangles (see pages 211–213).

Basic Transformations

A transformation of a graph of a function means moving it. Here are a few basic transformations that you might need to know:

Changing the basic function $y = x^3$

$y = x^3 + 5$	Graph is shifted *up* five units
$y = x^3 - 5$	Graph is shifted *down* five units
$y = (x + 5)^3$	Graph is shifted *left* five units
$y = (x - 5)^3$	Graph is shifted *right* five units
$y = (-x)^3$	Graph is reflected over the *y*-axis
$y = -x^3$	Graph is reflected over the *x*-axis

If you forget some transformations, do some trial-and-error on your graphing calculator, but only if you have time.

Some handy dandy example graphs:

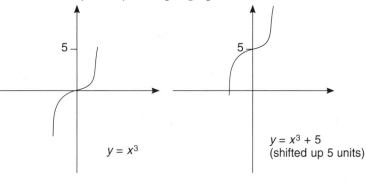

$y = x^3$

$y = x^3 + 5$
(shifted up 5 units)

THE FUNNY SYMBOL QUESTION

As if the SAT didn't already have enough ridiculous things on it, the Serpent came up with the funny symbol question. Here's how funny symbol questions work.

The Serpent gives you some symbol, like this,

★

and tells you what it does. You're supposed to apply it. Easy. Don't freak out and say, "Oh, no! We never went over ★ in my math class, I guess I can't do this one." The fact is that no one has ever seen that symbol in math class. The Serpent just dreamed it up. (Yes, he loses sleep at night thinking up funny symbols and how to make them exceptionally cruel.)

And he will tell you exactly what the symbol means.

The Evil Testing Serpent defines the symbol, usually using x and y (or a and b or whatever) in terms of arithmetic commands ($+$, $-$, $\times$, $\div$), which you know how to use. You take the numbers given to you in the question and do the arithmetic the funny symbol represents. Be careful that you do it in the *same order* as in the definition of the funny symbol.

Okay, here are some examples:

1. If $x \diamond y = x^2 + 2y$ then what is $3 \diamond 4$?
   (A) $6x$
   (B) 42
   (C) 3
   (D) 11
   (E) 17

Answer: (E). Plug in 3 and 4 where x and y were in the definition.

2. $\boxed{n} = 2(n^2 + n) / (n + 1)$. What is $\boxed{35}$?
   (A) 70
   (B) 64
   (C) 32
   (D) $35n$
   (E) 1

Answer: (A)
Note: $2(n^2 + n) / (n + 1) = 2n\,(n + 1) / (n + 1) = 2n$.

Take it from here.

3. $L @ K = L + K/L$. What is $L @ (L @ K)$?
   (A) $L + 2K + K/4$
   (B) $2L + K/4 + 1$
   (C) L
   (D) $L + 1 + K/L^2$
   (E) L/K

Okay. We know you're tired of this, so we'll give it to you:

$$L @ (L @ K) = L @ (L + K/L)$$

$$= L + \frac{(L + K/L)}{L}$$

$$= L + L/L + K/L^2 = L + 1 + K/L^2$$

Answer: (D)

Remember: Always do the stuff in the parentheses first.

PEMDAS!

−Ada

4.

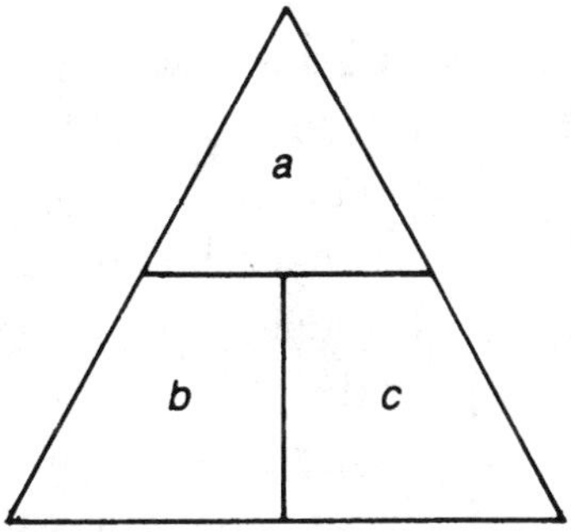

$= a \times b + c$

If

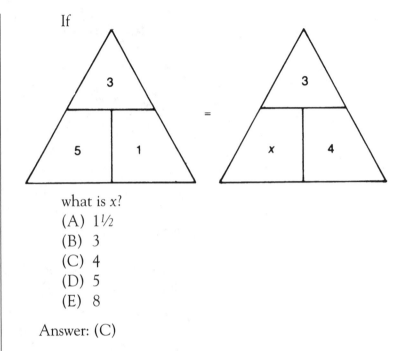

what is *x*?

(A) 1½

(B) 3

(C) 4

(D) 5

(E) 8

Answer: (C)

HEINOUS MISCELLANEOUS MATH

We're sorry to do this to you, but there are a few additional topics you should probably get familiar with. Don't worry, they're nothing you can't handle. So without further ado, we bring you the section of odds and ends that we like to call Heinous Miscellaneous Math.

Let's start with some definitions.

In mathematical terms, a **sequence** is a function whose domain is the set of positive integers. There are two kinds of sequences that you're likely to see—arithmetic and geometric.

Geometric Sequences

In **geometric sequences,** or **exponential growth sequences,** numbers change by a certain ratio, rather than by a certain difference. For example, the set {½, ¼, ⅛, ¹⁄₁₆ . . .} is a geometric sequence, because you can get each number by dividing the one before it by ½. On the other hand, the set {2, 5, 8, 11 . . .} is an arithmetic sequence because you get each number by adding 3 to the previous number. The Serpent requires that you know about geometric sequences, so we'll go into this a little more in-depth.

The formula for a geometric sequence is

$$a_n = a_1 r^{(n-1)}$$

where a_1 is the first term, r is the ratio of change, n is the number of the term you're trying to get, and a_n is the term itself.

Example: Find the eighth term of $\{\frac{1}{2}, \frac{1}{4}, \frac{1}{8}, \frac{1}{16} \ldots\}$

First, you should figure out the ratio, by dividing the second number by the first:

$$\frac{\frac{1}{4}}{\frac{1}{2}} = \frac{\left(\frac{1}{4}\right)4}{\left(\frac{1}{2}\right)4} = \frac{1}{2}$$

Then just follow the formula:

$$a_n = (\tfrac{1}{2})(\tfrac{1}{2})^7$$

$$a_n = \tfrac{1}{256}$$

Of course, the ETS is not going to be so nice as to say, "Hey, just plug numbers in!" No. The Serpent will probably sneak geometric sequences through the backdoor. Since they're frequently used to describe population growth, he'll probably ask something like this:

Example: A town now has a population of 100. A big company is to be moving in and the town's population is expected to double every six years. What will be the population of the town after ten years?

(A) 215
(B) 252
(C) 304
(D) 317
(E) 400

The tricky part of this problem is figuring out what the $r^{(n-1)}$ expression equals. The a_1 is obviously 100—this is the population that we're starting out with. Since the population *doubles* every six years, then r, the rate, should be 2. So what's $(n–1)$? Don't be tempted to subtract 1 from 10 and get 9. It wouldn't make sense because the population only doubles every six years, not every year.

So that's when you should ask yourself, "If six years is one cycle, then by the time we go through the tenth year, how much of the cycle have we gone through?" If we divide 10 by 6, we get the answer: ⁵⁄₃. We have gone through one and two thirds of the 6-year cycle of doubling.

Now you know all the numbers:

$a_n = (100)(2^{5/3}) = 317.4802.$

Since we can't have 0.48 of a person, we round down. The population will be 317.

Answer: (D)

Probability

Unless the SAT has made you that desperate. Then, Vegas it is!
      —Ada

Probability is one of those things you learn in school that is actually helpful in life. After you learn about it, you'll never want to go to Vegas again.

Probability of an event:

$$P(E) = \frac{\text{number of ways the event can occur}}{\text{total number of occurrences}}$$

The mathematical probability of an event that is certain to happen is equal to one. The mathematical probability of an impossible event is zero.

A fair die is rolled. (All dice are "fair" in SAT-land. It just means that all the numbers have an equal chance of being rolled.) What is the probability that the result is greater than 4?

Well, there are only two numbers that could make this event happen: 5 and 6. Meanwhile, you can actually roll any one of 6 numbers. So,

$$P(E) = \frac{2}{6} = \frac{1}{3}$$

Scatterplots and Best Fit Lines

A scatterplot is basically a graph without lines. Instead, dots are placed for the information that's available. The **best fit** line is exactly what it says—a line that best fits the graphed dots. The SAT won't ask you to draw this line, or figure out what the equation for it is. Instead, all you will have to do is know whether its slope is positive or negative. Sometimes the Serpent will tell you to get information from a scatterplot without asking for the best fit line. In this case, just treat every dot as a separate piece of information. These kinds of questions aren't that common on the SAT, but you should know how to handle them just in case.

Example: Five students were in a pie-eating contest, and the results were plotted in a graph of time versus pies eaten, as shown in Figure 1. Of the five students *A*, *B*, *C*, *D*, and *E*, which one ate the most pies per hour?

(A) A
(B) B
(C) C
(D) D
(E) E

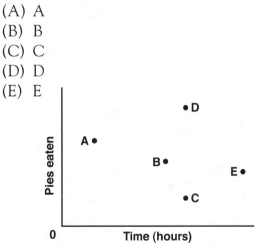

Notice first that the question asks for the most pies *per hour*, not the most pies overall. So, our goal is to find the most pies/hour. Since pies is the *y*-coordinate and time is the *x*-coordinate, the question is really asking you to find the *slope* of the imaginary lines that run from the origin to the point. If you draw these lines, you should be able to see that the line from the origin to A has the steepest slope.

Answer: (A)

GRID-IN PROBLEMS

Since the ETS doesn't offer you a multiple-choice option, they don't take points off your score for wrong answers on grid-in questions. (They're probably just trying to cover up the fact that they screwed up!)

Always at least guess! There is nothing to lose in this section.
—Ada

The SAT has math questions for which you produce the answer. No more stinking multiple choice—here's a chance for some creativity!

On the test, these problems will be called "Student Produced Answers." However, the ETS informally calls them "grid-in problems," and many of the questions will ask you to "grid" a number. Well, get this: **The ETS screwed up!** Let's say that again; it feels good. **The ETS screwed up!** You see, in every dictionary we've looked at, the word *grid* is used only as a noun. It doesn't exist as a verb! The ETS made up a word! We think it's pretty downright disgusting that the ETS will nail you if you don't know the meaning of the word *supercilious*, yet it has no qualms about making up its own word. **The ETS screwed up!**

Don't be thrown off by these problems: They test you on the same subject matter the rest of the test covers. Plus, you don't lose any points if you answer these questions wrong!

In fact, because the content is the same as the rest of the test, there aren't any special hints we can give you. The only tricky part of this section is knowing how to fill in the answers. There are directions for this on every test, but because you probably won't have time to read them, we've provided a summary.

First of all, take a look at a sample of the grid that will appear on your answer sheet. Notice that at the top is space to write in your answer. However, this is not required—the computer scores only what's in the ovals. So don't bother to write in the answer unless you're afraid you'll get confused otherwise.

You can start your answer in any column. Either of these positions is correct:

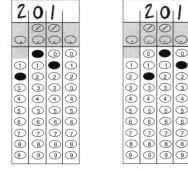

Both fractions and decimals are accepted. If the answer is ¼, you can use either ¼ or .25. But remember to make decimals as accurate as possible. For instance, ⅔ can be filled in as .666 or .667, but not .66 or .67. Because of this we think it's easier to stick with fractions.

Important: You can't state your answer in mixed fractions. For instance, 2½ would look like ²¹⁄₂ (twenty-one halves). So you have to use ⁵⁄₂ or 2.5.

For some reason, there is a decimal point in the last column: Ignore it. There is no possible answer that would use it.

If for some reason you forget, the largest possible answer on the grid is 9,999; the smallest answer is 0. There are no negative answers. If you get a negative number or a five-digit answer, try the problem again.

Here are two real SAT questions to whet your appetite (have you ever seen *whet* used in a sentence without *appetite*?).

1. If (⁹⁄₆) (12*b*) = 1, what is the value of *ab*?

Answer:

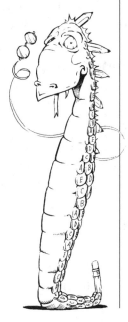

Mixed fractions are TOTAL deal breakers.

—Ada

(Remember: You don't have to write in the answer at the top; we did it for clarity.)

2. The lengths of the sides of a triangle are *a*, 9, and 17, where *a* is the length of the shortest side. If the triangle is not isosceles, what is one possible value of *a*?

Answer:

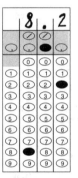

In this case, you could have written any number greater than 8 and less than 9. If *a* were 9 or greater, it wouldn't be the shortest side anymore. And if it were smaller than 8, you couldn't make a triangle out of it (just try drawing it).

What else do you need to know for the math section of the SAT? Not a whole lot, actually. Many of the questions just involve common sense. Notice that in some of the questions you don't have to waste time doing mathematical computations. Sometimes the choices listed aren't simplified—so why in the world should you simplify your answer? Look over the choices before you work the problem all the way out.

If you're constantly making stupid mistakes on problems you think you should know, you may want to try working faster. You might make a few more careless errors the first time around, but you'll be able to catch them when you check your answers. As with any strategy, try this on a few practice tests and see what works for you.

If you *do* have time at the end of a math section to check your answers, here's a little trick: Use a different method to get the answer than the one you used the first time. That way you won't make the mistake of doing it wrong the same way twice.

And remember, a good command of really basic things will make you work faster, and as we said earlier, speed and accuracy are essential to doing well on the math section.

Now go do the math sections on some practice SATs from the College Board's *The Official SAT Study Guide*. And make your grandmother proud!

CHAPTER 4

THE WRITING SECTION

THE STORY OF LITTLE-READ WRITING SERPENT

Way back in 1994, at a time when the ETS was revising the SAT, educators began to complain that there should be an essay on it. But at that point the stubborn Serpent didn't feel like putting an essay on the trusty SAT. Instead, he looked around his malodorous cave at the various rusty instruments of torture he had collected over the years and dug up the one he had once called "English Composition Achievement Test with Essay." Brushing off the remnants of decaying student flesh that coated it, the Serpent drooled, "Yes! This is it! This old test already has an essay on it. I'll rename it the SAT II Writing test! And I'll make a big fuss about it so most colleges will require it! And the high school students will continue to writhe in eternal agony!"

Fortunately, our intrepid authors quickly caught the Serpent, sending him whimpering back to his cave, and for years, *Up Your Score* helped students outsmart the SAT II Writing test. But then suddenly, thanks to the big mouths at the University of California, the SAT II Writing test wasn't good enough, and the Serpent had to come up with a new diabolical plot. An evil writing exam on the SAT I itself was the answer. After all, what could be nastier than topping off three hours of relentless passages and negative exponents with an essay? Oh, how the Serpent rejoiced! And although the new writing section is just the recycled SAT II Writing test, somehow this placated the Serpent's critics, and peace, for now, once again reigns in the kingdom of University Administrators.

But not to worry. The Serpent was neither smart enough nor creative enough to make the new SAT writing section more difficult than the SAT II Writing test, so we can use our knowledge to save a new generation of standardized test takers from the fear and nausea of the dreaded timed essay. *Up Your Score* will now show you how to outsmart the Serpent's puny excuse for a writing test, and you will all live happily ever after . . .

ENGLISH COMPOSITION ACHIEVEMENT TEST WITH ESSAY

The SAT writing section has an essay section that supposedly tests you on how well you can write, and a multiple-choice section (usage, sentence correction, and revision-in-context questions) that tests you on your ability to recognize and correct mistakes in grammar, sentence structure, and word choice. The Writing section allows you 25 minutes for the essay and 35 minutes (which is made up of a 25-minute section and a 10-minute section) for the multiple-choice questions. It's scored on a scale of 200 to 800.

In this chapter, we will explain the three types of multiple-choice questions and suggest strategies for attacking them. Then we will cover the 13 most important grammatical rules to know. Finally, we will tell you how to write a kick-butt essay. If you really want to kick butt on this test, it will help to find some practice tests. Ask if there are any practice tests in your high school guidance office. Also pick up a PSAT booklet, since the writing section on the PSAT is very similar to the multiple-choice section of the writing section. If you want to take any of the practice tests in the other review books (those not put out by the College Board), do so at your own risk. Most of the ones we looked at were stupid and quite different from the real thing.

Another way to hone your skills? Keep a journal or blog. Write constantly—not just about the things that happen to you on a daily basis but also about big ideas, current events, and your beliefs. Don't be afraid to express your most profound thoughts, such as, "I bought a new pair of jeans today, but I'm afraid they make me look fat." No, really, make a point of writing about complex ideas, with thesis statements and strong arguments. That way, when you sit down to write the SAT essay, it will come as naturally as blogging: "Over the centuries, great thinkers have asked many philosophical questions but none as vexing as, 'Do these jeans make me look fat?'"

As with the critical reading sections of the SAT I, a good way to prepare is to read a lot. The more you read, the more you will develop a sense for what sounds right and what doesn't.

THE THREE QUESTION TYPES

Type 1: Usage Questions (Identifying Sentence Errors)

These questions take less time than the other multiple-choice questions. A typical usage question looks like this:

> The <u>children</u> would <u>giggled</u> <u>as</u> they smeared
> 　　　　A　　　　　　　B　　C
> applesauce on <u>each other</u>. <u>No error</u>.
> 　　　　　　　　　D　　　　　　　E

You are to assume that everything that isn't underlined is the way it's supposed to be, and then find the error in one of the underlined portions. The answer to this example is (B), because *giggled* should be *giggle*.

Follow this procedure when doing usage questions:

1. Read the *whole* sentence quickly but carefully.
2. If you're positive that you see the error, mark it on the answer sheet and go on to the next problem.
3. If you don't see the error, look at each underlined portion very carefully; see if it follows 13 of the rules listed later in this chapter (Rule 9 doesn't apply to usage questions) or any other rules you might know. Something that sounds wrong probably is.
4. If you still don't find an error, mark (E).
5. If you have time left at the end of the test, go back and check all the questions for which you chose (E).

Type 2: Sentence Correction Questions (Improving Sentences)

These questions take more time than the usage questions but less time than revision-in-context questions. They also play with your mind. A typical sentence correction question looks like this:

> The doctor warned the students that <u>it are a myth that one cannot</u> get the swine flu for 24 hours after taking the SAT.
> (A) it are a myth that one cannot

(B) it are a myth, that one cannot
(C) it is a myth that one cannot
(D) it is a myth which one cannot
(E) its myths are that one cannot

Your job on this type of question is to select the answer choice that would best replace the underlined part of the question. The correct answer to this question is (C). Choice (A) is always exactly the same as the underlined portion of the sentence and is the correct answer whenever the original sentence is okay.

This is the procedure you should follow when doing sentence correction questions:

1. Read the *whole* sentence, not just the underlined part. Often the underlined part is grammatically correct by itself but is wrong in the context of the whole sentence.
2. Never read choice (A). Remember, choice (A) is always the same as the original sentence. Why read it again?
3. Even if you think that the original sentence is correct, check each one of the different answer choices to see if one of them is better than the original sentence.
4. If you still think that the original sentence is cool, then pick choice (A).
5. If you think that the sentence is wrong, look for the choice that will make it right.
6. If you can't decide which is the right answer, choose the one that is phrased closest to the way Dan Rather would phrase it.
7. If you can't figure out the answer, choose *the shortest one*. English is a relatively efficient language. Good writing often involves short, to-the-point sentences that don't go on for ever and ever talking about all sorts of things, and getting redundant, and being just generally too long, when they could be short but

The SAT is all about precision.

—Ada

aren't because they're long, in fact much longer than they have to be (like this sentence). So choosing the shortest answer works on an extraordinary percentage of questions. Take a look at this question:

Mr. Howe's class has organized a special program for our <u>school: the purpose being to</u> help us increase our understanding of Japanese culture.

(A) school: the purpose being to
(B) school and the purpose is to
(C) school, the purpose is to
(D) school, being to
(E) school to

The answer is (E).

Type 3: Revision-in-Context (Improving Paragraphs)

These questions are sort of a combination of sentence correction questions and reading questions from the SAT. A revision-in-context passage is a short essay full of flaws. It's supposed to be like an early draft of an essay that you would revise in school. Whatever.

The first thing you should do is read through the passage quickly, just to get a sense of what it is about. As you read it you will notice mistakes, but don't bother marking them down because any question that refers to a mistake will tell you where the mistake is.

Here's an example:

1. The jellator is unlike most animals. 2. It is known mainly for what it cannot do. 3. It is known less for what it can do. 4. It cannot reproduce. 5. It cannot hunt for its food. 6. It cannot walk on hind feet. 7. The one thing it can do is stop its own heartbeat.

8. When placed under dire conditions, such as when under attack, the jellator curls itself into a little ball and makes its heart stop beating. 9. The attacker, sensing that its prey is no

longer alive, will lose its desire to hunt and ran away. 10. The jellator then goes back to its own business of doing nothing in particular. 11. Scientists have many ideas about this unique skill.

12. Some believe that the jellator, possessing no other defense methods, evolved this ability over thousands of years.

13. Others believe that a meteor crashed eons ago, imbuing a jellator with magical skills. 14. However, the most common belief about the jellator's ability is that there is a little elf that lives inside the jellator's chest and holds the heart still when a predator is nearby.

Here are examples of three types of questions that would follow a passage like this:

1. Which of the following is the best way to combine sentences 1, 2, and 3?
    (A) The jellator is known mainly for what it cannot do, unlike most animals, and less for what it can do.
    (B) Known less for what it can do and mainly for what it cannot do, the jellator is unlike most animals.
    (C) Knowing what it can and cannot do, the jellator is unlike most animals.
    (D) Unlike most animals, the jellator is known more for what it cannot do than for what it can do.
    (E) The jellator is more like a dessert topping than an animal.

The correct answer is (D).

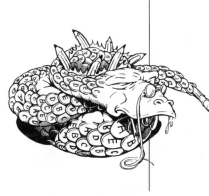

2. Which of the following is the best revision of the underlined portion of sentence 9 below?
    The attacker, sensing that its prey is no longer alive, will lose its desire to hunt and ran away.
    (A) will have run away and desired to hunt.
    (B) will lose its desire to hunt and run away.

(C) will have lost; its desire to hunt and
     ran away.
(D) will have lost it, and desired to have
     run away.
(E) will lose, desire, hunt and run away.
The answer to this question is (B).

Note: This type of question, which asks you to fix one sentence, is just like the sentence correction questions, except that choice (A) is not the same as the underlined portion of the sentence.

3. In relation to the passage as a whole, which
    of the following best describes the writer's
    intention in the third paragraph?
   (A) To summarize the rest of the passage
   (B) To illustrate an example
   (C) To provide theories for explaining the
        information in the second paragraph
   (D) To prove the existence of jellators
   (E) To titillate the reader with lewd,
        lascivious tales of bawdy lechers

The answer is (C).

Notice that while on the surface these questions look like the reading passage questions in the SAT critical reading section, these questions never ask you about facts and ideas in the passage. Still, you will have to more or less understand the passage, because fixing the mistakes requires knowing what the passage is trying to say and picking up on its main idea. (Sound familiar?)

THE 13 RULES OF THE WRITING TEST

These are the rules most likely to be tested for on the SAT I writing section. We won't give any in-depth explanations or use any fancy grammatical terms in this section. For each rule, we will simply make you aware of the concept and then give examples. Instead of being "textbookish" and going into the grammatical theory behind our rules, we will depend on your ability to "hear" when something "sounds" right or wrong.

Nevertheless, you will first have to understand the following basic grammatical terms that you probably already know. Sorry.

noun
Word that denotes a person, place, thing, idea (*joy*), quality (*stickiness*), or act (*drooling*).

pronoun
As Homer Simpson defined it when he was studying for his high school diploma, "A noun that has lost its amateur status." Actually, a word that takes the place of a noun. (Example: The Serpent is evil. *He* is cruel. *He* is a pronoun because it takes the place of *Serpent*.) *It, he, she, they, we, who,* and *them* are some examples of pronouns.

verb
Word that expresses action (*jump*) or a state of being (*be*). A verb tells what's happening in the sentence.

subject
Noun or pronoun that "does" the action of the verb in the sentence. (Example: *He* drooled. *He* is the subject because *he* is the thing that drooled.)

object
Noun or pronoun that the verb acts on. (Example: He tickled *me*. *Me* is the object because *me* is the thing that got tickled.)

preposition
Words like *to, at, in, up, over, under, after, of*. They go with objects. (For example, in the phrase "in the house," *in* is a preposition and *house* is the object.)

singular
Having to do with a single thing or single unit. (Example: *noodle*.)

plural
Having to do with more than one thing. (Example: *noodles*.)

Rule 1: Subject-Verb Agreement

Subject and verb must agree in number, so isolate the subject and the verb and make sure they match. If the subject is singular, the verb should be singular; if the subject is plural, the verb should be plural.

Example 1:

The proctor, as well as the students, were overcome by the tedious ticking of the timer and fell asleep.

Isolate: subject: proctor (singular)
              verb: were overcome (plural)
Combine: "The proctor were overcome."

This should sound wrong to you. *Proctor* is singular, so the verb should be singular—*was overcome*. Don't be tempted by the plural word *students*; it is set off by a pair of commas, so it's not part of the subject.

Correct: The proctor, as well as the students, was overcome by the tedious ticking of the timer and fell asleep.

Three expressions that are similar to the *as well as* in the above example are: *in addition to, along with,* and *together with*. When you see one of these expressions on the test, chances are the Serpent is trying to make you think that the subject is plural.

Example 2:

The anguish of the students have been a source of pleasure to the ETS.

Isolate: subject: anguish (singular)
             verb: have been (plural)

Combine: "The anguish have been a source of pleasure."

This should sound wrong to you. Don't get confused by the plural word *students*, because it isn't the subject. *Students*, in this sentence, is an object. You can tell because it comes after a preposition, *of*. Whenever a word comes after a preposition, it is an object, not a subject.

Correct: The anguish of the students has been a source of pleasure to the ETS.

Example 3:

Each of the streets were painted green.

Isolate: subject: each (singular)
             verb: were (plural)

Combine: "Each were painted green."

This one is a little trickier. You have to realize that the subject of the sentence is *Each* and not *of the streets*. (*Streets* is an object of the preposition *of*.) Anytime you see "of the _____," the word that goes in the blank is an object, not a subject. Although *streets* is plural, the subject of the sentence, *Each*, is singular. If you replace the "of the _____" part of the sentence with the word *one*, it is easier to see why the subject is singular: "Each one was painted green" sounds much better than "Each one were painted green."

Correct: Each of the streets was painted green.

There are 13 singular subjects like *each* that you should memorize: *each, every, either, neither, one, no one, everyone, everybody, someone, somebody, anyone, anybody,* and *nobody*. Whenever you see one of these words as the subject of a sentence

Flash cards
aren't just
for vocab.
—Ada

on the test, pay careful attention to whether the verb is singular. For example:

Incorrect: Neither of the streets *were* painted green.

Correct: Neither of the streets *was* painted green.

Again, it helps to replace the "of the _____" part of the sentence with the word *one:* "Neither one was painted green" should sound better to you than "Neither one were painted green."

Incorrect: Either this street or that street *were* painted green.

Correct: Either this street or that street *was* painted green.

Incorrect: One of the streets *were* painted green.

Correct: One of the streets *was* painted green.

Rule 2: Noun-Pronoun Agreement

Singular subjects take singular pronouns; plural subjects take plural pronouns. You know the list of singular subjects that you just memorized (*each, every, either, neither, one, no one, everyone, everybody, someone, somebody, anyone, anybody,* and *nobody*)? Well, each of these words takes a singular pronoun. Whenever one of the words on the list is the subject, the pronoun that refers to that word has to be singular. This is a hard rule to "hear" because so many people break this rule that we're used to hearing it the wrong way.

Example 1:
Not one of the boys read their SAT study guide.
Isolate: subject: one (singular)
                    pronoun: their (plural)

This sentence doesn't sound awful to most people, but it's wrong. The subject *one* is singular, but the pronoun *their* is plural. (*Boys* is plural, but it's an object. You can tell it's an object because of the "of the _____" construction.) The correct pronoun would be *his.*

Correct: Not one of the boys read his SAT study guide.

Example 2:

Each of the girls ate their lunch.

Isolate: subject: Each (singular)

pronoun: their (plural)

Each is singular, but *their* is plural. Try replacing the *of the girls* part of the sentence with *one* and you should see why the pronoun *her* sounds better than *their*.

Correct: Each of the girls ate her lunch. (Again, think "each one.")

There are also some pronouns that can go either way. These are *some, any, none, all,* and *most*—the SANAM pronouns (it's easier to remember when you realize that it sounds like Saddam). They can be either singular or plural, depending on the subject.

Example 3:

Kim Kardashian didn't know that some of the cameras was taping.

Ms. Kardashian might think this sentence sounds just fine, but *you* know that *cameras* is plural, and therefore *some* should be plural, too.

Correct: Kim Kardashian didn't know that some of the cameras were taping.

Example 4:

All of the pizza have been eaten.

Here, *pizza* is singular, so the verb should be singular, too.

Correct: All of the pizza has been eaten.

Rule 3: Pronoun Subjects and Objects

You must know when to use the words in the column on the left and when to use the words in the column on the right:

Subjects	Objects
I	me
he	him
she	her
they	them
we	us
who	whom

The words on the left are subjects, the words on the right are objects.

> *I* like hot dogs, but hot dogs don't like *me*.
> *He* pushed Susie, so Susie kicked *him*.
> *She* is good enough for Grape-Nuts, but are Grape-Nuts good enough for *her?*
> *We* all hate the ETS, because the ETS hates *us*.
> *Who* killed Bozo? Bozo killed *whom?*

Example 1:
Julio and me were down by the schoolyard.

Always simplify these sentences. Does "Me was in the schoolyard" sound right? No. "I was in the schoolyard."

Correct: Julio and I were down by the schoolyard.

Example 2:
The dog and him are eating pizza.

Does "Him is eating pizza" sound right? No. "He is eating pizza."

Correct: The dog and he are eating pizza.

Example 3:
The SAT writing section was easy for Huey and he because they had read *Up Your Score*.

"The SAT writing section was easy for he" should sound wrong to you. If it doesn't sound wrong, then recognize that the word *he* is an object in the sentence and therefore should be *him*.

Correct: The SAT writing section was easy for Huey and him because they had read *Up Your Score*.

Rule 4: Pronoun Consistency

Pronouns should be consistent throughout a sentence. When *one* starts with a particular pronoun, *one* should continue to use that pronoun, or a pronoun that is consistent with it, throughout *one*'s whole sentence.

Example:

The more you study for the SAT, the more one thinks about moving to Mongolia.

This sentence starts with the pronoun *you* and then ends with the pronoun *one*. This is inconsistent. It should be either:

The more *you* study for the SAT, the more *you* think about moving to Mongolia.

or:

The more *one* studies for the SAT, the more *one* thinks about moving to Mongolia.

Rule 5: Correct Tense

Make sure the time of an action is consistent. Look for key "time words" such as *when, while, as, after,* and so forth, and make sure the tenses make sense.

Example 1:

After he ate the newt and brushed his teeth, I will kiss him.

The problem here is that the verbs *ate* and *brushed* happened in the past, whereas *will kiss* is going to happen in the future. Change it to either:

After he eats the newt and brushes his teeth, I will kiss him.

or:

After he ate the newt and brushed his teeth, I kissed him.

Example 2:

While I was painting his feet, he had tickled me.

Presumably, he *interrupted* the feet painting with his tickling, so the sentence should read:

> While I was painting his feet, he tickled me.

This makes the sentence consistent. Never mind that it's weird—consistency is all that matters here. So, as the people in these sentences carry on with their mildly deviant activities, just go through and make sure everything is done in the proper time sequence.

Rule 6: Adjectives and Adverbs

Remember the difference between an adjective and an adverb? If not, your sixth-grade teacher will hunt you down and pinch you. The ETS likes to mix these two up.

Adjectives describe nouns. An adjective will always make grammatical sense in the phrase

> the _____ wombat (Example: the *lascivious* wombat)

Adverbs describe verbs or adjectives or other adverbs. They usually, but not always, end in "-ly." An adverb will always make grammatical sense in the sentence.

> The wombat did it _____. (Example: The wombat did it *lasciviously*.)

Example 1:
> I ran slow.

The word *slow* is an adjective. You can tell because it makes sense in the phrase "the slow wombat." However, in Example 1, it is being used to describe the verb *ran*. This is impossible. Adjectives describe only nouns. *Adverbs* describe verbs. Use *slowly* instead.

> *Correct:* I ran slowly.

Example 2:
> Poindexter juggles good.

Poindexter has problems. The word *good* is an adjective, but it's being used to describe the word *juggles*, which is a verb. Again, you have to use the adverb.

The "good" vs. "well" distinction is handy for the SAT... and life!
— Ada

Correct: Poindexter juggles well. (Notice that *well* is an adverb even though it does not end in "-ly.")

Example 3:

I hate lumpy fish on soporific afternoons.

The sentence is grammatically correct, not to mention worthy of analysis from a psychological perspective. If you immediately jumped on this sentence and tried to correct it, it means you're too tense. Eat some frozen yogurt.

Another tricky aspect of adjectives and adverbs is comparison of more than one person or object. Take the adjective *juicy*. If you're talking about only one object, you would use *juicy*: "This fruit is juicy." If you're comparing two objects, you would use *juicier*: "This apple is juicier than that pear." If you're comparing more than two objects, you would use *juiciest*: "Of the three fruits, the orange is juiciest."

Example 4:

Dan is the older of the four athletes.

Since there are more than two objects being compared, we can't use *older*.

Correct: Dan is the oldest of the four athletes.

Rule 7: Parallel Construction

Ideas that are parallel (related) should be expressed in the same way.

Example 1:

I like spitting, drooling, and to slurp.

Spit, drool, and slurp are parallel activities. They should be expressed in the same way:

Correct: I like spitting, drooling, and slurping.
Correct: I like to spit, to drool, and to slurp.
Correct: I like to spit, drool, and slurp.

Example 2:

You like spitting and drooling but not to slurp.

Beware! Parallel construction is one of the ETS's favorite tricks, and many students (who haven't armed themselves with Up Your Score) have trouble catching it. Good thing it's also one of the easiest tricks to defeat.

Just because you don't like slurping does not mean that it shouldn't be parallel with spitting and drooling, which you do like.

Correct: You like spitting and drooling but not slurping.

Example 3:

The juicer chops vegetables, squeezes oranges, and proctors can be liquefied with it.

Chopping vegetables, squeezing oranges, and liquefying proctors are all parallel actions. They should be expressed in the same way.

Correct: The juicer chops vegetables, squeezes oranges, and liquefies proctors.

Rule 8: Run-on Sentences and Sentence Fragments

A run-on sentence is usually two complete sentences that are incorrectly joined by a comma instead of separated by a period or a semicolon.

Example 1:

J.P. ate the mysterious object, it was a noodle.

This is a run-on sentence. It could be broken into two sentences:

1. J.P. ate the mysterious object.
2. It was a noodle.

It could also be combined into one sentence using a semicolon: J.P. ate the mysterious object; it was a noodle.

Sentence fragments are parts of sentences that are made up to look like real sentences. They are usually next to real sentences into which they should be incorporated.

Example 2:

All the kids had rashes on their bodies. Especially those with uranium lunch boxes.

The ETS has been known to concoct excessively long sentences. Sometimes it helps to cross out prepositional phrases that are only there to distract you.

In this example, the first sentence is complete, but the second is a fragment. The two could be combined like this:

All the kids had rashes on their bodies, especially those with uranium lunch boxes.

Note: You have to worry about run-ons or sentence fragments only when you're working on the sentence correction or revision-in-context sections. Usage questions don't test for run-ons or fragments.

Rule 9: Totally Bogus Sight Questions

These are absolutely the most ridiculous questions on the test. Including questions this ludicrous shows how deeply and utterly absurd the Evil Testing Serpent is. The questions don't test anything that has to do with your ability to write. They don't even test your ability to identify correct grammar. They just test whether or not you can see a single wrong or missing letter. For example:

Late in the war, the Germans, <u>retreating</u> <u>in haste,</u> <u>left many</u>
                                    A   B   C

of <u>their</u> prisoners go free. <u>No error.</u>
   D   E

If you didn't read the sentence carefully, you (like Larry and Paul) probably selected (E). Those of us who missed this question saw the word *let* where we should have seen *left*. With the word *let* the sentence is correct. With the word *left,* it is obviously wrong. In other words, we got this question wrong because we didn't see an *f,* not because we didn't know the grammar. In a sense, this question tests exactly the opposite of what it's supposed to test. People who are good writers know how the sentence is supposed to sound, so they imagine that the right word is there even when it's not. The moral of the story: *Read carefully.*

Rule 10: Dangling Modifiers

"Dangling modifier" is a fancy grammatical term for a simple concept. Here are some sentences with dangling modifiers.

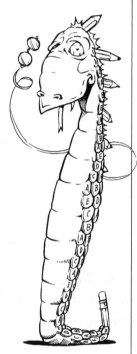

Always read the
sentence at least
twice before
picking Choice E.

      —Ada

Example 1:
Taking the test, his copy of *Up Your Score* was in his pocket.

This sentence does not mean what the person who wrote it wanted it to mean. This sentence implies that the copy of *Up Your Score* was taking the test. (This book can do many things, but it cannot take the test all by itself.) Whenever a sentence begins with a phrase like "Taking the test," which is supposed to modify (that is, describe) a word in the sentence, the word that it modifies must be in the sentence, and it must come right after the modifying phrase.

Correct: Taking the test, he had his copy of *Up Your Score* in his pocket.

The sentence can also be corrected another way.

Correct: While he was taking the test, his copy of *Up Your Score* was in his pocket.

Dangling modifiers will be on the sentence correction section of the test. Whenever you see a sentence with an "-ing" word in a phrase at the beginning, be on the lookout for a dangling modifier.

Example 2:
Conscientious about proper grammar, dangling modifiers were always on Bertha's mind.

Were the dangling modifiers conscientious about proper grammar? No, Bertha was. So she should come right after the comma.

Correct: Conscientious about proper grammar, Bertha always had dangling modifiers on her mind.

(Example 2 is an exception to the rule about dangling modifiers having an "-ing" word at the beginning.)

Example 3:
Parachuting over the Emerald City, the ant gasped in awe.

Was the ant parachuting? Hell, yes—so the sentence is correct.

Rule 11: Sentence Logic

On the sentence correction section of the test, there are often sentences that are grammatically correct but don't do a good job of saying what the writer wants them to say.

Example 1:

> There are often sentences that are grammatically <u>correct, and do not say what</u> the writer wants them to say.
>
> (A) correct, and do not say what
> (B) correct and do not say that which
> (C) correct but do not say what
> (D) correct, with the exception that
> (E) correct saying not what

The correct answer is (C). One would expect that if the sentences were grammatically correct, they would say what the author wanted them to say. *But* they don't. The word *but* indicates that the part of the sentence after the comma contradicts what you would expect after reading the first part of the sentence.

Example 2:

> <u>It was dark in the closet, and they</u> managed to find the exit.
>
> (A) It was dark in the closet, and they
> (B) It was dark in the closet, they
> (C) It is as dark in the closet, if they
> (D) Although it was dark in the closet, they
> (E) Until it were dark in the closet, they

The answer is (D). *Although* you would expect that in a dark closet the exit would be hard to find, they did find the exit. The word *although* correctly conveys the author's intent that the part of the sentence after the comma should say something contrary to what one might expect after reading the first part of the sentence.

Rule 12: Commonly Messed-up Expressions

Sometimes the ETS will deliberately mess up an expression to try to foil you. The only way to prepare for this type of question is by becoming familiar with standard, formal English and being able to hear or see which words or phrases just sound or look wrong. Like the Totally Bogus Sight Questions, these are pretty ridiculous.

Example:

Since it's a beautiful day, I'd just assume walk.

The expression is "just as soon," but it sounds a lot like "just assume." You have to be able to see that it's wrong.

Correct: Since it's a beautiful day, I'd just as soon walk.

Rule 13: Logical Comparison

Remember when your math teacher said, "You can't compare apples and oranges"? That's basically what this rule is about. Make sure that when you make a comparison, you compare two like things.

Example 1:

My mother's salary is higher than Jane's mother.

Your mother's salary is higher than Jane's mother's salary, not higher than Jane's mother. How could a salary be higher than a person?

Correct: My mother's salary is higher than Jane's mother's.

Example 2:

Harry raised more cows than Jim's ranch.

Again, Jim raised the cows; his ranch did not raise anything.

Correct: Harry raised more cows than Jim did.

A few more things to watch out for

- Don't split an infinitive. Instead of saying "to slowly walk," you should say "to walk slowly."

These are the grammatical equivalents of units.
—Ada

- Don't use slang or clichés.
- *Either* goes with *or*; *neither* goes with *nor*.
- When referring to a country, don't use *They*.

Example:

The United States is the richest country in the world. They have the highest GNP.

Correct: It has the highest GNP.

- You can prefer something to something, but you can't prefer it over or more than.

Example:

Correct: I prefer science to math.
Incorrect: I prefer science more than math.
Incorrect: I prefer science over math.

- Use the word *fewer* if you can count what you're describing; if not, use the word *less*.

Example:

Now that there are fewer elephants milling around, there is less dust being kicked into the air.

- Choices that begin a sentence with *being* are usually wrong.

Example:

Being that Larry is so old, he's never heard of Justin Bieber.

Ada says:
The SAT loves to test "idiomatic usage." This can come down to little tricks like knowing whether to say "different from" or "different than" (it's the first one). Additionally, watch out for similar words that are used differently, like "respectively" and "respectfully."

PRACTICE QUESTIONS

Okay—here are some pseudo-SAT usage and sentence correction questions. It's easier to practice the rules with these types of questions, although the revision-in-context section will also test the rules. There is one question for each rule and two sentences that is correct. (You caught that mistake, didn't you? It should be "two sentences that *are* correct.")

Usage

1. After many <u>people</u> had been <u>strangely</u>
                     A   B
   <u>painted</u> blue and yellow, the police <u>had</u>
     C   D
   <u>caught</u> the man with the spray can.

   <u>No error.</u>
       E

2. One <u>must listen</u> <u>carefully</u> to Ke$ha's
              A   B
   lyrics; <u>otherwise</u> <u>you</u> might miss their
                C   D
   thematic significance. <u>No error.</u>
                                E

3. Confucius <u>says</u> that people <u>who</u> <u>stand</u> on
                  A   B   C
   the toilet <u>gets</u> high on pot. <u>No error.</u>
                   D   E

4. <u>Sagacious</u> <u>individuals</u> do not <u>construct</u>
        A   B   C
   two-story <u>outhouses.</u> <u>No error.</u>
                  D   E

5. Every one of the <u>boys</u> in the class
                        A
   <u>must   have   their</u> elbows <u>fumigated.</u>
        B   C   D
   <u>No error.</u>
       E

6. Brian and Matt <u>are</u> practicing <u>because</u>
                      A   B
   <u>they</u> want to defeat Aliza and <u>she</u> in the
     C   D
   wrestling match. <u>No error.</u>
                          E

7. Oprah <u>ran</u> away as <u>quick</u> as <u>she</u> could <u>from</u>
             A   B   C   D
   the ravenous poodle. <u>No error.</u>
                              E

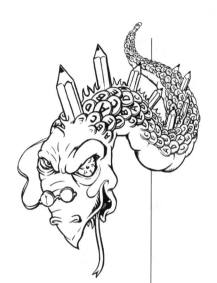

8. Eggshell <u>was</u> <u>scattered around</u> the spot
         A   B
<u>where</u> Humpty Dumpty <u>felt</u> to the ground.
  C   D
<u>No error.</u>
  E

9. Last year, Jesse's <u>toes</u> <u>yielded</u> twice <u>as much</u>
                A   B   C
toe cheese as <u>Jill</u>. <u>No error.</u>
           D   E

10. What's <u>your</u> attitude <u>on</u> this <u>year's</u> Grammy
            A   B   C
nominees? <u>Do</u> any of them deserve to win?
          D
<u>No error.</u>
  E

Sentence Correction

11. The most exciting thing about mushrooms
is <u>their texture, a mushroom</u> is mushy and
chewy.
(A) their texture, a mushroom
(B) their texture and mushrooms
(C) their texture; a mushroom
(D) their texture and that a mushroom
(E) its texture; a mushroom

12. Betty enjoys putting itching powder in
Chip's <u>jockstrap, and Chip does not</u>
enjoy it.
(A) jockstrap, and Chip does not
(B) jockstrap, but Chip does not
(C) jockstrap, being not as likely that Chip
will
(D) jockstrap, being as Chip will not
(E) jockstrap, and Chip does not to

13. The fish on your <u>couch, although not as
smelly</u> as might be expected, are making
this date unpleasant.

(A) couch, although not as smelly
(B) couch, but not as smelly
(C) couch, but quite that smelly
(D) couch, and smells
(E) footballed! It be greenly and whom that

14. The rock star <u>enjoyed singing obscene lyrics, breaking guitars, and to make videos.</u>
(A) enjoyed singing obscene lyrics, breaking guitars, and to make videos
(B) enjoyed singing obscene lyrics, breaking guitars, and to try to make videos
(C) enjoys singing obscene lyrics, breaking guitars, and to make videos
(D) enjoyed singing obscene lyrics, breaking guitars, and making videos
(E) enjoyed singing obscene lyrics, breaking guitars, and arrested for starting a riot

15. Scaling the fortress <u>wall, the boiling oil scalded me.</u>
(A) wall, the boiling oil scalded me
(B) wall, I was scalded by the boiling oil
(C) wall, the scalding oil boiled me
(D) wall, oil boiled and I was scalded
(E) wall, the boiling oil sure was hot

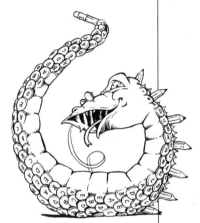

Following are the correct answers to questions 1–15 and the rules they test:

1. D, rule 5
2. D, rule 4
3. D, rule 1
4. E (sentence is correct)
5. C, rule 2
6. D, rule 3
7. B, rule 6
8. D, rule 9
9. D, rule 13
10. B, rule 12

11. C, rule 8
12. B, rule 11
13. A (sentence is correct)
14. D, rule 7
15. B, rule 10

THE ESSAY

The essay is your only opportunity in the entire SAT system to be creative—within limits. You see, the ETS graders are looking for certain qualities in each essay; if you deviate too much from those limits, the ETS will be frightened by your creativity and give you a low score. In this section, we will tell you how to write the kind of essay the ETS wants to see.

As in another important aspect of life, length doesn't matter, skill does. Don't worry about how much you write, as long as it's good. The essay graders look at thousands and thousands of essays. They spend a few minutes at the most on each one. If your essay is short but solid, they will be grateful.

Only you know how much time you have to set aside for planning the essay, writing it, and proofreading. But the time limit for the entire essay process is 25 minutes on the SAT.

Here are some examples of recent essay topics:

"Describe a previously undiscovered cause of Napoleon's defeat at Waterloo."

"Interpret Shakespeare's *The Tempest* from a Freudian standpoint."

"If sulfur were to mix with lithium in a heated, pressurized container, what would be the result?"

"What is the meaning of life? Show work."

Just kidding. No essay question will ever ask you for specific knowledge on a subject. The question will always ask you to write about a vague concept or to debate the validity of a statement. Here are some essay topics of the sort you might actually see:

We're mean,
we know.
But now the
real thing
will sound
too easy!

—Ada

1. "Progress always comes at a price." Use an example from literature, current affairs, history, or personal observation in which a difficult price had to be paid in order for progress to be made. Was the progress worth the price or was the price too high?

2. "The more difficult path can be the better path to take." Write an essay in which you explain why you agree or disagree with this statement. Support your argument with specific examples from history, current events, literature, or personal observation.

3. In a well-organized essay, describe a situation in which an individual or group at first resisted some form of change, then was convinced that change was necessary. Include in your essay
   a. what the change was and why it was resisted at first
   b. how the person or group was convinced to change
   c. a discussion of the results of the change once it was made
   Be sure to include examples in your discussion. The examples may come from personal observation, or from your reading in history, literature, science, or current affairs.

Ada says:
When planning your essay, pick the side that will be easier for you to support, even if it isn't what you would pick if you had a week (and the Internet) to work on the same topic for a class.

You'll notice that the subjects you can write about are extremely broad—"examples from history, contemporary affairs, literature, or personal observation"—basically anything except video games or your dog's habit of licking himself. So the first trick is to learn a lot about two or three subjects that interest you. Almost any will do. Read a few articles and books about these subjects and form some strong, well-thought-out opinions about them. Since the essay topics are so broad, you should be able to turn whatever you know into an essay that fits the topic.

Suppose you decide to become an expert on the civil rights movement in the United States. You could answer question 1 by talking about the great personal sacrifices made by people like Rosa Parks, Martin Luther King Jr., and Malcolm X. Then you could talk about whether the progress in civil rights was worth the high price they paid. You might give examples of the rights these people won for our generation (desegregated schools, affirmative action). For question 2, you could basically write the same thing—about how activists chose the difficult path of standing up for their civil rights.

For question 3, you could explain that racial intolerance and fear led many people to resist desegregation of schools, then outline how protests, court cases, and brave African American students who had to attend school with armed guards helped change public opinion. Finally, you could talk about some ways in which America has become a more diverse, more tolerant place as a result of desegregation.

As you can see, the questions are broad enough for you to adapt them to whatever you feel like writing about. The most important thing is that you not waste even five seconds asking yourself, "Hmmm . . . what should I write about?" Know in advance the subjects you are prepared to write on; then all you have to do is figure out how to apply your knowledge to the question.

Here is a secret weapon: Impress your essay grader by memorizing and including an obscure date or unique detail. This special knowledge will wow your grader and maybe even help you land a perfect score.

Write on One Subject

While the questions do not necessarily demand that you write about one specific subject, we think it is a good idea. If you take the first question and then say in your essay, "Everything has its price . . . when my gerbil died it cost a lot to freeze-dry it . . . and in the same way, Martin Luther King Jr. paid a great price for social change . . . and it should also be noted that the price of a movie ticket has increased markedly," then you will get a low grade for failing to make any sense at all. You should use multiple examples to prove your points, but they should all relate to a specific thesis statement. Don't write in general about how "everything has its cost" or your essay will wander. Your thesis statement should be quite specific: "The civil rights movement demonstrated that social change is accomplished at great cost."

"Personal Observation"

Can I call you back?

I learned something that day...

Unless your essay's thesis statement is "It's best to keep your email password a secret," avoid using examples from your recent dramatic breakup with your girlfriend or boyfriend.

If, as you read the remarks about the civil rights movement, you said to yourself, "Sure, that topic is interesting, but it isn't nearly as interesting as I am," then perhaps you should write an essay from "personal observation." Many of the questions will allow you to use examples from "personal observation." If you want to do this, then write about some issue in your own life or the life of someone close to you. Be sure to make it dramatic. Tell stories about the characters involved that illustrate the points you are making. Do not just blab your opinions without giving specific examples of why they are true. For example, if you are writing about how you have noticed that students do not show enough respect for the SAT, make sure to tell one story about how disrespectful the students are, and perhaps another story about how much joy and peace you have created by respecting the SAT.

It's definitely worth taking the time to review your life for good essay material. In the unlikely event that the Serpent's essay question is a poor fit for your areas of expertise, you can always turn to your own experience. Think back on times that were important to you—when there was a challenge you met, a moral quandary, a turning point in your life, some sort of realization. You know exactly the kinds of things we're talking about. (Hopefully you'll think of something that the essay readers haven't already read about hundreds of times that day.) But you don't want to find yourself thinking, "Oh, great, I can write about that time I saw Grandma shoplifting/hitchhiking/drinking margaritas," and then go blank on what to actually say about it, so determine what your central point might be, then take some notes on supporting material. Ask yourself "what happened," "what did I learn," "how did it change things?" And here's the bonus: Not only will this deep, introspective self-knowledge give you material for a strong SAT essay, but it will also be good practice for your college application essay, and a lovely little stroll down memory lane, to boot. Our next point—that it's okay to make stuff up—is particularly applicable to personal observation essays.

Making Stuff Up

HELPFUL HINTS:
When making up stuff for your "personal observation" avoid the opening "I learned a valuable lesson as admiral of the Spanish Armada..."

Suppose you are writing your essay and you are a little short of evidence. Our advice is to make stuff up. Because this test is not about how much you know but about how well you can write, don't worry if you fudge some of your facts. Your essay will not be graded on factual accuracy. Remember, the readers spend about a minute on each essay—they aren't going to spend that minute running to the encyclopedia to make sure you have your details right. They are just looking at the overall quality of your writing and organization.

This doesn't mean that you should say something that is obviously false. In the civil rights example, if you write, "The reason Malcolm X is still alive today is that . . . ," your grader will know you don't know what you are talking about. But suppose you write, "In 1961, 80 percent of taxpayers in North Carolina opposed desegregation, but by 1971, only 20 percent opposed it." Your grader will probably be impressed that you argue so convincingly (when actually you made the numbers up). The reason the second example works is that it isn't completely a fantasy; it is based on an awareness of a shift in public opinion that did occur during the sixties.

If you're writing about personal observations, feel free to make up characters and events as long as they're within reason. The SAT essay is not a truthful memoir, just a test of persuasive writing skills.

The ETS-Friendly Essay

In your essay, the ETS wants to see if you know the "rules" of good essay writing. The ETS does not care that the art of essay writing has been explored for centuries by great writers, each of whom discovered original ways of organizing and writing great essays. No, all the ETS graders care about is whether you know how to do the basic, no-frills high school essay. So, you should give them what they want and write an essay according to the formula they are expecting.

The formula they want is one that is organized just like an old-fashioned first date. Not a modern first date, which takes place over Facebook chat, but the kind you see in an old movie. An old-fashioned date has three parts: the introduction, the meal, and the good-bye.

Before you get down to your date, however, it's wise to spend a couple of minutes preparing. Organize your thoughts and jot down a few notes so that when you begin, you'll be smooth and polished and won't make a fool of yourself trying to sound intelligent when you aren't sure what you want to say.

1. The Introduction

a. This begins with a "pickup line" in which you get the prospective date's (the reader's) attention.

b. Next there is a provocative sentence that explains the pickup line and gets you talking about something you know about.

c. Then you invite the prospective date (the reader) to join you for a meal. (This is the thesis sentence.)

Look how applicable our analogy is!
—Ada

2. The Meal

We recommend that you divide the meal into three courses, during which you continue talking about the stuff you started discussing in the opening but now in greater depth so that you can show your date how knowledgeable and interesting you are. Make sure you move from one course to another by using smooth transitions. Remember to fill each course with substance and detail—unsupported opinion will leave your date hungry for more.

3. The Good-bye

You conclude by talking about what a lovely discussion you have had, you make a hint about your future together, and then, if you get the right signals, there should be one good-night kiss.

Now is your chance to do something you never get to do on a date. Review the experience a few times, correcting any part of it that didn't turn out exactly as you wanted it to. Add anything you wish you had said, and cross out anything you wish you hadn't said. As long as you do it neatly, no one will care that you didn't get it perfect the first time.

This isn't a *Gossip Girl* hookup.

—Ada

This has been a perfect evening— a true 800!

THE Good-bye

Some Insider Tips

Remember that a reader spends only a few minutes on your essay. Make it clear, concise, and, above all, *readable*. Although the ETS *says* the essays aren't judged on handwriting, it makes sense to write clearly. If the reader can't read what you've written, how can he or she grade it fairly? (And don't make the mistake of thinking that he or she will assume your illegible handwriting is hiding a brilliant essay—illegible handwriting just makes people *grumpy*. If you don't believe us, go ask any of your teachers about grading finals.)

Also, these slaves of the ETS do not have time to go back and reread your essay, so save your real creativity for English class. They're just looking for an understanding of basic essay structure, proper grammar, and good supporting details. Again, it's okay to make stuff up.

Reminder! All of your score recipients have the option of seeing your essay along with your scores. That means an admissions officer might be poring over that 25-minute essay you wrote a year before you started applying to colleges. Add that to the fact that the essay accounts for 240 points of your writing score, and you can see why you need to *do it well!*

The Do-It-Yourself Essay Formula

Follow this formula to an 800 OR a second date.

—Ada

To show just how easy it is to apply this formula to any essay topic, we have made a chart of the do-it-yourself essay. You'll see that no matter what the question is, you can write about whatever subject you planned to write about, and you can always make that subject fit the formula. We have written one essay about scientists, and one about the environment, but remember, you can write on almost any topic.

Note that Essay I agrees with the question, while Essay II disagrees. There isn't a "right" answer to any of the essay questions; remember, it isn't what you say that counts, but rather how well you say it.

	Essay I: Question: "Progress always comes at a price . . . " (question 1 discussed on page 268).	Essay II: Question: Depending heavily on others keeps us from realizing our own potential. Agree or disagree.
1. The Introduction—Opening Paragraph		
Attention-getting pickup line	There is an ancient Sudanese proverb that states, "To kill a tree is to kill oneself." (*We made this up. There's no such proverb, but how would the ETS know?*)	In tribute to the scientists who came before him, Isaac Newton said, "If I seem to see farther than others, it is because I stand on the shoulders of giants."
Explain your pickup line; get the discussion going	In the search for better transportation, homes, and defenses, human beings have drained the earth's resources.	Newton was aware that his deep insights into science came from his mastery of the works of his predecessors.

Invitation to the meal (a good way to do this is to restate the essay question in relation to your topic and then say how you are going to organize your discussion)

Has the progress we have made in our standard of living been gained at too great a cost to the environment? We can begin to answer this question by exploring three areas of human progress and their environmental repercussions.

Depending heavily on the work of other scientists does not keep one from realizing one's own potential as a scientist. In fact, three great scientists realized their potential by depending heavily on others.

2. The Meal—Paragraphs 2, 3, 4: Three Examples That Support Your Argument

First example that supports your argument (1 paragraph)

One area in which human beings have made enormous technological progress is in transportation. Only two centuries ago, the only means of land transportation were on foot or on the backs of animals. Now we have high-speed trains, automobiles, airplanes, and spaceships. However, the environmental cost of all of this transportation has been vast. The burning of fossil fuels is ruining the ozone layer and causing global warming. Roads now scar the land that was once wilderness.

When Copernicus suggested that perhaps the planets revolve around the Sun instead of the planets and the Sun revolving around the Earth, this was a new way of looking at the world. However, most historians of science agree that Copernicus's work depended heavily on Ptolemy and on contemporary mathematicians. Thus, while he had conceived of an entirely new way of understanding the shape of the solar system, he did so with the help of other scientists.

Another example that supports your argument (1 paragraph)

Humans have also paid a price for the improvements we've made in our dwellings. Once we lived in caves or in earthen huts. Now many of us live in manufactured homes in crowded cities. While this has brought us modern conveniences and greater protection from the elements, this lifestyle has ravaged the natural habitats of many animals.

Galileo also discovered new details of the universe— the moons of Jupiter, mountains on Earth's moon—which had never before been seen. Still, he was dependent on the scientists who preceded him. He used Copernicus's model of the universe to track the planets. Also, the telescope that he used was made possible by the work of other

Scientists speculate that American cities are a prime cause of the extinction of at least three species of birds each year. (*We made up this statistic.*)

scientists who had made progress in the field of optics.

Third example that supports your argument (1 paragraph)

Finally, human beings have always sought defense from one another and from animals. In pursuit of safety, we have advanced the science of weaponry to the point where our power to destroy the environment is absolute. If nuclear war should occur, the environment would pay the ultimate price—the end of life as we know it.

Even though Newton's work on gravity seemed to depart radically from that of the scientists who preceded him, it too relied on the work of his predecessors. As his "shoulders of giants" statement indicates, Newton was fully aware that his discoveries depended heavily on Galileo and other scientists who had advanced the idea that the universe follows mathematical laws.

3. The Good-bye—Last Paragraph: Conclusion

Summarize your argument (explain what you proved in the previous three paragraphs)

Look to the future (this is optional, but graders love it)

A good-night kiss (one last cute point, perhaps referring to your pickup line)

We have made great progress in the fields of transportation, housing, and defense, but the environment has paid a tremendous price.

If our planet is to survive, we will have to realize that some forms of progress are not worth the environmental cost.

To invert the Sudanese proverb: To save a tree may be to save ourselves.

Copernicus, Galileo, and Newton fully realized their potential as scientists by depending heavily upon others.

Those who will make future contributions to science will likely also do so through careful study of other scientists.

By standing on the shoulders of those other scientists, they will be able to see farther still.

Practice is the only way to learn time allocation. And don't peek at the prompt before you start!

—Ada

If you find that the time allotted is not enough for you to write an essay according to the formula, then just put two paragraphs in the "meal" instead of three. You don't necessarily need to write five paragraphs for your essay.

If you're saying to yourself, "I don't know enough facts about science to write an essay like the second one," don't worry. We didn't either. We just opened up our high school history book to the chapter about scientists and got our facts from there. Remember, because you are going to prepare your essay in advance, you can look up the facts you anticipate needing. And if you get to the test and forget some of those facts, you can just make them up. For example, you could have said, "After waking each morning, Isaac Newton allegedly spent four hours sitting in bed reading the works of scientists who preceded him." How would the test graders know that wasn't true?

The secret to the essay section is to write a couple of essays about two subjects that interest you before you even get to the test. Then, while everyone else is sweating over what to write about, you will just be tweaking your approach to a topic you have already prepared. As practice, why not write two essays about your chosen subject in response to the two essay questions here?

CHAPTER 5

GUESSING, OR THE ETS STRIKES BACK: IMPOSTORS FROM HELL

IMPOSTORS FROM HELL

The Serpent decided to include among the answer choices the wrong answers a student would be most likely to come up with.

Just when you thought it was safe to go back into the testing hall . . .

One day, soon after his self-inauguration as Supreme Commander of the High School, the ETS woke up in his comfortable and slimy bed and realized that he was dissatisfied with the SAT. Apparently, his torturous questions didn't always fool students. Scores were much higher than he wanted them to be. He felt very sad, as well as lugubrious, melancholic, despondent, downcast, doleful, woebegone, and disconsolate.

So, later that afternoon, he decided to pay a visit to one of his testing halls to see what the problem was. He actually overheard a student say, "Gee, this SAT really isn't that difficult." The Serpent felt his scales quiver in humiliation. Drastic action was necessary. The flaw in his SAT had to be discovered and corrected, and fast.

The ETS knew he had made the questions as mean and nasty as possible. But after weeks of rereading Slimy and Atrocious Torture and eavesdropping on students taking it, he realized what the matter was. Sometimes students would get math problems wrong and find that *their wrong answer* wasn't one of the choices. So they tried the problem again and got it right the second time. At other times, when they couldn't do one of the cruel math or critical reading questions, they would guess randomly and, out of sheer luck, get it right. This sort of thing just wouldn't do. But how could he possibly correct this flaw?

Then the Serpent had a brilliant idea that was also sagacious, discerning, perspicacious, and acute. He decided to put, in the list of answer choices, the wrong answers that students would be most likely to come up with if they made an error in figuring out the question or if they had to guess. That way, if a student made a mistake or had to guess, the student would choose one of the Serpent's wrong answers.

The ETS decided to call these tricky wrong answer choices Impostors. With this concept incorporated throughout the

SAT, students would once again live in fear. The Evil Testing Serpent chuckled hideously and its scales shone with proud energy because it knew that its delicious years of tyranny would continue . . . forever.

Okay, don't get frightened. We didn't mean to scare anybody. Actually, the plain truth is that the Evil Testing Serpent didn't plan on *Up Your Score*. We've psyched out his system of Impostors and discovered that, if you use them properly, they actually make the SAT easier. In this section we illustrate several techniques that we have developed to recognize Impostors, to avoid them, and to trick the Serpent by using them to help you find the right answer.

Impostors are used in both the critical reading and math sections. They are the tempting answers that look right but aren't.

For an example of a type of critical reading Impostor, look at this sentence completion question:

Although supporters hailed the Prime Minister as _____, others argued that he was too slow in recognizing problems.

    (A) autocratic
    (B) visionary
    (C) perspicacious
    (D) diplomatic
    (E) pusillanimous

This is the seventh question out of ten in a subsection, one that some people would get right but many may get wrong. Notice that the Serpent put two Impostors in there for people who don't know what the word *perspicacious* means. Since the sentence is talking about the Prime Minister, someone who doesn't know *perspicacious* might be tempted to choose either choice (A) or (D), since they both have to do with politics. In this case, however, we're talking about the Prime Minister's personal qualities, and the word *although* clues us in to the fact that supporters think he is not "too slow in recognizing problems." If you knew that *perspicacious* means "perceptive," you would have chosen (C). (Remember: This question was at the end of the section, so the obvious choices are wrong; for questions at the beginning of a section sometimes the obvious answer is right. For more on this, see Rule 2 on page 285).

Here's another example, this time from a reading passage:

"He is often lauded for pursuing a philosophy that is progressive in spirit and yet practical in application."

In line 15 (cited above), the word "spirit" means
(A) apparition
(B) psyche
(C) vigor
(D) disposition
(E) sentiment

To get this one right, you have to realize that the "spirit" of the philosophy is the essential disposition behind it. The correct answer is choice (D). But do you see how somebody who didn't like the passage could be misled? The Serpent deliberately put three Impostors in there—choices (A), (B), and (E). Some students might look at the word *spirit* and immediately connect it to ghosts, character, or emotions. So the three Impostors try to lure people into answer choices that relate to the kind of "spirit" that's in their heads.

In the math section, the ETS includes Impostors that are the answers students would get if they used the wrong method to solve a problem. The Serpent makes sure that if you screw up in the way he hopes you will, the wrong answer you get is one of the answer choices. For instance, the first question on one SAT math section reads:

If $x + y = 2$, then $x + y - 4 = ?$
(A) -2 (B) 0 (C) 2 (D) 4 (E) 6

The correct answer is (A), but the Serpent made sure that (C) was one of the choices in case some airhead left the minus sign out of the answer. He also made sure that (E) was there just in case some pasta brain added the 4 instead of subtracting it. He also made sure that (B) was there in case some goo-head decided that *x* and *y* were each equal to 2. So, in this example, the Impostors are (B), (C), and (E).

After the following dramatic interlude on the value of guessing in general, we will show you how to use Impostors to your advantage.

GUESSING, THE SAT, AND THE SPECTER OF WORLD DESTRUCTION

A Deep and Moving Play

C*ast*

A sagacious guru who has read *Up Your Score*
His naive disciple, who has not

Disciple: To guess or not to guess? That is the question.
Guru: Guess, my child, guess.
Disciple: But they take off a fraction of a point for each wrong answer, whereas they don't take off any points if I just leave it blank. So if I guess wrong, it's going to hurt my score.
Guru: Ah, silly child, how foolish you are. Even if you guess completely randomly, you should get a fifth of the questions correct just by the laws of chance (in the sections where there are five choices). So, the quarter of a point that the ETS takes off for each wrong answer is canceled out on the average by the number of lucky guesses you make.
Disciple: I'm so confused. Give me an example.
Guru: I would be honored. Imagine that there are 100 questions on the test and five answer choices for each question. If you guess randomly you should get 20 questions correct by the laws of chance. But then the cruel SAT graders take off a quarter of a point for each of the remaining 80 questions that you missed. In other words, they'll subtract $(\frac{1}{4}) \times 80$, or 20, points from the number of correct answers that you have. You have 20 correct answers, so you have a final score of $20 - 20 = 0$, which is exactly what you should get if you don't know anything and were guessing randomly. It is also exactly what you would have gotten if you left everything blank. So, my child, you see that guessing didn't hurt you.

Disciple: Yeah, but it didn't help me, either.

Guru: Right you are. But you were guessing randomly. If you can make educated guesses, or eliminate even one of the answer choices, then the odds will be decidedly in your favor and guessing can significantly increase your score.

Disciple: What about the grid-in questions in the math section? Should I guess there?

Guru: That is a different situation, my child. There is no penalty for wrong answers on those questions. However, that does not mean that you should automatically guess on every one. On the other questions there are only four or five answer possibilities, but on the grid-ins there are around 14,000. Therefore, you will probably be wrong if you guess randomly, and you will have wasted valuable time filling in all those circles. On these questions, guess if you have the slightest idea of what the answer is. Then, if you have plenty of time at the end, go back and fill in the blank ones with a number between 1 and 10, where the answer's most likely to be.

Disciple: Are there any secrets to being a sagacious guesser like you?

Guru: It's a good thing you asked. I can recommend an invaluable book that has an incredible section about guessing. It's called *Up Your Score.* It's a masterpiece, really. Buy some copies for your friends and family.

So, ignoring that pathetic excuse for a play, just how valuable is this guessing stuff, anyway?

Incredibly valuable. We did two experiments on the old SAT to prove that guessing really works. First, we took the test by only looking at the answer choices without reading any of the questions. We got an average combined score of 660. Although that's not going to get anyone into Harvard, it was 260 more points than would be expected from someone with no knowledge of the questions. In our second experiment, we had 10 kids take the test and leave blank all the questions they couldn't do. Next, we had them read this chapter and then guess on all the ones they had left blank. Their scores were increased by an average of 35 points, and they guessed correctly

On the grid-ins there are around 14,000 possible answers, so if you guess randomly, you'll probably be wrong.

what's the meaning of life?

Guess.

on 40 percent of the questions that they had left blank. ¡*Ay caramba!* Pretty good improvement for a simple application of the six basic guessing rules, which we'll now discuss.

THE SIX RULES OF GUESSING

This rule allows you to turn the ETS's favorite weapon against him!
—Ada

Rule 1: One of these things is most like the others.
If you have no idea what the correct answer is, choose the one that looks the most like all the other answers. This works because the Evil Testing Serpent is going to make his Impostors look as much as possible like the correct answer. Use the Impostors to show you the path to the correct answer.

For example, if the answer choices are

$$\text{(A) } \frac{\sqrt{3}}{7} \quad \text{(B) } \frac{\sqrt{3}}{2} \quad \text{(C) } \frac{-\sqrt{3}}{2} \quad \text{(D) } \frac{3}{2} \quad \text{(E) } 5\frac{\sqrt{3}}{2}$$

you should choose (B). Why? Because four out of five choices have a $\sqrt{3}$ in them, the correct answer probably has a $\sqrt{3}$ as well, so you can eliminate choice (D). Since four out of five choices have a 2 in the denominator, the correct answer probably does too; so eliminate (A). Since four out of five answers are positive, the answer probably is too; eliminate (C). None of the answers (A) through (D) has a 5 in it, so (E) is probably wrong. This leaves (B) as the best guess.

Rule 2: Problems increase in difficulty as you go along.
We have repeatedly pointed out that all of the subsections (with the exception of the reading passages) of the SAT get progressively more difficult as they go along. The first problem in the subsection should be easy; the last problem should be

hard. This should be taken into account when you guess. If, on one of the questions near the end of a subsection, the Serpent puts in an answer choice that can be arrived at through a simple calculation, it is probably an Impostor. Look at the following problem:

> What is the ratio of the area of a rectangle with width w and length $2w$ to the area of an isosceles right triangle with hypotenuse of length w?
>
> (A) $\dfrac{8}{1}$ (B) $\dfrac{4}{1}$ (C) $\dfrac{2}{1}$ (D) $\dfrac{1}{2}$ (E) $\dfrac{1}{4}$

If you do not know how to do this problem, or if you don't have time to do this problem, or if you have a personal grudge against the word *hypotenuse*, you should keep in mind Rule 2. This was problem 25—the last question in the section and therefore the hardest. According to this rule, you would eliminate answers (C) and (D) because they are both simple ratios of the two numbers that are in the problem (i.e., $2w/w$, or $w/2w$). If that was all you had to do to solve this problem, it would have been easy and therefore it wouldn't have been the last question in the section.

You could actually solve this problem by drawing the following sketch:

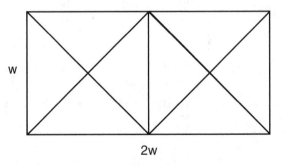

The sketch immediately shows you that 8 isosceles right triangles with hypotenuse w fit in 1 rectangle with width w and length $2w$. In other words, the rectangle is 8 times as large as 1 triangle. So the answer is (A).

Rule 3: Three's a crowd.

You know how you freak out when, for a couple of multiple-choice questions in a row, you keep getting the same letter for your answer? Well, the Serpent has been watching you and knows this. You'd think that he would use this information to cruelly blow your mind by making all the answers for the whole test (D). Yet he does not do this. Although it may seem that the Serpent decided to show some mercy to his victims, he knows that if nine times in a row the correct choice was (D), the students taking the SAT would panic and die from heart failure. That wouldn't be any fun for the Serpent because then they could never again be subjected to his torturous exams. Nice reptile, don't you think?

So, the ETS deliberately makes sure that there aren't many "runs"—three or more answers in a row that are the same letter. In a sample of 20 tests, there were only 9 triples; statistically there should have been about 24. Also, there were no runs of 4 or more, and there should have been about 9 according to the laws of probability (see page 234).

So if you pick (C) for two questions in a row that you think you got right, and you're not sure about the next one, don't guess (C). You should apply this rule if, for instance, you choose (D) on question 15, skip question 16, and then choose (D) again on question 17. When you go back to guess at question 16, don't guess (D).

Note: If somewhere in the test your answers form a triple but you are confident that they are correct, don't change them. It might, however, be wise to pay special attention to those questions if you have time to check your answers.

Rule 4: Choose an answer that contains the number represented in the most answer choices.

This rule pertains to a type of question that comes up occasionally in math and critical reading questions in the following nasty format:

> Based on what you read in the passage, which is true?

I.   Bart Simpson will be the class valedictorian.
II. MTV will stop showing music videos once and for all and become "Mime TV."
III. Bell-bottoms will come back into style every 20 years from now on.
(A) I only
(B) II only
(C) I and II only
(D) I and III only
(E) I, II, and III

Following Rule 4, in this example you should pick an answer that has a I in it because I shows up four times in the answer choices, whereas II only shows up three times and III only twice. This works because, if indeed I is true, the Serpent considers any wrong answer with a I in it to be an Impostor. If you have no idea at all about whether the other statements are true, select *I only*. However, if you have a hunch that statement II is correct as well, then you would go with (C) because that contains both I (which shows up the most) and II, which you think might be correct.

Sometimes there is a tie between two numbers. Say I and III showed up three times each. In this case, choose an answer that has both I and III in it, whichever one you think is correct.

Of course, if you think the best answer is one that I doesn't appear in, go with that. Don't use any of these rules against your better judgment.

Rule 5: Pick "nonanswers" at the beginning, not at the end.

In the math section, there will always be a few questions that have as an answer choice "It cannot be determined from the information given." The Princeton Review has devised a good rule for guessing on this type of question. They say that if "It cannot be determined . . ." is offered at the *beginning* of a math section, then it has about a 50 percent chance of being correct.

However, if it is offered near the *end* of the test, it's probably wrong. (Probably, but not *always* wrong; if you think it's probably right, then choose it.)

Why does this work? Well, the Evil Testing Serpent knows that most students will not be able to do the last couple of questions. He wants to make sure that there is a tempting answer choice for those students. So he makes one of them "It cannot be determined from the information given." Many students are conned into selecting this sort of answer at the end, when the problems are hard, because they are usually rushed for time and don't see a way to solve the problem right away, even though there is one. In other words, when a "nonanswer" is offered near the end of a section, it's probably a trick.

Rule 6: In the reading section, beware of answer choices that express an opinion too strongly or that make an absolute statement.

For example, without even reading the passage, we can make a good guess on this SAT question:

> The author's attitude toward Aristotle's writings is best described as one of
>
> (A) unqualified endorsement
> (B) apologetic approval
> (C) analytical objectivity
> (D) skeptical reserve
> (E) scholarly dissatisfaction

Choice (A) is making too absolute a statement. While the authors of SAT reading passages usually take a positive stance toward their subject, they almost never make an "unqualified endorsement." You might also eliminate choice (C) and choice (D) because they are redundant. To be "analytical" is pretty much the same thing as to be "objective"; to be "skeptical" is pretty much the same thing as to show "reserve." You can tell that the Serpent had to find two-word Impostors that would match the real answer, so he used redundant words in these choices. If "reserve" or "objectivity" had been the right answer, he wouldn't have bothered to make any of the choices have two words. So that leaves (B) and (E), but you can eliminate (E) because it is saying something negative about Aristotle, so the correct answer is (B).

A FINAL WORD ON GUESSING

Before we move on to the next chapter, you should know that guessing on a question is really no substitute for knowing the answer. Formally, we call this the Sponge Brain Rule, which says: "If you know the right answer, don't guess a different answer."

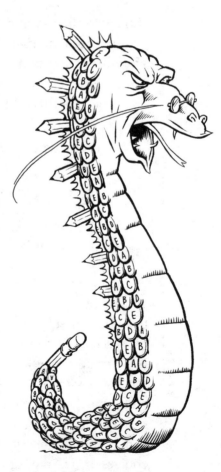

BUT
WAIT!
YOU ALSO
GET...

A man walks down the street
Says, "Why am I short of attention?
Got a short little span of attention
But, oh, my nights are so long."—Paul Simon

CONCEN-TRATION

Your *concentration span* is the length of time that you can direct your attention to a given task without spacing out. Every task also has what is called a *distraction potential*. The higher the distraction potential of a given task, the more difficult it is for you to concentrate for long periods. We all know that the distraction potential of the SAT can be very high indeed. Not only is the test itself difficult and boring, but the test hall atmosphere, complete with creaking chairs, strange odors, ticking watches, squeaking pencils, sneezes, and shuffling papers, can be distracting.

Imagine the following scenario. It's two hours into the test. You're on the second math section, and you get to this question:

If $a * b = 2ab$ and $a \dagger b = \dfrac{ab}{2}$, then what is the value of $a * (b \dagger c)$?

- (A) $4ab$
- (B) $4bc$
- (C) $2abc$
- (D) abc
- (E) ac

This is not too hard a problem to do when you're fresh, but after two hours it can be tricky. If someone were to take a "brain transcript" of you trying to do this problem, here's what it might look like:

"Okay, it's one of those weird problems with the funny symbol thingies. Let's see, what's the deal? . . . Oh, I got it. You stick in the moochie for $b \dagger c$, which makes $ab/2$, then . . . no, no, no, crap, it's $bc/2$ that you plug in. Then that leaves $a *$ $(bc/2)$. How much more time do I have left? Twelve minutes. That's ⅖ of the time for this section and I have more than ⅖ of the questions to do. Oh, no, I'm behind. Okay, okay, okay. Where was I? Oh yeah, you stick in $2a$, which makes $2abc/2$,

and then . . . I wish that idiot would stop tapping his foot. Tap. Tap. Tap. Tap. There he goes again. His hair is slimy. I wonder where he's applying to college. Tap. Tap. Why doesn't he wash his hair? Nasty! Okay, okay, okay. $2abc/2 = abc$, which is answer (D). Good. Fill in (D)."

Well, you got the answer right, but only after much wasted thought. The worst mistake was checking the time. Do this only between problems, never in the middle of a problem. And never let the slightest distraction bother you—foot tapping, slimy hair, or whatever. Of course, this is much easier said than done. Simply deciding to concentrate can leave you with a brain transcript that looks like this:

"Concentrate. Concentrate, damn it. Okay. I'm just gonna focus my brain like you wouldn't believe. This is the most important three hours of my life and I am going to concentrate intensely for the whole time. Ooooh, I'm really concentrating now. His slimy hair isn't bothering me a bit. This is total concentration—no distractions. The tap tap tap noise that his foot is making right now, which I wish he would stop, isn't bothering me either. You could stick me with pins and I wouldn't feel it. Okay, what problem am I on? . . ."

You're concentrating so hard on concentrating that you're not concentrating on the test. The trick is to learn to concentrate without thinking about concentrating. Your mind should be effortlessly focused. To learn to do this you must practice. Training your brain is just like training any other part of your body—you have to exercise it.

Concentration exercises are usually pretty lame. They're the kind of thing you read, then say to yourself, "That's lame," and move on without even trying them once. Typical concentration exercises are things like trying not to space out while running through the multiplication tables in your head. Any mental task that can be done for 20 consecutive minutes but is tedious enough that your brain is tempted to space out makes for a good concentration exercise.

We have discovered that drinking games make excellent concentration exercises. If you practice these games for

Practice makes perfect. Concentration is no exception. The earlier you hone your concentration abilities the better.

20 minutes a day for a month, you will find that your concentration span will improve dramatically. You will also be admired when you go to parties at college because you will be so good at these games.

Important Note: Usually these games are played in groups, and whenever someone screws up, that person has to take a drink. You, however, should play them alone and without doing the drinking. You will kill the whole value of the concentration game if you stop every few minutes to drink. You will also kill off so many brain cells after a month of these games that you will have no brain left with which to concentrate.

We've provided you with guidelines for two drinking games. We suggest that you play Game 1 for 10 minutes, then Game 2 for 10 minutes. It is good practice to try to do these games with the television on to see if you can concentrate so intensely that you are not even aware of the TV.

Game 1: Kerplunk!

This one starts off simply but gets difficult. Say to yourself, *in a steady rhythm*, the following sequence of sentences:

1. One frog—two eyes—four legs—in a pond—kerplunk!

(Then multiply everything by two.)

2. Two frogs—four eyes—eight legs—in a pond—kerplunk! kerplunk!

(Then do it with three frogs.)

3. Three frogs—six eyes—12 legs—in a pond—kerplunk! kerplunk! kerplunk!

As you can see, the basic pattern is

X frogs—two X eyes—four X legs—in a pond—repeat "kerplunk" X times

Keep doing the sequence. Whenever you say something wrong (i.e., saying 12 legs when you should have said 16 legs or forgetting to say "in a pond" or not knowing how many times you have said "kerplunk" or forgetting which number is next) or whenever you lose the mental rhythm and have to pause to think of what to say next, you have to divide the nearest even number of frogs that you are on by two and then start again. For example, if you were on 10 frogs and you said that they had 40 eyes, you would have to go back to "five frogs—10 eyes—20 legs—in a pond . . ."

Game 2: Buzz

This is a counting game. Pick a number between 2 and 10, not counting 2 and 10. Then start counting *in a steady rhythm*. Whenever you come to a number that

or is a multiple of the number
    has the number as one of its digits

you don't say the number; instead you say, "Buzz." The best way to explain this is to give an example.

Suppose the number is 4, then you count

1, 2, 3, buzz, 5, 6, 7, buzz, 9, 10, 11, buzz, 13, buzz, 15, buzz, 17, 18, 19 . . .

If you miss a "buzz" or lose the rhythm, you have to go back to the number that is half of the nearest even number that you screwed up on.

Game 3: SAT Practice Tests

This game hasn't gained widespread popularity in bars, but it is the most useful concentration game. If you take a lot of practice tests and really concentrate on each section for the entire half hour, you will concentrate better on the real test.

Moving On

Another concentration problem you might have is an inability to move right on to the next question if you have not been able to solve the previous one. This difficulty arises because your mind is unwilling to accept that it is unable to do the problem and wants to keep working on it. A brain transcript might look like this:

Old Problem

"Okay, screw this. Too difficult. Can't figure it out."

"But wait! I can do this one. If I just knew what this part was. I've already spent two minutes on it. I might as well finish it. No. That's stupid. Move on to the next question."

"Hey, maybe choice (D) is also right on this problem. No, that can't be right. Move on to the next problem."

New Problem

NOT LOOKED AT YET

"This one looks easy. I can do this one. Choice (D) looks good but . . ."

"Where was I? Oh yeah. Choice (D) looks good."

"Okay, it was (D). I'll fill that in on the answer sheet."

This sort of zigzagging really wastes time. When your brain tries to occupy itself with two problems at the same time, it doesn't work well on either of the problems. You have to trick your subconscious mind so that it will move on to the next problem without trying to go back. Three things will help you do this:

1. Guess—This is another good reason for guessing on all questions you can't answer. When you guess, your subconscious is satisfied that it has found an answer and is more willing to move on.

2. You shall return—Tell your brain that you're going to come back to the problem after you've finished the test. Then your brain will be more willing to leave the problem temporarily. (Put an X in the test book next to a

problem you think you can't get, a ? next to one you think you might be able to get with more time.)

3. Practice—The more timed practice tests you take, the more relaxed your brain will become with moving on.

Keeping Track of Time

Just as the "Fashion and Beauty Tips" say on page 321, wear a good watch. A darn good watch. In unfavorable circumstances, there might not even be a clock in the testing area. In any case you don't want to keep looking up nervously at the clock and risk spraining your neck. Also, remember the start time! A nice proctor (isn't that an oxymoron?) who knows what she's doing will write the start time on the blackboard, but since you'll mostly be staring at the test booklet, write the start and end times there at the top for easier reference. Or on your hand. But don't smudge it on your sweaty forehead. Check the time on your trusty watch regularly, with increasing frequency near the end of a section. But don't freak out— it's only to help you pace yourself better.

Done early? Go back and check your answers, duh. Still have time left? (Wow!) Check them again. Sometimes neuroticism works to your advantage . . . and you're stuck in that chair with nothing else to do anyway.

PROCTORS: MINDLESS SLAVES OF THE ETS

SAT proctors tend to be selected haphazardly, and for the most part they do not give a flying poo about your life or your problems. They're paid only a pittance, not enough to make them care.

Sure we're being harsh, but we've interviewed students at many schools, and we have heard some nasty horror stories about incompetent and ignorant proctors. On each test date, students across the nation go in to take the SAT in what they hope will be a fair environment. Instead, some of them must cope with bumbling idiots who forget to read instructions, eliminate break time, talk while you work, or give incorrect responses to student questions (responses like "No, you

The Greek word proktos means "anus." So does the English word proctor.

shouldn't guess"). Many proctors simply haven't learned how to do their job. They are given a proctor's manual with specific instructions on what forms of ID are acceptable, how far apart to seat people, what to do if there's a fire alarm, etc. But since their wages are not incentive enough for them to read it and no one ever checks on them, they usually are left to say and do whatever they want. Here, once again, we discover the Evil Testing Serpent doing his foul work. He insidiously fails to insist on the quality of the proctors he selects.

Proctors come in three varieties. The first and most prestigious model is the Test Center Supervisor—a popular item, but available only in limited quantities. The TCS is in charge of the whole test center. She's supposed to find all of the underling proctors, procure rooms, and maintain contact with the ETS.

Next in the pecking order is the supervisor, the bigshot in each room. The supervisor is the dude who reads the directions in a clear and carefully modulated voice ("Please read the directions as I read them aloud to you . . ."). The supervisor is in charge of all the proctors in his room.

The plain old proctors are the people who hand out the tests and answer sheets and make sure you don't cheat. (Sometimes the proctor is the same as the supervisor.)

Proctors are selected by the test center. Often local teachers are chosen as proctors—people whose faces are familiar to students. Supervisors are paid in proportion to the number of students taking the test, and proctors are paid a flat fee.

Because your proctor may not know all the facts, it is necessary for you to find out everything you need to know about the SAT before the test date. We hope this book has answered all of your questions. If it hasn't, read *The SAT Practice Booklet*. If that doesn't help, go to collegeboard.org. If you still have an unanswered question, get a life.

If you happen to get good proctors, thank them, kiss them, and offer to nibble gently on their earlobes. (They'll love this.) However, you should be prepared for a bad one and know how to cope. This will save you from getting screwed.

To be on guard against a bad proctor, to misquote the Beastie Boys, "You've Got to Fight for Your Right to SAT." Your liberties, so generously granted to you by the ETS, include the following:

1. You have the right to 25 (or 20, or 10) *silent* minutes to work on each section. The minutes begin *after* the proctor has finished reading all instructions, not before!

2. You have the right to a 5- to 10-minute break at the end of each hour.

3. You have the right to use the test booklet as scrap paper.

4. You have the right to have your seat changed for a legitimate reason. The proctor, of course, decides whether your reason is "legitimate" or not. Being placed at a right-handed desk when you are left-handed, having the sun in your eyes, and sitting with water dripping on your head from a ceiling leak are all examples of legitimate reasons. Wanting to sit next to your girlfriend is not.

5. You have the right to retain what you've stored in the memory on your calculator.

6. You have the right to breathe.

If any of these rights is violated, *speak up*. If one of the proctors says something you think is questionable or even admits that he doesn't know something, go ask the supervisor, who we can only *hope* knows what she's doing. Never be afraid of "authorities" who actually know less than you do about their own jobs. Be polite, but insist. Remember, it's your future, and you don't want to spend it as an SAT proctor, do you?

RELAXATION

Welcome to our section about relaxation. Sit back, close your eyes, and imagine that you are on a beach next to the bluest of oceans. The sun warms your skin and your toes wriggle in the soothing sand. The smell of coconut suntan lotion washes over

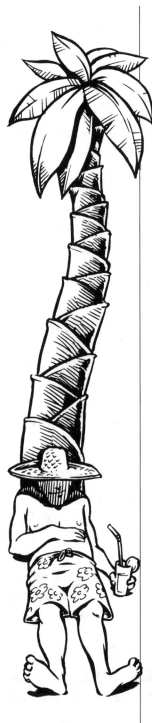

you in a delicate sea breeze. As you take deep breaths of this beautiful air, you feel more and more at peace.

That sure would be relaxing. But the SAT isn't anything like that. The SAT is when you get up from the beach and stroll into the blue ocean and a black cloud of stingrays surrounds you and stabs you until ravenous sharks smell your blood mixing with the saltwater and begin a feeding frenzy on your flesh.

Nevertheless, there are ways to become a little bit more relaxed while taking the SAT. Although the SAT will never be a day at the beach, it doesn't have to be a gruesome drowning either. If you learn how not to panic, it can be sort of a lukewarm, slightly grimy, but not uncomfortable bath. Scientists have made considerable progress in recent years in the field of "stress management." In consultation with some experts in the field, we have developed the *Up Your Score* Lower Your Stress Plan™.

Because people are frightened of the unknown, the best thing you can do to lower your stress is to prepare yourself. If you've memorized the test directions, know how to approach all the question types, and have practiced on numerous old SATs, then there won't be any unknowns to stress you out. (You can even pick a Saturday morning to get up early, go through the routine you have planned for test day, and take a full practice test. There, there, it's not that bad.) And this might sound pretty stupid, but a lot of people forget to just breathe during the test because they are so nervous. If you find yourself holding your breath subconsciously, take some long, deep breaths. A pretty useful method is "square breathing": First, exhale all of the bad air out of your lungs. Hold that for four seconds. Then, slowly inhale all of the air you can for four seconds. Hold it for four seconds. Then, repeat the sequence. (Four-four-four-four—that's why it's called Square Breathing, get it?)

Another way to reduce your anxiety is to do what is called "positive visualization." In the weeks before the test, each night before you go to bed, make a movie in your mind about exactly what it will be like to arrive at the test center, show your admission ticket and ID, sit down, get your answer sheet, listen to the incomprehensible proctor read the directions, hear the smelly kid in front of you crack his knuckles. Then visualize yourself being completely relaxed throughout the whole ordeal. No, you are beyond relaxed—you are totally focused with intense energy on the test. Yet your body is not showing any signs of stress. You are breathing deeply, your palms aren't sweaty, your pulse is slow. If you visualize this scenario numerous times before the real test, you'll be amazed at how similar to your visualizations the real test will be. Of course, you'll be more nervous than you were in your imagination, but you won't feel any need to panic, and that extra bit of nervous energy might help keep you alert.

Another relaxing thing to remember is that you are *not supposed* to know all the answers. Sure, an occasional whiz gets a perfect score, but the SAT is not like a classroom test on which your teacher will be disappointed in you for each question you get wrong. In fact, you can get tons of questions wrong and still do okay. For example, you can skip 30 questions and still score around 2000. You can skip about half the questions and still get a score that is around the national average. So, don't worry about whether or not you can solve a particular problem. Work on it for a reasonable amount of time, then say, "It just doesn't matter. I'm not supposed to know all the answers," mark it in the test book so you can come back to it if you have time, use one of our guessing techniques to make an educated guess for the time being, and then go on with the test.

Finally, we checked with the heads of the world's major religions and they all agree that while a poor performance on the SAT might make it less likely that you will get into the college of your choice, it will not have any effect on your chances of getting into the heaven of your choice.

So enjoy your bath.

Even those who get perfect scores don't feel like it on test day, I promise!
—Ada

Endurance

Yes, you have to sit through a longer test than your predecessors did. Boo-hoo for you. Take five minutes to lament your fate, then suck it up. It's time to build up your stamina. You don't want to pass out halfway through the test and get carried away on a stretcher.

A great way to improve stamina is simply to calm down. Don't distractedly look up (or sideways or over your shoulder) too often. Force yourself to look only at the test—and your trusty watch (see page 322). Practice also helps. The more practice tests you take, the more ready you'll be to handle the ordeal. Discipline yourself with daily routines. Do lots of push-ups. Finally, if all else fails, bring a camel-pack backpack filled with 5-hour ENERGY Shots to the test. This helped Ada. Good luck going to sleep that night, though.

YOGA AND THE SAT

A Body-Oriented Experience

In order to succeed on the SAT, it is most important to use your *mind*. If you arrive at the testing area without your *mind*, you are sure to do poorly on the test. (There have been reports of test takers in California who scored above 800 without their minds; these rumors have been investigated and have been found to be vicious hoaxes.) Most of this book is devoted to training the mind to meet the intellectual challenge that the SAT presents. However, a certain amount of physical conditioning is necessary as well. Each year thousands of students all across the nation suffer from muscle fatigue, leg cramps, and spinal curvature as a direct result of the SAT. Yes, the SAT can be a grueling, bone-breaking, lung-collapsing experience for the ill-prepared. How can this be? How can taking a test be so physically draining? Simply stated, all the misery is caused by the beastly little desk pictured on the next page.

And well you should gasp! This demented version of a chair, or one much like it, will be your home during the three most important hours of your high school career. Equipped with hardly ample desk space of about one square foot, this chair undoubtedly will have you making a fool of yourself as you attempt to keep your test booklet and answer sheet together on the desk and not let them fall all over the floor. They will fall on the floor anyway, making a rustling sound, and you will wind up annoying everyone in the testing hall.

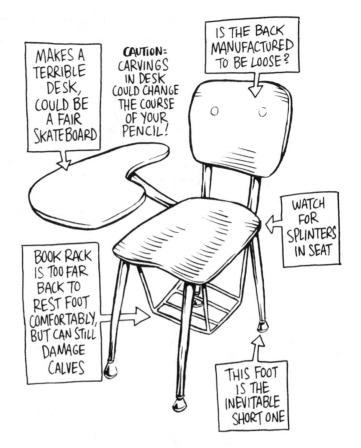

If you are left-handed, the situation will be even worse—you will wind up with the book on your lap and the answer sheet on the desk—leaving your left arm wrapped across your body to mark the circles. This is misery. Demand from the proctor a more appropriate place to take the test. He will probably just laugh wickedly and enjoy watching you suffer.

To make matters worse, the legs of the chair are usually too short and the edges too sharp. If you're not careful, you'll cut yourself and there'll be blood everywhere. And if you don't keep your posture (practically impossible to maintain), you'll wind up in traction with a slipped disc. Only the strong survive.

But there is hope. For help, we suggest you turn to knowledge that has existed for centuries in the eastern regions of the world. The ancient art of yoga, we have found, offers the most relevant conditioning for the serious-minded. If you practice the following "sun salutation" sequence, starting at least a month before the test, you will suffer minimal discomfort from your immediate surroundings during the test.

Concentration Meditation

In addition to doing yoga to improve your concentration for the SAT, try some concentration meditation. It's simple and could really help you home in on what's important—like the history of celery.

To meditate, simply focus your attention on a single object (say, the tree outside your window, your bedside lamp, or even this wonderful book) and sit in a relaxed, but upright position. Focus your attention. Increase your awareness of the object. Think of it as zoning in, not zoning out. Do this for ten minutes twice a day and you'll be surprised at what it can do for you.

Unlike the SAT math section, there is no "right" way to relax.

—Ada

CHEATING

Cheating is rampant at many test centers. Among the cheating methods we have encountered are sharing answers during the breaks between sections, peeking at other people's answer sheets, communicating answers through sophisticated body language codes, leaving a dictionary in the bathroom and looking up words during the breaks, and even having one student take the test for another student.

Two kids with whom we went to high school cheated by using the following method. Since their last names were Basset and Bates (the names have been changed to protect the guilty), they knew that they would be sitting near each other during the test. Basset was a math whiz and Bates was a vocabulary guru. So Basset did both of his own math sections while Bates did both of his own verbal sections. When the proctor turned around, they traded tests. Basset did Bates's math sections and Bates did Basset's verbal sections. They both did very well and—what a surprise—they both got exactly the same score.

Another way of cheating that we heard of involved using M&M's. Throughout the test, one kid would eat different-colored M&M's, each one standing for a letter—yellow for A, green for B, etc. The other kid would watch him and know what the right answer was.

Some years back, the ETS lost a lawsuit to a high school student it suspected of cheating. Brian Dalton's score rose from 620 in May 1991 to 1030 (out of a possible 1600) in November 1991, and the large increase caused ETS to withhold his score from colleges until it had "investigated" further. Dalton explained that he had been sick the first time he took the test, and that he had subsequently completed a prep course. But the ETS still refused to release his scores because a handwriting expert suggested that another person might have filled out his answer sheet. Dalton took the ETS to court, and the judge ruled in his favor because the ETS hadn't thoroughly investigated information that Dalton had submitted, including testimony by proctors and another handwriting expert. However, it

Cheating by glancing at a neighbor's answer sheet is likely to be a losing proposition; not all tests have the sections in the same order.

was too late for Brian: St. John's University had already rejected him due to his initially low SAT score.

Should you cheat? *No. You should not cheat.* You see, there's nothing wrong with beating the system by learning what you've learned in this book because, although we do teach you a lot of tricks, we don't break any rules. But if you beat the system by breaking the rules, you are doing something that's wrong. You will feel guilty and wish you hadn't done it. When your friends who didn't cheat don't get into their first-choice colleges and you do, you will feel awful. Just ask Basset and Bates.

So why did we write this section? To make you aware that cheating is a reality and that you shouldn't let people cheat off you. In fact, you should screw them over when they try. Suppose that during the break someone asks you what you got for number 22. Even though you know that the answer is (B), tell them that you got (C) and that you're totally sure you got it right. Then after the test say to the person, "Did I tell you (C)? I meant to say (B). Golly, I'm really sorry."

Note: If you were planning to cheat by looking at the answer sheet of the person next to you (which you shouldn't have even thought of doing!), you should know that while all the tests on a given test date have the same sections, they are in different orders. While your first section may be a math section, the first section of the person next to you may be a verbal section. The ETS devised this plan to thwart cheaters.

A Gray Area

Cheating by getting answers from other people is clearly wrong. The most common form of cheating, however, does not involve getting answers from others. The most common method of cheating is working on a section of the test after the time allotted for that section is over. At the bottom of every section the Evil Testing Serpent warns you in big, bold letters:

STOP

IF YOU FINISH BEFORE TIME IS CALLED, YOU MAY CHECK YOUR WORK TO THIS SECTION ONLY. DO NOT TURN TO ANY OTHER SECTION IN THE TEST.

At many test centers, no one checks what section you are on. We would estimate that about half the kids at our test center cheated by using this method. The five of us were good kids and didn't. But after the test, when we realized how many of our friends had done this, we felt we were at an unfair disadvantage for not having done it.

Clearly, this kind of cheating is not as bad as getting answers from other people. You could argue that when your future is in the balance, why not borrow a minute from the math section to work on the verbal section that you didn't quite finish, especially if half your classmates are doing it? On the other hand, it's still cheating.

Note: The parents of one of our past guest editors dabbled in the dark art of proctoring and would like to point out that the Evil Testing Serpent instructs all proctors to expel from the testing center anyone who cheats using this method. Also, doing so is immoral and will outweigh the advantage garnered by high SAT scores when applying for admission to heaven.

Bottom line: Don't do it.
—Ada

LITTLE CIRCLES

Robert Southey, the author of *The Three Bears* and arguably the worst poet ever, once said, "The desert circle spreads like the round ocean." He was referring, of course, to the metaphorical relationship between circles and the SAT.

Circles are quite significant in that there are many of them that you will have to fill in during the course of the test. This is about how to fill in those little circles. (Actually, they're not really circles, they're ovals.)

Undoubtedly, you've had to fill in lots of little circles in your life. You probably never gave much thought to technique or speed. In fact, until the publication of *Up Your Score*, no one had ever researched the science of filling in circles. We were the first.

Our original groundbreaking study showed that some students spend an unimaginably wasteful 2.3 seconds per circle. At that rate, they will spend 7 minutes and 4 seconds of their total testing time filling in circles. For O-lympic competitors, we developed the In-to-Out Circle Method, which enabled students to reduce their time to an unprecedented 0.4 seconds per circle, saving almost 6 minutes of time to spend working on the test.

In-to-Out Circle Method

So how obsessive do you have to be about filling in the circles? As it turns out, optical scanning machines are far more advanced than anyone could have possibly imagined. Advances mandated by Congress after the 2000 Florida election fiasco have created machines capable of reading people's minds before they even select an answer. One such machine narrowly missed being elected president of Bolivia. The machines used to grade SATs employ a similar technology. They scan through your answers and search for a pattern—for instance, if you decide to fill in only the left half of every circle, the machine will recognize this pattern and realize that it is your way of marking an answer. As long as you are consistent, you could draw a phallic picture in every little circle and the machine would not give it a second thought. Still, doing so drastically increases your likelihood of ending up in prison, so we wouldn't recommend it.

Whatever you do, avoid the following time-wasting methods of high school students who are not familiar with our groundbreaking research:

Vertical Lines Method

Horizontal Lines Method

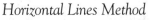

Out-to-In Circle Method

Artist Cross-Hatching Method

Unfocused Method

Moron Dot Method

Unclear on the Concept

Uh, What Was the Question?

Suicide Doodle Method

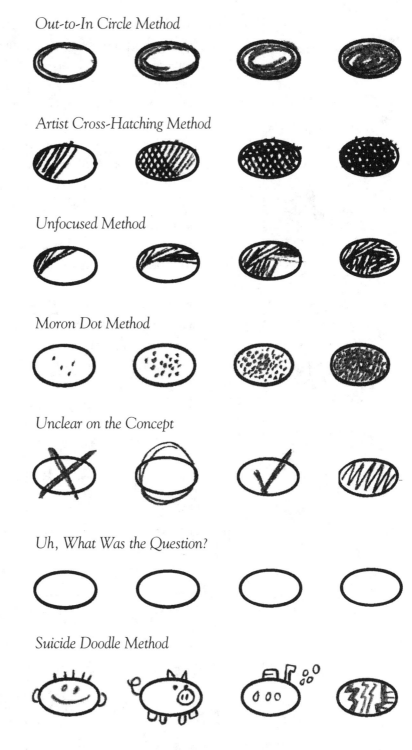

To perfect your technique, follow these rules.

1. Leave the point of one of your pencils *dull*. Although you don't want to use a dull pencil on the math section (you want a good pencil for scratch work), it will save you time on the verbal section because the more surface area the point of your pencil has, the better coverage a single line will provide.

2. Although you don't want your arm to be too stiff, you should press hard on the answer sheet. The darker the mark, the more likely the scanner is to see it. This is an important factor since you won't necessarily be filling in your circles all the way.

3. On the math grid-in questions, there is space above the grid to write in the answer. But the computer only registers the circles, so you don't have to waste time writing in the answer.

4. Practice, practice, practice. Try to get your time below 0.3 second per circle. Following are a bunch of circles for you to practice on. If you get your time below 0.1 second, you may be able to qualify for the O-lympics.

(A) (B) (C) (D) (E)   (A) (B) (C) (D) (E)   (A) (B) (C) (D) (E)
(A) (B) (C) (D) (E)   (A) (B) (C) (D) (E)   (A) (B) (C) (D) (E)
(A) (B) (C) (D) (E)   (A) (B) (C) (D) (E)   (A) (B) (C) (D) (E)
(A) (B) (C) (D) (E)   (A) (B) (C) (D) (E)   (A) (B) (C) (D) (E)
(A) (B) (C) (D) (E)   (A) (B) (C) (D) (E)   (A) (B) (C) (D) (E)
(A) (B) (C) (D) (E)   (A) (B) (C) (D) (E)   (A) (B) (C) (D) (E)
(A) (B) (C) (D) (E)   (A) (B) (C) (D) (E)   (A) (B) (C) (D) (E)
(A) (B) (C) (D) (E)   (A) (B) (C) (D) (E)   (A) (B) (C) (D) (E)
(A) (B) (C) (D) (E)   (A) (B) (C) (D) (E)   (A) (B) (C) (D) (E)
(A) (B) (C) (D) (E)   (A) (B) (C) (D) (E)   (A) (B) (C) (D) (E)
(A) (B) (C) (D) (E)   (A) (B) (C) (D) (E)   (A) (B) (C) (D) (E)
(A) (B) (C) (D) (E)   (A) (B) (C) (D) (E)   (A) (B) (C) (D) (E)
(A) (B) (C) (D) (E)   (A) (B) (C) (D) (E)   (A) (B) (C) (D) (E)
(A) (B) (C) (D) (E)   (A) (B) (C) (D) (E)   (A) (B) (C) (D) (E)
(A) (B) (C) (D) (E)   (A) (B) (C) (D) (E)   (A) (B) (C) (D) (E)
(A) (B) (C) (D) (E)   (A) (B) (C) (D) (E)   (A) (B) (C) (D) (E)
(A) (B) (C) (D) (E)   (A) (B) (C) (D) (E)   (A) (B) (C) (D) (E)
(A) (B) (C) (D) (E)   (A) (B) (C) (D) (E)   (A) (B) (C) (D) (E)
(A) (B) (C) (D) (E)   (A) (B) (C) (D) (E)   (A) (B) (C) (D) (E)
(A) (B) (C) (D) (E)   (A) (B) (C) (D) (E)   (A) (B) (C) (D) (E)
(A) (B) (C) (D) (E)   (A) (B) (C) (D) (E)   (A) (B) (C) (D) (E)
(A) (B) (C) (D) (E)   (A) (B) (C) (D) (E)   (A) (B) (C) (D) (E)
(A) (B) (C) (D) (E)   (A) (B) (C) (D) (E)   (A) (B) (C) (D) (E)
(A) (B) (C) (D) (E)   (A) (B) (C) (D) (E)   (A) (B) (C) (D) (E)

HANDWRITING PRACTICE

In recent years, the SAT has started asking students to certify that they aren't cheating by copying down a statement in cursive. Since many kids barely ever use script these days (or never learned it in the first place), here's some space to practice.

I hereby agree to the conditions set forth in the test regulations and certify that I am the person whose name, address, and signature appear on this answer sheet.

IS THE SAT BIASED?

In recent years, the SAT has been called unfair. Why? Because of its alleged bias against women, minorities, and the poor, all of whom consistently do worse on the tests than rich white males. (If you're rich, white, and male, shame on you!)

In previous editions of *Up Your Score*, we gave you statistics on specific questions that were proven to be biased by gender, race, or income. But because so many people recognized the obvious biases in these questions, the ETS has stopped publishing statistics for specific questions. It has also tried to eliminate openly biased questions, and, in fairness, we could not bring ourselves to lambaste them for questions they used years ago.

Because of the nature of the SAT, however, many still consider it biased. Basically, the test is a fast-paced game that

The College Board's slogan is "Inspiring Minds." More like suppressing minds . . . Oh, the irony.

stresses speed and strategic guessing. (Unfortunately, it's used to predict success in college, which does not necessarily depend on speed or strategic guessing.) This type of test favors the way archetypal American boys behave. Female students and students from homes that don't place an emphasis on speed and guessing are therefore at a disadvantage when taking the SAT.

Gender Bias On average, girls score about 30 points lower on the SAT than boys do, with most of the points lost on the math section. While many people argue that boys are better math students or girls' grades are inflated, research has shown that girls perform better in both high school and college courses. The SAT, therefore, consistently underpredicts the performance of female students in college. (The only thing the SAT claims to do is predict college performance.) Because of objections to a perceived gender bias, the ETS has added the writing section to the SAT. This section is supposed to boost girls' scores, but it doesn't really address the real problems of standardized tests. But by learning how to take the test, girls can score higher than boys—it is just a matter of developing skills that aren't generally encouraged in girls (cockiness, rushing through things, guessing, etc.).

Another ironic stereotype, perfect!

—Ada

Race Bias On the class of 2013's SATs, the following were the average scores (out of a possible 2400) for various racial and ethnic groups:

Asian Americans	1645
Whites	1576
American Indians	1427
Mexican Americans	1355
Puerto Ricans	1354
Other Hispanics	1354
African Americans	1278

Minorities may do worse on the SAT because of income bias (see below); in general minorities have lower incomes than whites do.

The ETS tried to bridge the racial gap in 1970 by the lame gesture of adding one reading passage per test concerning minorities. However, the benefit of the passage is questionable, except for *Up Your Score* readers who use it to their advantage (see page 48).

Income Bias Richer kids tend to do better on the SAT than poorer kids. This may be the most difficult bias to overcome; it is certainly the most blatant. First, low-income students frequently do not have the educational opportunities that more privileged students have. Another very widespread problem is SAT coaching. Many people who can afford it shell out about $900 to take an SAT prep course. This gives those students a huge advantage. However, you, the informed consumer, paid only $13.95 for this book and will have your score, and your consciousness, raised immensely.

Overall, these biases are mean and nasty and we wish they'd go away. But don't be too discouraged. You've read *Up Your Score*, and therefore can overcome any SAT hurdle that comes your way.

Most of the information for this section came from FairTest (the National Center for Fair and Open Testing), which leads the fight against the ETS. If you have any questions or would like to subscribe to their newsletter, go to fairtest.org, call (617) 477-9792, or write to FairTest (P.O. Box 300204, Jamaica Plain, MA 02130). Tell them *Up Your Score* sent you.

SATING FOR DOLLARS

After you ace the SAT, you will decide that, because you are such a good, involved student with a kick-butt SAT score, you could get into a prestigious college. You will develop a passion for this particular college, but your dreams of attending will be crushed when you learn that it costs about three times as much as you can possibly afford.

At this point you have several options. You could turn your back on the material world and join a socialist commune where money is not an issue. You could create a Kickstarter charity campaign called Educating Our Future Leaders and solicit everyone in your address book, then take their donations and spend them on your college education. (This is probably illegal, by the way.) You could sell your little brother, but you probably wouldn't make enough money.

Or you could try to win some scholarship money. Ask your guidance counselor about scholarship opportunities and research them online or in the library in the most recent scholarship books you can find. Many of these books are huge and daunting, but you will soon realize that you don't qualify for many of the scholarships in them unless you live in Santa Fe, your birthday is February 29, and you're a direct descendant of an original signer of the Declaration of Independence. You can also try searching the Internet and using a site like fastweb.com. Although scholarship applications are less fun to fill out than tax forms, they can be much more rewarding. Please note that the cost of a college can be a misleading indicator of whether you can afford it. Some of the most expensive colleges have the best financial aid options.

DON'T LET YOUR PARENTS READ THIS!

Sorry. This section is unfortunately not about "Sex and the SAT." It is, however, about the next best thing: money. You see, a good SAT score can be worth lots of money. Not only could you get more scholarship money and maybe a better job because you went to a better college, but now, thanks to us, you may be able to get your parents to pay you for a good score. This is how the devious plan works: Some parents are willing to spend up to $1,000 on an SAT prep course. And comparatively this book costs next to nothing! So you could tell your parents that they are saving roughly $990 and you are getting excellent preparation for the SAT. See where we're going with this?

Sit your parents down. Tell them you think your SAT score will be the deciding factor for colleges. Discuss what you think your score goal should be. Say how your friends are taking prep courses, and you might need to do the same to reach your score goal. Then, when the moment feels right, spring "The Deal."

The Deal is this: "If I reach my score goal using only *Up Your Score*, practice, and hard work, how about you reward me with a relatively small percentage of what you would spend on a prep course . . . say, $400?" Work from there. Negotiate. Eventually you might get a good $250 out of it. Or a new iPhone. The possibilities are endless.

But what if you think you really want to take a prep course? Well, you can still do it without having to spend $1,000. Try visiting collegeboard.org where, in addition to a free practice SAT, for $69.95 they also offer an online course and other services to help you improve your score. Your parents will be so impressed with your initiative—and by the money you've saved them—that they may just go ahead and buy you a new toy! So go out there and siphon from your parents!

Just don't blame us.
—Ada

SATITIS

What if you wake up on test day and don't feel well? Panic, beat your fists against the wall, and shriek, "Why me?"

Then sit back and assess how you feel. If you really feel vile, consider postponing the test and asking the ETS for a refund. If, however, you just have a cold, slight nausea, and a mild headache, you should still take the SAT. First of all, your "illness" could just be nerves, in which case it might go away after you take a shower. Even if it doesn't, adrenaline might well carry you through the test (you can come home and allow yourself to wallow in your symptoms afterward), and you won't have the SAT looming in front of you for another few months. Take some cold or headache or tummy medicine as long as you're certain it won't make you drowsy. (It's very difficult to succeed on the SAT if you take the test while you are sleeping.) Try to relax and breathe deeply and focus on the test, not on your scratchy throat, runny nose, watery eyes, throbbing head, clogged sinuses, or aching stomach. And remember, the SAT nauseates everyone. Finally, if you know you didn't do well, just cancel your scores.

CANCELING COUNSELING

If, after the test, you think you might have screwed up, that's only natural, and you shouldn't worry about it. However, if you *know* you screwed up, you should cancel your scores. If you made some grievous error like choosing (E) for all the sentence completions or falling asleep during a section, then it is probably wise to cancel. But don't cancel just because you made a few stupid mistakes.

The simplest way to cancel is to fill out a Test Cancellation Form before you leave the test center. However, if you decide to cancel after you've left the center, you must notify the ETS by the Wednesday after the Saturday or Sunday you took the test. (For details, go to collegeboard.org.)

If you're set on getting an amazing score, memorize all the problems that you weren't sure about and then go home and see if you guessed correctly. If you did guess correctly, keep your score. Otherwise, cancel. (We recommend this only if you want to take the test over and over again until you get a perfect score.) If you cancel, your score report will read "Absent or Scores Delayed." Important note: If you took multiple SAT IIs on one test date and you cancel one score, you're really canceling them all. So think twice!

THE SSS AND THE SDQ

In his spare time, the Evil Testing Serpent likes to play matchmaker. This is why he invented the Student Search Service (SSS). The SSS (sounds like something the Serpent would say) is like a computer dating service, except that instead of matching sexually frustrated singles, it matches colleges with potential students. It's free, and it's a good way to get lots of mail, so you might as well do it. However, if you're eco-conscious, you may not want to waste all that paper. One way to save trees is to share college brochures with your friends. Just make sure you have your own application when the time comes.

In order to enroll in the program, you have to fill out the Student Descriptive Questionnaire (SDQ) in the Student Bulletin for either the SAT or PSAT (both of which are available in your high school guidance office) or you can enroll when you sign up for an Advanced Placement test. By the way, doing this questionnaire is a great opportunity to practice filling in little circles.

Unless you're a compulsively ethical person, there is no reason why you have to tell the truth when answering the questionnaire. If you have no artistic ability, but you still want to see the pretty pictures in the brochures that the art schools send out, then fill out question 6 to say that you got an "A or Excellent in Art and Music." Also, do not be modest when answering the questionnaire. If you're good at something, say that you're great at it. That way you'll be sure to get mail from the colleges that are interested in that skill. The way it works is, the colleges send the ETS a list of characteristics that they are looking for in their students, and the ETS sends them the name, address, sex, date of birth, Social Security number, high school, and intended major of students who match those characteristics. The college doesn't know your answers to individual questions; it only knows that the matchmaking Serpent thought you might be compatible.

Another similarity between the SSS and a dating service is that they both make mistakes, matching you up with some real losers. The "Registration Bulletin" claims that you will get mail only from schools with "the academic programs and other features you find important." This is false. If you put on the questionnaire that you are an Alaskan native who wants to study philosophy and has no mechanical ability, you will still get mail from the Mormon School of Interplanetary Auto Mechanics.

THE SAT AND THE INTERNET

Most of you already know all the fun stuff you can do on the Internet. You can download any One Direction or Macklemore song you want, you can play Grand Theft Auto with someone in New Zealand, you can even flirt with 40-year-old men. Now, for your extreme convenience and pleasure, you can also prepare for the SAT on the Internet.

We've spent countless hours checking what's out there. Here's what we've found.

As we've mentioned one million times already, the College Board (collegeboard.org) has a site on the Web that is surprisingly peppy for such a stuffy organization. You can register for most of the SAT services mentioned in Chapter 1 (see page 24), and it offers advice not only on test taking, but choosing a college and getting financial aid. There's even a "store" where you can buy books and software and a "library" where you can review documents. If you have any practical questions about the SAT, a visit to this site might be helpful. There's a free full-length practice test available at sat.collegeboard.org/practice/sat-practice-test. They have a "Question of the Day" that is a good place to see SAT practice questions. You can view it online, or you can sign up to get one emailed to you each day—which is an easy way to integrate SAT prep into your routine. The College Board even provides an analysis of your score and suggests areas where you need work. We recommend that you save this for a Friday or Saturday night when you're looking for a good time. You might be a little hungover the next morning, but with words like *licentious* and *bacchanalian*, the rush is worth it.

Several SAT schools now have online versions of their courses that are less expensive than their classroom offerings and have the excellent advantage that when you get bored (and you will get bored if you expect the other guys to be as witty and charming as we are), you can always log off.

The Princeton Review (princetonreview.com) also has a pretty good site. You can take a practice test, read some sample questions, and get lots of college advice. It has one promising feature—online dissection of recent tests—but unfortunately the dissections are pretty superficial. They tend to say things like "The critical reading section had no particular surprises" without getting down to details about specific questions.

Kaplan's website (kaptest.com) covers territory similar to The Princeton Review's—analysis of the recent tests, lots of college advice. Their SAT course itself seems solid enough.

And, of course, you should be sure to follow *Up Your Score* at upyourscore.com and on Facebook, where Ada will post the latest and greatest SAT tips and you can commiserate with fellow test prep sufferers.

SNEAKY SNACKING

Never forget a water bottle.
—Ada

Ever since the ETS increased the length of the SAT to practically three days long, he so generously allows students to bring in snacks. (We know this is just to keep his victims alive longer in order to continue torturing them.)

You shouldn't eat the food during the test because that would waste valuable time. Instead, snack between sections. Choosing your SAT menu can be lots of fun. Here are a few guidelines and suggestions:

1. Nothing noisy: no potato chips, carrots, or tuna casseroles (at least not the kind with cornflakes on top)
2. Nothing sticky: no cookie batter, maple syrup, toffee, or superglue
3. Nothing big: no turkeys, cotton candy, or melons
4. Nothing smelly: no Limburger cheese, kimchi, or fried fish

As long as you stay within the guidelines, we leave the specific choices up to you. However, we do recommend the following recipe.

Sweet and Tasty 800 Bars
½ pound butter
1 (1-pound) box dark brown sugar
3 cups flour
3 eggs
1 teaspoon vanilla extract
2½ teaspoons baking powder
2 jumbo Hershey bars (the kind with the little squares)

Melt the butter and let it cool until you can put your nose in it for three seconds and feel no pain. Stir in the brown sugar. Then add the flour slowly. Beat the eggs and add them one at a time. Add the vanilla and baking powder. Break the chocolate bars into _____ squares with your _____ and add them to the batter.

(A) Hollywood . . . remote
(B) little . . . fingers
(C) liquid . . . fly swatter
(D) gaseous . . . squirt gun
(E) coconut . . . willpower

Answer: (B)

Take a big handful of the batter and eat it. (Don't you wish all recipes said that?) Pour the batter into a buttered baking dish with a volume of 216 cubic inches. If it's 2 inches deep and 12 inches long, how many inches wide is it?

(A) 8   (B) 9   (C) 10   (D) 25   (E) $8x - 5$

Answer: (B)

Preheat the oven to the average of 100°F and 600°F. Place the pan in the oven until the bars turn golden brown on top—35 minutes in a standard oven, 40 minutes in a slow oven.

When the bars are golden brown, remove the pan from the oven. Now you can cut them into whatever shape you choose.

In terms of getting your food into the test center, we recommend one of those hooded sweatshirts with the pockets in the front. These can hold a lot of food, and the food is easily accessible because it's in your front pocket. It also keeps the food hidden from all the other starving test takers around you. It's a jungle in the test center. Ladies, pocketbooks are also useful. Do not do what Larry did. He cleverly stashed a chocolate bar in his back pocket. Before he had a chance to eat it, two of the Musketeers had melted, leaving an embarrassing brown stain.

FASHION AND BEAUTY TIPS

Just as it's important not to be hungry during the SAT, it's important to be comfortable. You don't want to waste time wishing you'd worn looser jeans or that your shirt wasn't scratchy. Make sure you dress in layers no matter when your test date is. The test room could be heated, air-conditioned, both, or neither. Be prepared for any climate. Bear in mind that cardigans and sweatshirts that zip up the front are easier to wriggle out of quickly than garments you have to pull over your head. Avoid loose, floppy sleeves; as fashionable as they may be, you don't want to have to keep swishing them out of the way to fill in your answer sheet. The same goes for bangle bracelets (which also have a tendency to jangle annoyingly). Finally, a lucky pair of socks or the underwear you wore when you won the basketball tournament couldn't hurt.

Hand care is crucial to the SAT. Your hands will grip your pencil, they will punch numbers on your calculator, they will write out the certification statement in cursive even though no one ever uses cursive anymore, they will strangle the proctor if he or she is absolutely incompetent and unreasonable. Cut your fingernails so you don't waste time biting them; the same goes for your cuticles. If you like, paint your nails a soothing color like a pastel green or a blue that reminds you of the ocean. Begin treating your hands with natural minerals and creams at least one week before the test and do isometric hand exercises in order to increase the ease with which you grasp your pencil.

Hair care is also very important. Even if you're otherwise attired in your oldest floppiest sweats, go to the test with squeaky clean hair—it'll make you feel pulled together and competent. Plus, its brilliant shine might distract other

Go to sleep as early as possible the night before, so you're well rested, and shower on the morning of the test. It'll wake you up, and you'll feel fresh and ready to show the ETS what you're made of. Plus, you don't want to be that stinky kid in the room whom everyone else despises.

students and therefore increase your percentile score. Also bear in mind that the month before the SAT is no time to start growing your hair out. The last thing you want is to be constantly pushing your hair out of your eyes and cursing yourself for ever cutting it in the first place.

Finally, choose the watch that you wear carefully. Some proctors will write updates on the board about how much time is left, but having your own watch is a better bet. Because you will constantly be checking how much time is left, you want to feel comfortable with your watch. Digital ones are preferable because in the heat of the moment you could forget how to tell time. Also, make sure your watch doesn't beep, or if it does, that you know how to turn off the sound. Otherwise you risk being the object of intense hatred by the other test takers.

STICK IT IN YOUR EAR

At this point in the book, we would like to recommend that you find two cylindrical objects, rub them back and forth between your fingers, and then insert them into two of your body's orifices simultaneously.

The orifices are your ears and the cylindrical objects are foam earplugs. These little squishy thingies are great. They cost about a dollar a pair at your local pharmacy—a small price to pay for cutting out most of the distracting noises in the testing hall. They are comfortable once you get used to them. In fact, some people we know at college have become addicted to them and can't study without them.

When you put in the earplugs, you suddenly hear your own breathing more intensely and sometimes even your own heartbeat. These are precisely the things that you are supposed to listen for when trying to meditate. So once you get used to them, you'll find yourself concentrating and relaxing with a meditative intensity.

Earplugs are also helpful for blocking out those annoying teacher noises in classes you'd prefer to sleep through.

SOME OTHER THOUGHTS ON GETTING INTO COLLEGE

Remember, the SAT is only one aspect of your college application. If your score isn't that strong, make sure the rest of your application is.

Grades and Courses These should always be your first priority. Colleges usually insist on a minimum standard of grades and courses before they even look at the rest of an application.

Essays College admissions officers read hundreds of essays— your goal is to write one that will stick in their minds. You might want to reveal something about yourself in your essay that didn't come out in the rest of your application. You can write about your summer job as a camp counselor, but remember that many others will probably write similar essays about their summer experiences. Make yours stand out. Humor can be effective, but if the admissions committee doesn't find your witticisms funny, it's worse than not using any humor at all. So make sure you get feedback on your essays before you send them in. (This goes for all essays, not just humorous ones.) Show them to your family, your friends, your teachers, your plumber. However, don't let them write the essay for you—it should always reflect you.

Extracurriculars These are secondary to grades, but they are becoming more important. No one wants a school full of do-nothing dweebs. (If you are a do-nothing dweeb, change your ways now. There is still hope!) One extracurricular that is irresistible to colleges is organizing and leading something socially responsible. Ask yourself what your school or community needs and then get your friends to work with you on a project, such as a recycling program. This is not only a good deed, it may get you into college. Admissions officers also love self-propelled activities—one kid we know organized his own summer trip to work at a Moscow newspaper, and he got into Harvard. Conversely, bear in mind that dinky extracurriculars aren't that impressive. Being a leader (editor of the school paper, captain of the basketball team) is more impressive than just being a member of a club that meets once a week.

Recommendations A great recommendation can make a big difference. Ask teachers who know you well and who you think have good things to say about you. Try to choose someone with whom you have a real connection—the teachers you actually think you'll want to see at your high school reunion in ten years.

Special Talents Colleges need running backs for their football teams and violins in their orchestra. Even if you haven't been recruited by the Bears and aren't the next Itzhak Perlman, make sure your colleges know about any special talents that you have. One of our past guest authors, who originally was deferred Early Action at MIT and Cal Tech, got into both Regular Action after sending an application update that included info about the guest authorship and a percussion audition tape for the band and orchestra conductors at each school. Of course, we at *Up Your Score* believe that *we* were the deciding factor, but the tapes couldn't have hurt, either.

Note: If at first you don't succeed, try, try again. If for some reason you have your heart set on one school (although there is usually no good reason for that) and you don't get in, think about taking a year off to make yourself fascinating and smart, and apply again.

PARTING WORDS OF ADVICE

(To Be Read the Night Before the Test)

Dear Reader,

Congratulations! You've made it through (or else you're peeking at the end of the book). You know what the word *cerebration* means, and you're all set to be cerebral. You have your ID, your admission ticket, three sharp pencils and one dull pencil, a calculator or two with charged batteries, and some good food to bring into the test all waiting by the door. Maybe you've studied everything in a day; maybe you started with verbal flash cards four and a half years ago. Who cares? It's over now; no amount of studying the night before the test is going to help you significantly.

If you need a boost of confidence, just remember that there are people out there who will be taking the test tomorrow without having read this book first. (Unthinkable, isn't it?) If you botch the test, you'll just take it again on the next test date. If you don't get into the college of your choice, you can choose another one that probably doesn't cost as much and has a better football team.

We hope you enjoyed our book and learned a lot. Our objective was to teach you how to take the SAT, but we hope that along the way you learned some stuff that will help you for the rest of your life. At the very least, you now know a lot of new vocabulary words, but if we did our job right you are a more clever test taker and a better thinker than you used to be.

All of us authors went through the same thing you're going through right now. We know how you feel. There is a lot of pressure. It feels as if someone is scratching fingernails on your mental chalkboard.

So go outside and look at the stars. There are lots of them and they're trillions of miles away. In the Grand Scheme of the Universe, how big a deal can the SAT be? Chill. You're going to cruise tomorrow. Sit back. You only live once . . . and then they send you your score report.

Good luck,

Larry, Manek, Paul, Michael, Ada

Larry, Manek, Paul, Michael, Ada

P.S. You do know what the word *lamia* means, don't you?

We'll look this one up for you. According to *The American Heritage Dictionary*, it's "a monster represented as a serpent with the head and breasts of a woman; reputed to prey upon humans and suck the blood of children." Sweet dreams!

Larry Berger

Larry Berger is the president of Amplify Learning, a division of Amplify Education, a digital education company. He cofounded Wireless Generation, an educational software company, in 2000. He has written two other books: *I Will Sing Life*, a book about children and poetry, and *Tray Gourmet: Be Your Own Chef in the College Cafeteria*. He graduated summa cum laude from Yale and went on to be a Rhodes Scholar at Oxford. At Yale, he codirected the Children in Crisis Big Sibling Program and the Booksgiving Book Drive. He expands to three times his normal size when placed in water.

Michael Colton

Michael Colton is a screenwriter in Los Angeles. His projects include the feature film *Penguins of Madagascar* for Dreamworks Animation and the animated series *Zoolander: Super Model*. He also appeared regularly as a panelist on *I Love the '80s*, *Best Week Ever*, and other shows on VH1. Before moving to L.A., he cofounded the web magazine Modern Humorist; before that he was a staff writer for *The Washington Post*. He graduated from Harvard University, where he wrote for the *Lampoon* and the *Crimson*. Check out michaelcolton .com for more info and a pretty picture of doves.

Manek Mistry

Manek Mistry grew up in Ithaca, New York. He graduated from Cornell University in 1990, with a degree in biology. He then switched course and spent the next three years at Cornell Law School, receiving a JD in 1993. Now that he's out in the real world (after 20 long years of schooling, heading in many different directions), he's realized that the only thing he really wants to do is write. Of course, he knew that in first grade, too. He's had short stories published in a number of literary journals and (like everyone else in the world) is working on his first novel. No, really, he's going to finish it someday. He lives in the Pacific Northwest.

Paul Rossi

Since graduating (with distinction) from Cornell University, Paul Rossi has traveled to several cities, searching for permanent employment. In the process, he has discovered that the street value of his education in French literature and nineteenth-century European history is not easily convertible into U.S. currency. Currently he is living in San Francisco, writing experimental fiction and (yes) poetry while trying to keep his houseplants from dying on him. His friends consider him to be a fine and peace-loving citizen.

Ada Throckmorton

Ada grew up in the cow-tipping town of Leawood, Kansas (just kidding, it's really just a suburb like any other), but doesn't mind straying from the yellow-brick-road state to visit the mountains or the coast. Ada has had a number of career aspirations over the years—from novelist to doctor to neuroscientist—but is planning on studying environmental engineering at Stanford University. When not imagining her future career, Ada enjoys participating in debate and speech competitions. If she can manage to tear herself away from debate work, homework, and Netflix, Ada enjoys going on runs, kicking around a soccer ball, and hanging out with friends. Additionally, Ada has a special appreciation for bursts of spontaneity in the form of either crafting or two-minute dance parties with her mom.

W<small>HIZ</small> K<small>IDS</small> W<small>ANTED</small>

Join the *Up Your Score* team!

Attention high schoolers: The search is on for guest editors of *Up Your Score*! Are you a culturally savvy and articulate student who used *Up Your Score* to achieve a perfect (or near-perfect) SAT (or ACT) score? Are you interested in fame, fortune, and the rest of the prodigious perks that go along with revising and promoting upcoming editions of the series? Then we want to hear from you! For more information, visit upyourscore.com or write to info@workman.com.